DRAWING THE LINE

DRAWING THE LINE

Public and Private in America

ANDREW STARK

BROOKINGS INSTITUTION PRESS

Washington, D.C.

ABOUT BROOKINGS

The Brookings Institution is a private nonprofit organization devoted to research, education, and publication on important issues of domestic and foreign policy. Its principal purpose is to bring the highest quality independent research and analysis to bear on current and emerging policy problems. Interpretations or conclusions in Brookings publications should be understood to be solely those of the authors.

Copyright © 2010
THE BROOKINGS INSTITUTION
1775 Massachusetts Avenue, N.W., Washington, D.C. 20036
www.brookings.edu

Library of Congress Cataloging-in-Publication data
Stark, Andrew, 1956–.
  Drawing the line : public and private in America / Andrew Stark.
     p.   cm.
  Includes bibliographical references and index.
  ISBN 978-0-8157-0333-4 (alk. paper)
  1. Community development—United States. 2. Public-private sector cooperation—United States. 3. United States—Social policy. 4. Right of property—United States. 5. Government ownership—United States. I. Title.
  HN90.C6S72 2010
  320.60973—dc22   2009042013

9 8 7 6 5 4 3 2 1

Printed on acid-free paper

Typeset in Minion

Composition by Peter Lindeman
Arlington, Virginia

Printed by R. R. Donnelley
Harrisonburg, Virginia

For Rachel and Zoe

CONTENTS

WELFARE

ACKNOWLEDGMENTS

I am indebted to the Donner Canadian Foundation, the Social Sciences and Humanities Research Council of Canada, and the AIC Institute for Corporate Citizenship at the Rotman School of Management, University of Toronto, for their generous research support, and to Raha Bahreini and Frances Boquiren for their exceptionally able research assistance. Keith Banting, Peter Euben, Anne Fadiman, Nathan Glazer, Steve Lagerfeld, Tod Lindberg, Joshua Marshall, Jim Morris, Paul Starr, Philip Stenning, Michael Walzer, Joe White, and Adam Wolfson provided valuable comments on earlier versions of various chapters; Don Herzog and Mark Lilla read the entire manuscript, offered penetrating criticisms, and gave vital guidance. I am grateful to them all, as I am to Chris Kelaher of the Brookings Institution Press for his interest in and support for the project, and for shepherding the manuscript through the review process. My wife Deborah's sense of prose style, eye for a weak argument, and understanding of what really matters in a political issue are unsurpassed; the book is better in innumerable ways thanks to her impeccable judgment. It is dedicated, with love, to our daughters Rachel and Zoe.

Earlier versions of chapters appeared as follows: chapter 1 as "America, the Gated?" *Wilson Quarterly* (Winter 1998); chapter 2 as "Arresting Developments: When Police Power Goes Private," *The American Prospect* (January-February 1999); chapter 3 as "Forever—Or Not," *Wilson Quarterly* (Winter 2006); chapter 4 as "What's Wrong with Private Funding for Public Schools?" *Dissent*

(Winter 2001); chapter 5 as "Moving the Baseline: The Contradiction at the Core of Constitutional Discourse over State Aid to Parochial Schools," *William and Mary Law Review* (April 2001); chapter 6 as "Pizza Hut, Domino's and the Public Schools: Making Sense of Commercialization," *Policy Review* (August and September 2001); chapter 7 as "Getting the Health Care Debate Right," *The Public Interest* (Spring 2003); chapter 8 as "What's Natural?" *Wilson Quarterly* (Spring 2003); chapter 9 as "In Sickness and in Health: What to Do about Private Health Insurance in America," *Dissent* (Fall 2005); chapter 10 as "Morality Plays," *The American Scholar* (Winter 2000); and chapter 11 as "The Consensus School, Its Critics, and Welfare Policy: A Study of American Political Discourse," *Journal of Politics* (April 2009).

INTRODUCTION

State legislators sometimes say the most revealing things.

In October 2007 I interviewed Missouri representative Cynthia Davis, a conservative Republican from Jefferson City and a member of her state legislature's human services and welfare committee. My purpose was to sound out her views on Missouri's version of workfare—the idea that while someone is receiving welfare payments, she should be required to work, whether at a community service position or a private sector job subsidized by the welfare check.

Representative Davis, like most conservatives, is happy with workfare, which was introduced nationwide through the welfare reforms of 1996. She praises it for confronting welfare recipients with the same kind of stark private market reality that faces most of the rest of society, requiring them to expend effort for what they receive. "No longer is [welfare] a public entitlement, a handout," Davis told me approvingly, on which "participant[s] get something for nothing . . . they have to work just like anyone else if they are going to get anything. They get the satisfaction and sense of self-worth of knowing they can earn money and develop real work habits."

Yet seconds after taking this position, Representative Davis proceeded to undermine it. It would be "a mistake," she declared, "to view workfare as real work," or to think that the workfare participant somehow "earns what she is receiving." Real work provides "a paycheck for an employee who is performing a service that the private market values." The welfare recipient, however, is "getting the check from the public purse in the first place only because she is temporarily needy, not because she has been hired for a job. She can't be allowed to forget that. . . . We can't let workfare be seen as real work because that will encourage dependency . . . it [would be] insulting to those who have gone into the workplace to get real jobs."[1]

In virtually the same breath, then, Representative Davis describes workfare as an enterprise governed by the norms of the private market (recipients receive assistance only because they work for it, thus gaining the sense of self-worth that comes from supporting oneself) and those of the public sphere (recipients receive assistance only because they are needy and thus remain stigmatizingly dependent). This conceptual inconsistency, however, seems unavoidable for Davis, as long as she is going to advance what is a recognizably conservative position: that workfare should carry all the stringency of the private market sphere and all the stigma of a public program.

What is more, both these values, public and private, get turned right around by liberals seeking to make workfare less stigmatizing and less stringent. On the one hand, liberals insist that workfare be viewed as a full-fledged private market relationship. They do so to claim, for the participant, the dignity that comes from her being said to earn what she gets. As Democratic state senator Dale Miller of Ohio told me, workfare participants should be seen as "receiving a paycheck, not a welfare check—if anything, given the pitiful amount they're receiving, they are probably earning more than they're getting. They should [be accorded] the dignity of anyone who works at a job."

Seconds later, however, Senator Miller reversed himself. It is a "trap," he told me, "to view workfare as a job," because doing so "obscures the fact that the state must do much more to get the participant ready to get a real job" than she "could ever recompense" by the value of her work. Workfare is a "civic compact, not an employment contract," he emphasized, not a private market arrangement but a public sphere one based on the idea that the recipient cannot yet fend for herself. That is what obligates the state to furnish the child care, training, food aid, housing allowances, and transportation assistance that is necessary for the recipient to become a functioning citizen—and that no private market employer could be expected to supply.

Senator Miller thus struggles to depict the workfare participant as both a respectably self-supporting private market agent earning (if anything) more than she receives, and as a public sphere occupant whom the state is obligated to aid with whatever is necessary to render her independent, which is certainly much more than she could ever earn. However conceptually ill at ease these two ideas may be, at the political level they come together in a robust liberal position on workfare, in which we should afford as much private market dignity and extend as much public sphere generosity to the workfare participant as possible. But, as Senator Miller acknowledges, this liberal position embodies a conceptual "tension."[2]

A traditional understanding of the debate over workfare does not pick up these tensions. Instead, it casts liberals as the exclusive champions of the values of the public sphere: compassion, concern for others, redistribution according to need. It is those public sphere values alone on which liberals rely in arguing for as generous and unstigmatizing a workfare program as possible. Meanwhile, conservatives are portrayed as marshaling exclusively the values of the private market sphere: earn what you get, deserve what you earn, dignity of work. In the traditional view, it is by appealing only to those astringent private market values that conservatives argue for the virtues of a less generous and more stigmatizing program.[3]

But as I interviewed legislators and activists on both sides of the workfare issue, a different picture of the debate emerged. Each side, liberal and conservative, in fact draws equally and unstintingly on both public sphere and private market values to defend its position, dividing with the other over what policy course those values *together* imply—one that is more generous and less stigmatizing or one that is more stigmatizing and less generous. Liberals want to construe workfare as a regular private market contract to drain it of any capacity for creating stigma, but as a public sphere compact to ensure that it will be sufficiently generous to meet genuine needs. Conservatives, by contrast, want to locate workfare within the private market realm to require recipients to work for what they get—and instill the pride that comes from being self-supporting—and yet every bit as much in the public sphere, to remind recipients that they remain dependents on the state, with the hope that the resulting stigma will encourage them to get a real job.

It turns out that what is true of these debates over welfare is true too of a large number of intensely fought grass-roots American political battles over the border between the public and private realms, battles that I explore in the chapters that follow. These debates concern not just welfare but education, health care, and the use of space. They center on questions such as: Should parents be allowed to privately pay for extra teachers at their children's public schools? Should residents of private communities receive tax deductions from the public treasury for the homeowner dues they pay to build their own private roads or parks? Should the public treasury support private, faith-based welfare services? Should public police officers, moonlighting in a private security capacity, be permitted to wear their police uniforms while doing so?

When should public health insurance end, leaving families to rely instead on their own private resources to meet their health care needs? Should Medicaid, for example, pay for Viagra? Should we be concerned that more and more private individuals are getting a piece of public space—a building, a walkway, a bench, or even a brick—named after themselves in exchange for a financial contribution?

All of these debates, and many others that I examine, are typically portrayed as conflicts between one side championing the values of the public sphere, whether civic equality, communal obligation, or secular neutrality, and the other those of the private realm, whether market, family, or religion. In the following chapters, I refer to this kind of portrayal as "the traditional approach." But in each case, I argue, there is a deeper and more politically helpful way to view these conflicts. A closer look shows that each side asserts and relies coequally on both sets of values—on the exact same public and private values—but applies them in inverse or opposing ways. Some of the debates vary this theme along lines that I note, although the very fact that the theme emerges in these different variations underscores its persistence.

Such an understanding, I argue, can provide new ways of moving these debates forward. That is because often, one side or another—and sometimes both—in calling equally on public and private values, does so in a way that leads to an unsustainable contradiction. As Senator Miller conceded, for example, his position in the workfare debate is in "tension" with itself. So is Representative Davis's, which suggests the need for a rethink on both sides. And yet, because the two sides divide over the application of values that each side accepts, we might be able to find in those mutually accepted values a path to principled compromise. After all, both the liberal Senator Miller and the conservative Representative Davis, though at one level locked in debate over workfare's generosity and stigma, nevertheless seem agreed—at a more fundamental level—on how to describe workfare. Yes, workfare is "work," but it can also be a "trap" and a "mistake" to so view it. Are there grounds for building a consensus position, then, in the fact that both sides use almost exactly the same language, drawn equally from private market and public sphere norms, to frame and justify their views?

My claim here is different from other recent interpretations of American public debate. To take one example: Alan Wolfe argues that many Americans, because of the public and private values they consensually share, in fact come down in the middle, moderate position in most debates.[4] I maintain that such public and private values together actually sustain the polar positions in these debates, too, albeit in diametrically converse ways. At a moment when national politicians and commentators are searching for new ways of framing disagreement or forging consensus, the experiences of "Main Street" Americans can shed new light on this quest.

My interest lies in exploring *how* Americans argue when they use concepts of public and private to contend over welfare, health care, education, and space. It is not to explore *what* they argue about as a whole when they dispute approaches to welfare, health care, education, or space. For example, racial and gender issues—issues such as whether urban public education is sufficiently integrated, or whether the welfare system embodies gender stereotypes—are not my focus here; they have been well examined by others.

Within any given debate, *public* and *private* are to be understood in relative terms—by comparison with each other. For example, in the debate over workfare, as just discussed, *public* betokens "redistribution according to need," while *private* denotes the value of "earning what you get." And both sides, I argue, want to see workfare embody each value equally. But in the debate over parents raising private money for their own children's public schools, when participants make use of "public values," they mean "concern for the community as a whole," while "private norms" mean something more akin to "concern for one's own." And in the debate over barricading public streets against outside traffic and crime, to take a final example, *public* principally signifies "equality of treatment," while *private* connotes "property rights." Sometimes the public and private values being invoked are moral principles; at other times they are legal rules derived from each sphere, public and private; and on still other occasions they take the form of constitutional norms appropriate to each realm.

As Jeff Weintraub says, "Any notion of 'public' or 'private' makes sense only as one element in a paired opposition," and that is my orientation here. I agree with Weintraub when he goes on to say that "attempts to use the public/private distinction as a dichotomous model to capture the overall pattern of social life in a society . . . are always likely to be inherently misleading."[5]

Much of the analysis in what follows goes beyond the public record.[6] It also draws heavily on phone interviews I conducted with hundreds of officials and citizens around the country—police chiefs, welfare activists, HMO managers, state legislators, PTA presidents, homeowner association leaders, mayors, health insurance executives, school board trustees, church-based social service providers, state insurance commissioners—allowing me to explore their arguments in depth.

In some cases, as with debates involving gated communities, a particular set of localities stood out. In others—as with debates over workfare—the two sides were found pretty much everywhere. In some cases, the debate was joined and well documented. In others it was more diffuse or, absent a detailed public record, manifested itself more fully only as I interviewed people. I note as well that these debates, located as they are in disparate policy domains, deal with a range of subject matter: from the spiritual to the everyday, from the official to the intimate, from the quietly deliberative to the loudly emotional; and the textures of the different chapters reflect this. I confine myself throughout largely to the state and local level, because I wanted to explore diversity in debates across localities. But of course state and local policy is not hermetically sealed from national politics or federal programs, and so my interviewing and discussion reflect that fact.[7]

Earlier versions of several chapters were published as articles over the past ten years, some in liberal and social-democratic journals such as the *American Prospect* and *Dissent*, others in conservative journals like the *Public Interest* and *Policy Review*, and still others in journals of no fixed political address, such as the *Journal of Politics*, the *Wilson Quarterly*, and the *American Scholar*. Each of the chapters is a snapshot in time, covering events that are more or less recent. Consequently, David Kirp's observation of his work in *Almost Home* applies to my own work: "These pieces were written over the span of a decade. In some instances, factual material has been updated, but the core meanings of these stories remain unchanged."[8] Their core message is that many a grassroots policy debate is shaped not so much by the line dividing public and private values as by a line cleaving two inverse interpretations of those same jointly held public and private values. And that has consequences for how we might move these debates forward in a new direction.

SPACE

1

AMERICA, THE GATED?

The Los Angeles suburb of Hidden Hills, a handful of Mediterranean-
and ranch-style mansions scattered amid rolling, lightly wooded hills fifteen
miles inland from Malibu, boasts one of the highest incomes per capita of any
community in California. It is the kind of place where live-in gardeners and
six-car garages are taken for granted and where bridle paths outnumber streets.
The community is home to fabulously successful business executives and pro-
fessionals as well as a curious collection of aging pop stars: Frankie Avalon, Neil
Diamond, Tony Orlando, and John Davidson. It is also one of the nation's
oldest gated communities, part of the vanguard of what has become a controversial national trend.

In 1961, however, ten years into its existence as a private enclave, Hidden
Hills took a step that moved it well to the front of the vanguard. Even though,
like other gated communities, it had a thriving, well-managed private homeowners association that oversaw many of its affairs, Hidden Hills incorporated
itself as a full-fledged city but left its gates and private homeowners association
in place. Ever since, Hidden Hills has been a city with two governments, one
private, one public. "It is odd," says Fred Gaines, a lawyer from nearby Wood-
land Hills, "to have an entire city that's gated."[1]

Odder still is the way in which the two governments have divided their
powers. In Hidden Hills, the city government, the public entity, carries out
building inspections, provides security, issues licenses, and sponsors some

9

adult education programs, funding them all through property tax revenues; it also manages the local trash collection franchise. These are precisely the kinds of services that governments around the country, after decades of nagging by economists, are now rushing to fund through user fees or to privatize entirely. Meanwhile, the Hidden Hills homeowners association is very busy with other matters. In Hidden Hills, this private government controls the community's quintessentially public spaces and events—its parks, its roads and horse trails, even its annual Fourth of July parade.

There is one more oddity, perhaps the crowning one. In 1995, after thirty-four years of sharing a sleek wood-and-glass low-rise on Long Valley Road in the center of town, the two governments split up. Hidden Hills' public government moved to a renovated slate-roofed garage on Spring Valley Road, just twenty-five feet inside one of the community's three gates. Then the homeowners association moved the gate. Today, the city hall of Hidden Hills stands seventy-five feet outside the town's own gates.

There is method to Hidden Hills' various madnesses. Consider, first, the advantage the town derives by publicly providing an array of easily privatized services. Residents can claim their property tax payments as deductions on their federal and state income tax returns. If these services were funded out of private homeowner dues, however, they would not get the same deductions.

It is not only the rich who have discovered the benefits of this arrangement. The few other private communities that have managed to replicate Hidden Hills' twin-governments trick have embraced the same financial logic. In suburban Pittsburgh, a 500-unit middle-class townhouse community called Pennsbury Village became, in 1977, the only private condominium complex in the United States ever to form its own municipality. After the bitterly litigated separation agreement with the local township was signed, borough manager Irv Foreman recalls, "We sat down, the condo association and the municipality, to divvy up powers, and for tax reasons we gave everything we might otherwise have purchased privately, such as trash collection, sewer, water, and animal control, to the municipality, to the public government."[2]

All this seems clear enough. But why, we might ask, has Hidden Hills placed its most public functions, including the Fourth of July parade, in the hands of its private government? Because if these things were furnished by the public government, paid for out of tax-deductible property taxes, they would have to remain open to all. They would have to be public, because, through the deductions, every American taxpayer would be contributing to their support. That would be anathema to the residents of this very exclusive private community.

There is only one public space that Hidden Hills could not privatize, could not fund and operate through its private government: city hall, the seat of its public government, an ineradicably public place where anyone from anywhere can legally demand to go. That is why it had to be moved outside the city's gates. "If people could get into town just by saying, 'We're going to city hall,'" explained city attorney Amanda Susskind, "then the residents of Hidden Hills could have no security."[3]

Hidden Hills' municipal building stands as an ironic counterpoint to a much better known town hall on the other side of the continent. There, in its model town of Celebration, Florida, the Disney Corporation has erected a splendid Philip Johnson–designed town hall smack in the middle of the community. But Celebration is a private community, with no intention of incorporating as a municipality. Its impressive town hall, as critics have pointed out, is nothing more than an architectural bauble; totally without political function, it serves as the administrative base for the private homeowners association. Both cases suggest that public buildings will find a place in private communities only if no public business is conducted in them.

Curious as it is, Hidden Hills may be pointing the way to some of the more fundamental dilemmas and conflicts of the American future. Americans today are caught in an array of forces pushing, at the grass-roots level, to redraw the boundary between public and private spaces. Gated communities are only the most obvious example. Public-private boundaries are also being redrawn in tens of thousands of ungated communities—planned developments, condominiums, cooperatives—managed by various kinds of private governments grouped under the rubric *homeowners associations*. Ill-equipped to form their own public governments Hidden Hills-style, many of these communities have begun demanding tax-deductible status for their private homeowner dues. They argue that they are privately shouldering an array of traditionally public sanitation, security, transportation, and recreation responsibilities— assuming burdens that municipal governments bore before the age of retrenchment.

Public-private borders are also being shifted in hundreds of poor and middle-class city neighborhoods, where aroused residents fighting crime, traffic, and blight are demanding to have their public streets barricaded or gated against drug dealers and other outsiders. Unable to totally privatize their streets, as Hidden Hills has done, they seek barriers that would impede public access without wholly prohibiting it. These efforts have provoked bitter debates. "Whose streets are these, anyway?" critics ask. And in more than a thousand American towns and cities, private downtown property owners have banded together to form business improvement districts (BIDs), paying for and providing street cleaning, landscaping, security, and other services that were once the exclusive province of municipal governments.

Each of these trends grows out of eminently defensible political concerns. But each also raises difficult practical and philosophical questions about the public-private border. BIDs, for example, are in many ways an impressive response to the failings and financial straits of municipal governments. Many BIDs have worked wonders, rescuing entire urban cores from decay and bringing public streets back to life. Unlike the residential neighborhoods that seek gates and barricades on public streets, BIDs welcome the public—paying customers—to their domain. And unlike private residential communities, from which they have learned a lesson, BIDs insist that municipalities continue to provide a full complement of services, supplementing them with their own efforts rather than replacing them. But in preventing city governments from shifting scarce resources to needier neighborhoods, BIDs combine private advantage with their share of the public weal to make themselves privileged zones.

In key ways, today's border wars are confounding traditional political ideologies and coalitions. Among those leading the charge to allow residents of private communities to write off their homeowners association dues as income tax deductions, for example, are liberal Democrats, who see granting such tax breaks as a way of emphasizing that building parks and maintaining roads, two functions of the associations, are really public responsibilities. Among those most fiercely opposed to gating public streets are staunch libertarians, many of them local Republican politicos. They view public street barriers as infringements on their personal freedom.

Until now, most media and scholarly attention has focused on the rise of gated communities—"privatopias" that are said to herald a future "fortress America" in which the private simply secedes from the public.[4] These are cogent critiques, but a more complex reality is being forged by ungated private communities seeking quasi-public status for their expenditures, by public neighborhoods seeking quasi-private status for their spaces, and by business improvement districts seeking a role for the private in the midst of robust public expenditures *and* public spaces.

BOOSTING PRIVATE COMMUNITIES

One of the stormier of these contemporary public-private border debates concerns whether residents of private communities should be allowed to deduct their homeowners association dues from their federal and state income taxes.

Around sixty million Americans live in such private communities, and their numbers are rapidly growing (at least seven million of these people live in gated communities).[5] Currently, residents are barred from deducting their association dues, as Yale law professor Robert Ellickson explains, "because it is assumed that the value of the association services they receive equals the value of the assessments they pay."[6] Tax deductions are usually available only in situations in which there is no necessary equality between what one pays and the benefit one personally receives. Deductible expenditures have a public purpose or a redistributionist or altruistic cast. And until recently, it has generally been assumed that there is nothing altruistic or public spirited about paying for your own amenities through a private homeowners association.

But private communities have been challenging that view. In 1990 Robert Figeira, executive director of Woodbridge Village in Irvine, California—with 9,300 households, then the nation's second-largest private community—made the case for deductions in his testimony before a California State Assembly committee: "We have open space areas . . . parks, roads, bicycle trails, [and] recreation programs," Figeira told the committee. "We believe half of the people that enjoy [them] are from outside. . . . We maintain the lake and yet the people that live there get no credit for it. It's just, again, part of their association dues, yet it's all open to the public." Assemblyman Gil Ferguson, a southern California Republican, drove home the point. "And you might explain to the committee that not one penny of that is deductible," he said. "Not one penny, not one," Figeira agreed.[7]

In its report the committee endorsed the notion that residents of private communities—the majority of them ungated in California—are indeed "private[ly] maintain[ing] a number of essentially public facilities."[8] The legislature never acted. The argument, however, is certainly not implausible, and it continues to be a political lightning rod. "The politician who manages to capture this constituency, speak to its needs, and offer it a voice will be amply rewarded," says Robyn Boyer Stewart, president of Common Interest Advocates, the California lobbying group for private communities.[9]

A self-described "Zen soldier" who carefully evokes her past association with progressive causes, Stewart offers a liberalism-tinged defense of tax-deductible homeowner dues. "By placing severe limits on government's capacity to raise property taxes" when it was passed in 1978, Stewart says, California's Proposition 13 "made it impossible for local governments to continue providing the basic kinds of public services they always had, and so they foisted the responsibility on new developments to privately maintain an array of new roads, parks, streetlights, medians, recreation facilities, all of which [where the community remains ungated] the general public uses." Many private communities in fact "don't want to be doing this," Stewart adds, "but they have had to because government is now so constrained in its capacity to provide services that broadly benefit the public."

What particularly galls liberals on Stewart's side of the issue was the sight, all through the 1980s, of California's municipal governments insisting that their revenue initiatives were less like taxes than private assessments. Proposition 13 contained a loophole (closed by Proposition 218 in 1996) that allowed cities to raise money more easily if they could show that the levy was not a tax—defined as a revenue initiative devoted to broader public purposes—but a "benefit assessment," designed specifically to improve the private property values of those paying. But if California's public governments had come to protest that their main purpose was to look after private interests, while its private homeowners associations had begun claiming to pursue the public interest, it is easy to see why Stewart and other liberals might find themselves on the private side of the divide.

The drive to make private homeowner dues deductible would seem to run into obstacles when gated private communities try to join in. In a very few gated communities (and Hidden Hills happens to be one), private homeowner dues are apportioned on the basis of property values, much like deductible property taxes. In effect, this means that some kind of redistribution is going on behind the gates. Those with $5 million estates, for example, are subsidizing the capacity of their poorer neighbors, those living in $2 million homes, to enjoy the private equestrian trail. And this leads some residents in gated communities, even in Hidden Hills, to claim that their homeowner dues ought to be deductible.

In the vast majority of gated communities, however, each property owner pays an equal amount to maintain the common spaces, and no internal redistribution takes place. Instead, to justify deductibility residents of these communities must argue that their private expenditures somehow benefit the public beyond the gates. To see how they might do so, consider the dissenting opinion advanced by Judge Hiram Emery Widener Jr., a conservative Nixon appointee, in a 1989 tax case involving Flat Top Lake Association, whose members live in a gated, lakeside, white-collar community near Beckley, West Virginia.

The private dues paid by Flat Top's homeowners "do benefit the public," Judge Widener contended, because they protect "the public purse by performing activities which the taxpayer would otherwise have had to pay for."[10] In other words, a single mother in nearby Beckley benefits from Flat Top's artificial lake, even though she cannot swim in it, because had Flat Top not been a private, gated community—had it been a development reliant on public infrastructure—she and other taxpayers would have had to help pay for it. By Judge Widener's logic, the very fact that the lake is private is a public benefit: a gift (hence deductible) from Flat Top homeowners to the Beckley public. The rest of the court, however, found this argument a bit too metaphysical for its taste.

As in most other things, California is the cutting edge of the movement to make the dues paid by private homeowners deductible. This is not surprising, since these particular homeowners have the most to gain. Homeowner dues are comparatively high in California, partly because the state encompasses America's wealthiest homeowners associations but also because its private communities have all had to make up for the effects of Proposition 13. Elsewhere, though, private dues are lower and property taxes higher. In states such as Connecticut, Maryland, and New Jersey, residents of private communities have been trying to win rebates of city or county property taxes instead of seeking deductions for their dues on their state and federal income taxes.

Like the western case for tax deductions, the eastern brief for tax rebates displays a certain cogency within bounds—especially when the community seeking them is not gated. Consider the argument for rebates advanced by Benjamin Lambert, an attorney whose firm has represented about forty New Jersey private homeowners associations: "Almost all municipal governments still tax local private community residents for whatever public services the municipality provides, whether it be trash collection, snow removal, hydrant repair, sewer maintenance, or street lighting. But many municipalities don't supply those services to private communities, because private communities, through their homeowner dues, already provide them for themselves."[11] Hence, Lambert concludes, "private community residents have been paying twice—through their dues and through their taxes—for services they get only once."[12]

According to Doug Kleine, former head of the research arm of the Community Associations Institute (CAI), the national umbrella organization for private homeowners associations, rebaters believe that "the purpose of government is to give you back everything in services that you give it in payments, not to take your money and use it for the benefit of others."[13]

In the mid-1980s Lambert and like-minded colleagues began asking New Jersey municipalities to rebate some fraction of property taxes to dues-paying private community homeowners. Things did not go well at first. The effort stirred opposition in a surprising quarter. Just as the cause of private communities found unexpected liberal support in California, so in New Jersey it stirred the opposition of conservatives. The voters of Mount Laurel, the town made famous by its twenty-year fight against court orders requiring it to support low-income housing, rejected a mid-1980s referendum proposing rebates for the area's private communities. The United Taxpayers of New Jersey, a leading organization in the tax revolt that brought Governor Christine Whitman to power, also opposed rebates, which it saw as giveaways for the few instead of tax relief for the many.

Nevertheless, New Jersey's private homeowners associations pressed on and in 1990 pushed the Municipal Services Act through the state legislature. Under its provisions, those who pay homeowners association dues now get rebates on the property taxes they pay to support municipal trash collection, snow removal, and street lighting. In its first year, the act cost New Jersey's municipalities some $62 million.

The rebate movement has not stopped there. The next step, says David Ramsey, former president of the New Jersey chapter of CAI, is for private communities to obtain rebates for the taxes they pay to maintain public roads, on the analogous grounds that they are already maintaining their own private roads. I asked Ramsey if there wasn't an important difference. After all, those who pay for their own trash removal don't use the public system, and so arguably should not have to pay for it. But those who pay for their own private residential roads still have to drive on public roads. Shouldn't they have to pay at least some property taxes for public road maintenance?[14]

"No," Ramsey said. "Private community residents may use public roads, but remember too that the general public can use most private roads, any that remain ungated. And since the general public doesn't pay even a cent toward the maintenance of any of the private roads they are able to use, there's no reason why private community residents should pay for the maintenance of the public roads they use." Rebates, Ramsey says, would simply "even the score."[15]

Whether that is true depends on whether the public actually uses private community roads as much as community residents use public roads. In some New Jersey locales where private community residents make up close to half the population, Ramsey's argument begins to acquire a certain plausibility. Where the demand for rebates becomes distinctly less plausible, however, is precisely where the quest for tax deductions gets shaky: where gated private communities try to get in on the act.

Consider, for example, the argument Maryland attorney Steve Silverman advances in favor of granting residents of gated communities rebates on the taxes they pay to maintain public roads. True, acknowledges Silverman, who represents homeowners associations in the Washington, D.C., area, the general public cannot use gated private roads. But then again, residents of private communities actually never use most public roads, he claims, because the majority of these roads are not major thoroughfares but neighborhood crescents and cul-de-sacs.

"Most people tend to use the neighborhood streets where they live," Silverman says. "You're not going to drive on someone else's public street unless you're going to visit them. In which case they've invited you, so they should pay for your use of the public road in front of their place, just as, when you invite someone to visit you in your gated community, you pay for whatever wear and tear they inflict on your road."[16]

Though the gated community resident may actually be the one driving along those public roads, Silverman in effect claims, it is really others—those whom that resident visits, buys from, works for—who are the beneficiaries, and they are the ones who should pay the freight. On this argument, however, a nation of citizens and publics risks becoming a nation of hosts and guests.

There is a striking resemblance between Silverman's argument for rebates and Judge Widener's case for deductions. In Silverman's argument, a resident of a gated community does not benefit from a public road even though he drives on it; in Widener's argument, a member of the outside public somehow benefits from a gated private lake even though she cannot swim in it. Because each case for tax breaks so radically severs the notion of personal use from personal benefit, neither cuts much ice. The arguments ungated private communities mount for deductions and those they assert for rebates, however, are each at least plausible when taken separately. The problem with them is that each argument undermines the other.

In essence, the Californians are saying that their homeowner dues underwrite services that benefit many others beyond themselves. Hence the altruistic tenor of deduction talk: we are providing public services well in excess of our own personal benefit, they say, and thus deserve tax deductions. What the eastern-based rebate advocates find outrageous, by contrast, is precisely that their property taxes do underwrite services that benefit others. Rebate talk has a distinctly self-interested twang: residents should get back any amount that goes beyond what they receive. You get rebates when you act as a consumer in the private market sphere and overpay for the value you get, not when you act as a citizen—a taxpayer in the public realm—where even if you do not use a service, you can legitimately be called upon to underwrite it.

This ambiguity allows public governments—municipalities—a couple of strong ripostes to private community complaints. Suppose, as California private communities argue, that their private homeowner dues should be understood as altruistic, intended to purchase municipal services that in part benefit others. Then surely one's public tax payments must be so understood—in which case, what is the justification for the New Jersey rebate? Alternatively, suppose, as New Jersey private communities argue, that their public tax payments should be understood as self-interested private-market-style user fees for road repair and park maintenance, whereby one properly pays for no more than one gets. Then clearly one's private dues should be so understood—in which case, why should those dues, as Californians demand, be made deductible?

Conflicts between private communities and public governments, as they get reported in the press or portrayed by social critics, are traditionally depicted as straightforward incursions by the private realm into the public realm. They are represented as incursions of private homeowner associations, staking their claim on the private market right to look out for one's own and get what one pays for, into the public realm, with the one-for-all-and-all-for-one obligations it struggles to defend.[17]

But at another level, the private community movement relies equally on public sphere and private market values—values that are in tension with one another—and hence, to borrow Sandra Day O'Connor's famous description of *Roe* v. *Wade*, it is on a collision course with itself. Stewart of California's Common Interest Advocates views the eastern rebaters as dangerously "secessionist"; Jeff Olson, a California private community manager and supporter of tax deductions, told me he doubts that the rebate drive can get off the ground.[18] New Jersey rebater Ramsey takes the same view of the West Coast deduction forces. As they assemble their debating points, private community leaders have yet to make up their minds about some of the most basic questions a community can ask itself: Are the vital, commonplace acts of purchasing trash collection, parks, roads, and sewage services ones we undertake in our public or in our private roles? Do we perform them as citizens who have shouldered the broader public purposes of government, or as consumers who need look out only for ourselves?

BARRICADING PUBLIC ROADS

Gates are appearing not only on the streets of exclusive private enclaves such as Hidden Hills. All over the country local residents are seeking to gate the public streets they live on, hoping to keep out gangs, drug dealers, traffic, and litter.[19] Nobody knows how many public streets have been restricted, but every year residents on thousands of public streets reportedly seek such controls.

There are important differences between barriers on public streets and those on private streets. Private gates enforce both inequality and exclusivity. They not only distinguish between insiders and outsiders but completely bar the outsiders. Barriers on public roads, by contrast, perform only one or the other function. In one common model, a gate or guardhouse allows local residents to pass through unimpeded while requiring nonresidents to explain themselves to a guard or else be photographed by a camera mounted on the gate. There is unequal treatment but no exclusivity. "In the final analysis," according to Tom Benton, manager of Miami Shores Village, a mostly Anglo upper-middle-class community of 2,500 households on the northern edge of Miami, "gates and guards will slow you up, but if you want to proceed, no one can stop you from going on a public street."[20]

The alternative to the gate is the barricade: a string of orange cans, a line of concrete cylinders, or a row of shrubs placed at the mouth of a public street, requiring the general public and residents alike to take a detour. This is the approach favored by Miami Shores, where Spanish-style mansions on Biscayne Bay give way by degrees to less exalted dwellings. Feeling threatened by rising crime, the community bankrolled professionally designed landscape plantings to close off several streets connecting it to some poor neighborhoods to the west. Barricades are exclusive; they block entry. But they are also egalitarian, blind to the difference between residents and the public at large. Indeed, they often work their greatest hardship on residents. In Oak Forest, an affluent suburb north of Miami, a barricade separated William Matthews's front door and his garage, requiring the 84-year-old retired restaurateur to drive a half mile to park his car after dropping off his groceries.

Each of these methods of limiting access to public streets thus manages to avoid one of the two most maligned features of private gates. Each offers a legally acceptable method of taking public streets some distance toward the private. Each has gained a certain measure of popularity in Dade County, Florida, where many of the twenty-eight municipalities, including Miami, not only continue the upkeep of public streets that have been restricted but have actually helped finance the construction of gates and barricades. In Dade the most powerful argument in favor of such barriers on public streets has been a kind of egalitarian one. "Why should the protection that gates provide from crime and traffic be available only for those who can afford private communities?" asks Silvia Unzueta, a local pro-barrier leader.[21]

Unzueta and others have been seeking barricades on the older, grid-patterned streets in the poorer north end of Coral Gables, a town of 42,000 immediately west of Miami. They point out that residents in the newer and wealthier south end live largely on cul-de-sacs, which afford much the same kind of security as barricades. "Why should others be denied these basic public goods simply because of an inability to pay?" Unzueta asks. It is a theme that comes up repeatedly in pro-barrier arguments.

The notion that there are certain goods that government ought to provide more or less equally to all—health care, perhaps, or education, or police protection—grows a little forced when the list expands to include street barriers, the ultimate socially divisive mechanism. Many barrier opponents hold that barriers are less like education than they are like Cadillacs and caviar, market commodities that government has no obligation to provide. Monique Taylor, a property owner living just outside Miami Shores, represents a brandnew hybrid in local politics. She has absolutely no problem with private gated communities. "What people do with their own property is their own business," she says. Yet Taylor is fiercely opposed to the gating and barricading of public streets, and for much the same reason: what people do with their property is their own business, and the public streets belong to everyone. "I have a right to drive my preferred route,'" Taylor told me. "Barriers impinge on my freedom of travel, forcing me to go where I don't want to go."[22]

Taylor's argument is echoed by other barrier opponents. Mike van Dyk, a Dade County Republican activist, is head of a private community homeowners rights group and a leading local opponent of barriers on public streets. "I pay for those streets," van Dyk told me. "I don't like someone telling me I can't go on public property."[23] Some barrier opponents, in a strange twist on a popular libertarian argument, have even spoken of public street barricades as a kind of "taking," in which the state—simply by allowing the barriers—unconstitutionally deprives citizens of their property rights, albeit their rights to public rather than private property.[24]

Barrier advocates scoff at the idea that there are any great principles at stake. "What's all the fuss? So you can't always take your chosen route to get somewhere," says Randall Atlas, a safety and security consultant who has studied the impact of barriers in some Dade municipalities and believes that they reduce crime. "You might, heaven forbid, have to go on a crowded street or around the block.... It's about convenience, not freedom."[25]

Like many barrier advocates, Atlas depicts his opponents as efficiency-driven neurotics who would be better off if they occasionally stopped and smelled the roses. This is an interesting critique, since barrier advocates just as often portray their foes in precisely the opposite terms: as aimless wanderers who have nothing better to do than drive through other people's neighborhoods. "There are always oddball people coming in," complains Carol Pelly, a barrier advocate in Thousand Oaks, California, "and they don't have any purpose here."[26] A "big pastime" in Addison, Texas, says local realtor Mickey Munir, "is going out just gawking at [other people's] houses. People [who want barricades] just don't want gawkers looking at their houses, that's all."[27]

Ironically, the debate over public street barriers inverts the terms of the controversy over private gated communities. That controversy typically pits egalitarian gate critics against freedom-loving gaters, who cite their rights to do whatever they want with their own private property. On the public streets, however, the egalitarians favor gates and the more libertarian-minded oppose them.

Indeed, the egalitarian argument used to defend gating on the most modest of public streets can be turned around to attack gates at the ritziest of private enclaves. Several communities in suburban Dallas—Addison, Plano, Richardson, and Southlake—have shown how.[28] All four towns at one time or another decided to ban barriers on public roads, believing that they project the image of a divided city. But the towns went further. They also effectively banned or placed moratoriums on the construction of gated private communities. If residents on public roads are going to have to do without barriers, the towns concluded, it would be unfair to allow them in private communities. "I am offended," Addison city manager Carmen Moran told me, "by the concept that some should take for themselves security that others don't have."[29] To be an egalitarian might dispose one to insist on gates for public streets, as it does Silvia Unzueta. But it can just as easily impel one to attack the gates erected by private communities, as it does Carmen Moran.

On a traditional understanding, the clash between gating advocates and opponents is a straightforward battle between the forces of privatization and the defenders of the public realm. Whether the streets are in public or private communities, to gate or barricade them—to inhibit what would otherwise be free public access—is to bring them a good distance into the private domain.

But at a deeper level, each side in fact rests its case equally on the assertion of both private market and public sphere values: the private market value of property rights, and the public sphere value of civic equality. Silvia Unzueta supports gating across the board because she applies a property rights norm to private streets—residents of private communities should be able to do what they want with their own property, including gating it—but a civic equality approach to public streets—if private communities are allowed to gate, then less-well-off public neighborhoods should be enabled to do so as well.

Carmen Moran, by contrast, opposes both forms of gating, because she applies a property rights norm to public streets—public streets are owned by everyone and gating them is a form of taking—and then turns around and asserts a civic equality norm for private streets: private community residents should not be treated as first-class citizens, and so if public street residents are not allowed to gate, private community residents should not be either.

Understood in this way, each side appeals equally to two basic sets of values that are clearly divergent: the private market value of property rights (the right to do with one's possessions as one pleases), and the public sphere value of civic equality (the idea that those who are less able should be brought to a plane of equality with those who are more so). Where they differ, often passionately and sometimes bitterly, is over how to pair these two values with private streets and public roads.

In debates in which one side is seen as advancing only public sphere values and the other exclusively private market values—that is, in many debates as they are traditionally understood—any grounds for compromise would have to embrace—pay due homage to—both sets of values, public and private. But in the debate over gating, the reverse is the case. Each side rests its arguments equally on values drawn from both the public sphere (civic equality) and the private market realm (property rights). Accordingly, any compromise position would rest on only one of those two values, whether the public or the private, bringing together each side's usage of it. The position taken by Monique Taylor and Mike van Dyk represents such a compromise. Resting solely on the private market value of property rights that both sides—Silvia Unzueta's and Carmen Moran's—share, it splits the difference by holding that gates should be permitted on private but not on public roads. It is no surprise that this third force has emerged in the gating wars.

BUSINESS IMPROVEMENT DISTRICTS

In a mid-1990s essay on community spirit in America, *Time* editor Richard Stengel claimed that neither "gated suburbs [nor] business improvement districts" could be "considered salutary for the republic." Both, Stengel noted, "represent the secession of a smaller, more privileged community from the larger one." Each is "in some respects driven by fear." Neither, he said, is all that different from the "recently arrested Viper militia in Arizona."[30]

Three weeks later, *Time* published an angry response from Andrew Heiskell, the magazine's former editor in chief and a former board member of New York's Bryant Park Restoration Corporation, a BID. Heiskell did not take the Viper militia comparison particularly well. Noting that Bryant Park itself had been rescued from a reign of drug dealers and vagrants and restored to its long-forgotten status as a lively six-acre oasis in midtown Manhattan, he wrote that the "major BIDs in the New York area have vastly improved the quality of life" there.[31] Indeed, BIDs around the country can boast an impressive record of achievement: crime down 53 percent in the area served by Central Houston, Inc., and linear feet of graffiti down 82 percent in Philadelphia's Center City District.[32]

Some of the districts have been so successful that their managers suspect local politicians of BID envy. At a meeting some years ago of BID directors, recalls Terry Miller, former chief financial officer for the Association for Portland Progress, in Oregon, "several of the most well-established and powerful directors acknowledged nascent tensions caused by mayors' suspicions that they [the BID directors] somehow wanted to be mayor themselves."[33]

To hear some BID managers talk, Stengel missed the mark as badly in comparing BIDs to gated communities as he did in comparing them to the Viper militia. "I don't like gated communities," Philadelphia BID director Paul Levy told me. "Private, gated communities want to keep people out; BIDs want to welcome them in," he says. "Gated communities are devoted to private spaces; BIDs are dedicated to the improvement of public spaces."[34]

True enough. But there is another and more important difference. The great fear BID founders had, Levy says, is that once their new organizations started to provide their own private security, street cleaning, and trash removal, municipal governments would begin withdrawing public services from the downtown, much as they have done in private residential communities. So nearly every BID in America negotiates a "baseline service" agreement with its city government, obliging the municipality to maintain the level of services it would have deployed regardless of how much extra the BID is able to provide privately. If the BID is paying for ten private security agents, this is understood to be in addition to the forty police officers the city would furnish anyway. Clearly this arrangement serves the interest of property owners, but it is also intended to ensure that they retain a stake in the public system and have no incentive to agitate for tax rebates. After all, as Times Square BID director Gretchen Dykstra says, the districts "continue to get their money's worth from the city."[35]

It is possible, BIDs seem to be saying, for a private government to lightly overlay an undiminished public sphere, a sphere of fully accessible public space and full-service public government, enhancing public life at no cost to the community. In this way, BIDs are different from restricted public streets and private communities that seek tax rebates.

Or at least in theory. In 1994 John Dyson, then New York's deputy mayor for finance and economic development, called on the city council to rebate a portion of property taxes to dues-paying BID businesses. Dyson's proposal didn't go anywhere. It would have cost the city $7.5 million annually, which even Dyson acknowledged it could ill afford. But the very fact that he could have made such a suggestion (and that some BID managers nodded in agreement when he did, as one told me) suggests that the baseline principle might not hold. For if a BID is sweeping its own sidewalks every two hours, what is really left for the city to do? If it fills its own potholes, scrubs its own graffiti, or reduces its own crime, what added value do the city department of public works and other municipal service agencies provide? And after a while, won't hard-pressed cities feel an irresistible urge to reduce services in areas where BIDs are flourishing? "I don't buy the baseline," New York city councilman Andrew Eristoff told me. "BID businesses are going to start asking 'What are we paying our taxes for?'"[36] "The baseline," says Dave Fogarty, coordinator of a BID project in Berkeley, California, is a "myth."[37]

But if the baseline is a myth, it is a double-edged one. While cities might sometimes trim services or fail to provide value for tax dollars within BID perimeters, they can also wind up putting even more resources into a BID than the area would have received had the district never been formed. Center City District, Philadelphia's BID, provides any municipal constable patrolling the area with free use of a radio, TV camera, pager, and other amenities. It also built a storefront police substation, on the principle of "If you build it, they will come." And they did: the Philadelphia Police Department began deploying thirty officers over and above what the Center City baseline required.[38]

There are other examples. Instead of paying for its own private graffiti removal, a prototype BID in San Francisco established a "graffiti hotline," which regularly contacts the public graffiti removal service to have freshly spray-painted scrawls and screeds removed. Public service to the area has "improved immensely," says a pleased Jim Flood, a local property owner and BID activist, because "nobody else is calling" the removal service.[39] BIDs were meant to use their wealth to supplement city services, but many are actually using it to become more adroit consumers of those services. "In my mind," Randall Gregson, director of the New Orleans Downtown Development District told me, "I am always trying to draw the line between what the BID should do and what the city should do."[40]

And understandably so, for if the BID experience offers one clear lesson thus far, it is that the notion that these private governments can lightly overlay the city's public government, each abiding peacefully by the baseline, is something of a chimera. Private government has a tendency either to repel or attract public government. It is not neutral. Either the businesspeople who belong to the BID will begin agitating for rebates, because they are getting a lower level of public services than they should, or critics outside the BID will start attacking it, because it is enjoying a higher level of public services than it should.

But BIDs go beyond bringing a measure of instability to the relationship between private government and public government. They might actually lead the two to change places entirely.

For more than a century, judges have prohibited municipal governments from taxing or otherwise assessing federal government properties such as federal courthouses, post offices, and passport bureaus, for the street-cleaning, snow-removal, and other services that municipalities provide for these properties. The reason is that federal revenues must not be siphoned off to public purposes set by other levels of government. The question, though, is: What if those municipal services are provided by a BID?

BIDs raise similar questions for nonprofit organizations. Though they generally pay no municipal taxes, many hospitals and churches have begun making voluntary contributions to local BIDs. And when they don't, says BID consultant Larry Houstoun, the BID in certain cases should consider "taking them to court to challenge their nonprofit status."[41] Thus BIDs, business-controlled enterprises that enjoy nonprofit status, may find themselves in court energetically trying to depict other nonprofits as businesses.

As for BIDs' relationship with federal-government properties within their perimeters, David Barram, then administrator of the U.S. General Services Administration, the agency that manages all federal nonmilitary property, declared in early 1996 that the federal government would not pay anything to BIDs. By September of that year, however, after some vigorous internal debate (which revealed that federal managers in some cities were already contributing to BIDs), Barram reversed himself, announcing that the federal government would begin negotiating payment schedules.

If Barram found himself torn between these two different positions, it was understandable. Bob Jones, a member of the federal Empowerment Zone Task Force involved in helping to launch the District of Columbia's first BID, expected that critics might well claim that federal payments to BIDs "quack like a local property tax" and ought to be prohibited. Jones, though, had a reply. Federal payments to BIDs are less akin to taxes than they are to user fees for services. And, Jones says, government properties "pay private firms to fix our sidewalks or pick up our trash all the time."[42]

But if the BID is a private business taking fees for services rendered, don't federal regulations require the government to go through a process of competitive bidding? This problem initially caused concern for federal officials. What resolved it was the recognition that BIDs have no private competitors.

Municipal governments, in effect, grant BIDs local monopolies to provide certain kinds of services. Furthermore, BIDs do not generally charge property owners fee-like amounts commensurate with the services they render. Instead, they assess properties on the basis of their size or value. But doesn't that take us right back to square one, where BIDs once again look more like tax-levying public governments than fee-collecting businesses?

Business improvement districts traditionally get attacked as dangerous (or defended as welcome) encroachments of the private onto the public realm. And they do represent such an encroachment, but underlying both the attack and the defense is a simultaneous description of the BID's relationship with government as both a private market one and a public sphere one. For BID defenders, viewing the transaction through public lenses allows it to escape the requirement of competition; viewing it through private lenses allows it to evade the charge of violating sovereignty. For BID critics, the public framing delegitimizes the arrangement as an illegal tax, while the private framing delegitimizes it as a noncompetitive procurement contract. Government's payments to BIDs are like a vibrating cord alternating faster than the eye can see between public and private, never firmly fixed in one realm or the other.

THE LURE OF HIDDEN HILLS

Decades ago, Hidden Hills achieved for itself the best of both worlds by securing tax support for whatever it chose to fund through its public government and total exclusivity for whatever it assigned to its private government. That tidy division is impossible for the vast majority of private communities, which provide their own municipal services but cannot form their own public governments. Nor is it a possibility for the vast majority of public neighborhoods that would like to exclude outsiders but cannot completely privatize their streets. And such a tidy division is not even a desire of BIDs, which say they want to carve out a role for private government in the midst of a vibrant public sphere, neither supplanting the existing public government's provision of municipal services nor excluding the public.

As Americans involved in each of these movements grope toward the promised land represented by Hidden Hills, trying after their own fashion to wring the best from both private and public, they find themselves having to navigate a daunting set of private-public contradictions and conundrums. At one and the same time, private homeowner associations classify their purchase of basic municipal services as a private market act that justifies a tax rebate and a public-spirited act that merits a tax deduction. Residents seeking to barricade public streets argue that the private realm values of property rights justify gating on private streets and that the public realm values of civic equity should therefore require cities to pay for barricades on public streets. And BIDs, at one and the same time, must characterize the payments they get from federal properties as private market fees that escape being illegitimate taxes, and as public-style taxes that elude being noncompetitive fees.

On a traditional interpretation, all three—private communities, public street barricaders, and BIDs—present privatizing incursions into the public domain. But at a deeper level, they each rely on marshaling values and norms drawn equally from both the public and the private realms, as do their critics.

Hidden Hills was spared such conundrums because its political arrangements, self-serving though they may seem, still respect one of the fundamental distinctions between public and private: if a facility is going to be subsidized through the public tax system, then the public must, at least in some fashion, be able to enjoy its benefits. It must serve some public purpose. Conversely, if something is going to remain wholly private or exclusive, then no public tax support should be available to it or even be sought. There is no question that some of the more private communities that now pursue tax deductions and rebates, or the public neighborhoods that now seek to shore up their privacy, often test, tweak, or even blur this public-private distinction. But to their credit, none have flouted it utterly.

Yet even this last firewall has been showing signs of strain. In 1996 the Panther Valley Property Association, a gated private community near Hackettstown, New Jersey, transferred responsibility for its road maintenance to its own newly created special taxing district. Such districts are not full-fledged municipalities, but they are public entities nonetheless, with the right to tax residential properties for particular services, such as water, sewer, or, in this case, roads. Panther Valley homeowners now deduct what they spend for local road maintenance from their federal and state income tax returns. But those roads remain wholly closed to the general public. Any outsider seeking to drive on Panther Valley's public roads will be turned away.

Panther Valley, in effect, has moved beyond Hidden Hills. David Ramsey, the attorney who represented the Panther Valley homeowners, describes their agreement with the local township as a "unique settlement, the first of its kind." That is almost exactly the same language that Peter Pimentel, executive director of the Northern Palm Beach County Improvement District, uses to characterize several nearly identical arrangements recently concluded in Florida. "It's pathbreaking," Pimentel says, although he adds that "no one wants to take this to the IRS, because they're afraid of what they might say."[43]

Pimentel defends the practice of using the tax system to support roads that are not open to all. After all, he says, municipal parking lots and toll highways are public facilities, but you cannot just waltz onto them as you please; you have to pay. The analogy, though, is misconceived. As long as you are willing and able to pay, public governments cannot bar you from such facilities just because you are not a local resident—as Panther Valley can. Nor, for that matter, as long as you are a local resident, can America's public governments bar you from voting simply because you are unwilling or unable to pay for a home or a piece of property—as Panther Valley can. Private governments have been turning both of these established principles of American public life on their heads. Until not long ago, in the struggle over the border between public and private space, some lines had yet to be crossed. Now they have been.

2

ARRESTING DEVELOPMENTS

For six hours every month during 1997, Lieutenant Rick Lewis of the Jacksonville, Florida, sheriff's department moonlighted at the Jacksonville Golf and Country Club, a lush eighteen-hole course located in the heart of the city's wealthiest gated community. As a moonlighter, Lewis did exactly the sort of things he did as a cop. For five dollars an hour, he donned his police uniform, got in his cruiser, and patrolled the clubhouse and grounds. Five dollars an hour might seem a little low for Lewis's services, and, in fact, it barely covered the rental fee the sheriff charged him for use of the car and uniform. But the money wasn't his real remuneration. His "principal form of payment," as Lewis told me, took the form of free golf privileges at one of Florida's finest and most exclusive golf courses—something that would otherwise be available only to those who had spent several hundred thousand dollars for a home within the community's gates.[1] Sergeant Norm Brewer, who has participated in a similar deal with Jacksonville's Deer Creek Country Club, calls it the "club cop program."[2]

In 1991 Robert Reich, soon to become labor secretary in the Clinton administration, coined the phrase "secession of the successful" to describe the growing tendency for wealthy Americans to opt out of the public system and instead pay privately for their medical treatment, their children's schooling, their roads, their green spaces, and even their policing.[3] But policing is special. It is not that policing is somehow a more public function than, say, education or health care. What distinguishes policing, as we shall see, is that it implicates both the world of raw physical reality (the realm of physical force and space) and the world of pure social construction (the realm of laws and rules) in a fashion simply not replicated in education, health care, or any other comparable sphere. Policing, moreover, lends itself to peculiarities like Jacksonville's club cop program. Paying moonlighting cops in golf passes that cannot otherwise be purchased not only takes policing into the marketplace, it takes the mode of payment out of the marketplace. It doesn't just privatize policing, it privatizes the currency as well.

In a variety of gradual and unnoticed ways, new policing practices are subtly transgressing the traditional boundaries between the public and the private. Three practices in particular are noteworthy: the increasing use of public police officers to enforce privately established rules; the enforcement of public traffic, parking, littering, and loitering ordinances in private spaces; and the real possibility of public funds being used to underwrite police forces that are under private control. In many cases the nation's 150,000 private communities are taking a leading role. But owners of malls, parking lots, and other private businesses are also involved, vigorously contesting, and indeed transgressing, the traditional public-private border in policing.

PUBLIC ENFORCEMENT, PRIVATE LAW

On January 2, 1998, Miguel Valdes, a private security guard working for a Florida bank, shot a customer for double parking.[4] Nobody would disagree that Valdes went way over the line. In contrast to public police, private police possess a clearly circumscribed set of powers to enforce public laws. They have the power of citizen's arrest and the authority to eject trespassers from private property. Beyond these, private police may not use physical force, pursue, detain, search, or seize.[5] Overzealousness may be a constant temptation for what some people derisively call "cop wannabes," but we usually know overstepping when we see it. But now reverse the private-public arrow and consider another problem: *public* police enforcing *private* rules. Put away the image of a liveried private security guard brandishing a gun at you for double parking and imagine instead a uniformed police officer coming to your door and telling you to mow your lawn.

All across the country, police officers are working off-duty as private security personnel—for private communities, shopping centers, hotels, and restaurants. In that capacity they do nothing beyond what an ordinary private security guard would do to enforce the private rules of an employer. They utter verbal warnings, and, in the case of guards working in private communities, they might issue citations from the homeowners' association that can be "enforced" (because no public law has been violated) only by pursuing the violator through the civil courts.

But there is a difference. These police officers are very frequently allowed to wear their official police uniforms and drive in their official police cruisers while working at off-duty jobs. Steve Teal, who manages 130 private communities in the Phoenix area, regularly hires uniformed moonlighting cops to enforce homeowner association rules. Teal's moonlighters can tell residents and visitors not to fish in one place, for example, or picnic in another, or swim in the pool past ten o'clock; and none of these are acts that violate any *public* ordinance. Everything the guards do is totally private; the only thing public about them is their uniformed physical presence. And that is the point. Teal has tried "pure" private security patrols from Brink's and Pinkerton, but, he says, "they just aren't as effective as a policeman wearing a city uniform." Uniformed public police "have an authority image," Teal observes. "People don't question them—that's the point of it."[6]

The same logic applies in the case of mall managers who hire moonlighting police in full uniform to speak to teenagers flouting the mall's private rules against running, yelling, or roughhousing—none of which are illegal acts. The manager has always been able to ask patrons to stop violating shopping center rules or tell them to leave if they don't behave. Should miscreants refuse to leave, the manager can even call the police, because trespassing is illegal. But more and more often these moonlighters convey in every respect the "authority image" of regular police officers, with all that entails, even before the matter has risen to the level of a public offense.

As long as the moonlighter does nothing that exceeds the bounds of what a private security guard would do in enforcing private rules—as long as he arrests no one, detains no one, issues no public citations—what difference does it make what he is wearing? Consider the example of Black Butte Ranch, a private, gated community near Bend, Oregon. In 1990 Black Butte created its very own special services district, a governmental entity that uses residents' property taxes to fund a fully equipped, fully empowered *public* police force with a jurisdiction that happens to coincide precisely with the borders of the private ranch. This newly minted public force then contracted with the community's homeowners association to enforce a number of the association's private covenants, among them its curfew and golf course rules.

In principle, the distinction between public laws and private rules remains intact. When the Black Butte police enforce private rules they do not issue official police citations. Instead, they hand out private homeowner association citations, which are enforceable only through small claims court. The real tickets are reserved for violators of the county ordinances the Black Butte police are also obligated to enforce.[7] Yet when they stop a private rule violator and hand him a private ranch ticket, they have all the appearance of public cops. In fact, they would be impersonating police officers if they weren't, in fact ... well, police officers.

An impressive diversity characterizes the ways in which American police departments approach this issue. On the one hand, a large number of departments permit uniformed moonlighting. In fact, because off-duty cops immediately become on duty if they witness a crime, some departments *require* moonlighters to wear their public uniforms. "If you have to take police action," says Phoenix police sergeant Mike Torres, "you might as well be in your uniform from the get-go."[8] On the other hand, many departments—including Paradise Valley, right next door to Phoenix—absolutely prohibit moonlighters from wearing their uniforms. Chief John Winterstein decries wearing uniforms off duty because it creates "the impression that the arrest authority is being used for private purposes."[9] Uniformed moonlighting even makes some private community leaders quail. "When a cop wearing full regalia says, 'You're violating our pet rule,'" worries Bob Diamond, former national president of the Community Associations Institute (CAI), the nation's umbrella association of private communities, "clearly it's troubling."[10]

As if in poignant testimony to the issue's conflicting tugs, the St. Louis police department at one point embarked on an ultimately vain attempt to make it possible for moonlighting cops, in effect, to wear two uniforms at once. Originally the department required uniformed cops to display a little white spot on their collars when moonlighting ("It looked like a bird dropping," according to security consultant Cliff van Meter).[11] More recently, moonlighters came to sport a discreet red bar on their lapels. The uniform provides the public presence necessary should the moonlighter have to enforce a public ordinance, while the bar is meant to somehow drain the uniform of its public authority if the rule being enforced is a private one. The problem, however, as St. Louis police sergeant Daniel Nicholson acknowledges, is that "no member of the public notices the bar—or would understand it even if they did."[12]

In the face of such conflicting opinions among police departments themselves, one might think to look to the courts for guidance. But most court decisions involving moonlighting cops actually turn on a very distinct but equally important question—whether moonlighters can do things in their private capacity that they could never do in their public capacity without a warrant, even if those activities then lead to an arrest for a public offense like drug trafficking. Courts have ruled, for instance, that cops moonlighting for FedEx may open packages at the company's behest in order to verify contents, which is something they could never do without a warrant while on duty as policemen.[13] But permissive as these decisions are, they focus on moonlighters who adroitly use the trappings of their private role to enforce public laws; hence they say nothing about whether moonlighters can use the trappings of their public role to enforce private laws.

There is a several-decades-old case that speaks to this latter question. In 1963's *Griffin v. Maryland*, the Supreme Court found that a uniformed police officer moonlighting as a security guard had acted under color of public authority in asking five black teenagers to leave a Maryland amusement park in compliance with the owner's policy of racial segregation.[14] The Court found that the off-duty cop's deputy-sheriff's badge alone sufficed to place his actions on the public rather than the private side of the divide, even though he used no enforcement techniques that could not have been employed by a garden-variety security guard.

There is an added wrinkle in *Griffin* that is likely responsible for limiting the case's influence over recent instances of police moonlighting: the discriminatory private policy in question would have been unconstitutional if it had been a public law, something that is seldom the case in the instances currently under discussion. The rules that private communities and shopping malls promulgate could be public laws; they just are not. Yet that does not vitiate *Griffin*'s essential relevance: the determination that for moonlighters the uniform, even with no arrests, no detentions, and no searches or seizures, suffices to bring the color of public authority to the enforcement of rules no public body has passed. The Supreme Court has held that the uniform converts what would otherwise be a private act into a public one. The rationale is simple: as Jeremy Travis, former head of the National Institute of Justice, says, "Publicly uniformed police will be given greater latitude by those who are the recipients of enforcement. . . . They intrude a zone of public enforcement into the private."[15]

PUBLIC LAW, PRIVATE SPACE

Now consider another permutation of the public-private policing question. In 1993 a middle-class private community in St. Louis called Maryland Estates tired of paying high maintenance costs for the private roads weaving through its property and returned them to the public domain through a formal dedication to the city. As private roads, they had been governed by Maryland

Estates' covenants, one of which banned parking by oversized vehicles. But even though the roads were now part of the public domain, the Maryland Estates homeowners association saw no reason why its private rules should not continue to govern them. Marvin Nodiff, the attorney who represented the homeowners association, says that *Maryland Estates* v. *Puckett* is the only reported instance in which a private group has sought to extend its rules concerning speeding and parking to public roads.[16] A test case was provoked when Christopher Schallert, a local resident, insisted on parking his RV on what was now a public street. The homeowners association sued, and in December 1996 Judge Robert Campbell of the St. Louis county circuit court decided that private rules cannot bind the behavior of any person on public space unless that person has agreed to those rules. Thus while no members of the association could park a Ford Explorer on the now public streets, any member of the general public would be free to do so.

Now consider another question. What happens when private communities or businesses try to reverse the arrow and have a host of minor public laws, like those concerning speeding, parking, littering, or loitering, enforced on their private roads and spaces? The question highlights an important distinction in the rationales behind different sorts of law enforcement. Crimes like murder, theft, and drug trafficking threaten the public good no matter where they occur. But petty infractions like exceeding the speed limit, parking in the wrong space, or littering do not. They may cause harm, but the harm is necessarily limited to the particular space in which the infractions occur. Because of this reasoning, police have traditionally not enforced these laws in private areas. "Even if the cops happen to be present for some other reason," says Marjorie Meyer, a Houston private community manager, "they won't give you a ticket for speeding on a private road."[17] While cops can generally ticket cars for parking in fire lanes or disabled spaces even in privately owned parking lots—because there is a broader public health and safety interest involved— they cannot, says Dallas police officer Kenneth Seguin, "ticket the guy from apartment 202 for parking illegally in apartment 203's spot."[18] Likewise, the police or public authorities typically enforce dog license laws on a private space but not dog litter laws, where the injury, in a sense, is done *to* the space. The difference lies in the rationale for these two separate kinds of laws. Unlike assault or theft laws, laws concerning traffic offenses, littering, and loitering are tied to a particular space. And thus we feel that it matters whether that space is public or private.

American courts have long affirmed this distinction. Yet many private communities and businesses have begun exploring ways of sheltering their private spaces under the umbrella of the public police power. After all, says Florida attorney Chuck Edgar, "If the cops will deal with a speeder for free and through the traffic courts, but your homeowners association must bear the burden of chasing him through the civil courts, who ya gonna call?"[19] True, police will only enforce laws covering the more serious public offenses in private areas. But they can find a way around this problem. Cops can enforce minor speeding and parking laws by citing the offender for graver public violations that are more directly threatening to public health and well-being.

"A clever cop," says former Seattle police chief Mike Shanahan, "has a bag of tricks whereby he can forge such links."[20] "If someone was exceeding a privately posted speed limit in a private street," claims Boston sergeant Kevin Jones, "I couldn't get him for speeding, but I would consider arresting him for 'operating to endanger'; I'd go to court, if necessary, and if I lose, I lose."[21] "If you're parking in the space reserved for the law firm in a private parking lot," says David Brennan of the Anchorage Parking Authority, "they can get you for trespass but not illegal parking."[22] Similarly, as New Jersey private community attorney Ron Perl points out, if young people gather on a private community's lakeshore or golf course, "the police can't get them for loitering per se; it would have to be trespass."[23] The space between recklessness and speeding or between trespassing and illegal parking is, Bob Diamond says, "full of sticky wickets."

Or consider another trick: zoning ordinances are direct expressions of the police power, the state's capacity to regulate in the name of public health, safety, and welfare. Yet in some cases, says Steve Hovany, former town planner of Schaumburg, Illinois, the zoning ordinance that creates a private community will incorporate parking regulations. "The police enforce them," Hovany says, "but when you park illegally on a private road you get cited for violating a zoning ordinance, not a parking ordinance." In this way, Hovany says, the public regulation of parking on private spaces finds "some kind of stretch to the police power."[24]

Lately, however, a few bellwether states and municipalities have taken the final step and eliminated any last vestige of daylight between public law and private space. Instead of fancifully using the guise of recklessness or trespassing, they have dispensed with all pretense and begun directly enforcing public speeding, parking, and pet litter ordinances on private roads and common spaces. "Until recently," Chuck Edgar says, "cops in Florida wouldn't enforce traffic laws in private communities; now, by contract, they'll come into the community, whether gated or ungated, and enforce all the traffic laws that previously applied only on public streets." Some Florida private communities have to pay for the service. But in Illinois, California, Maryland, New Jersey, and Virginia, the public picks up the tab. Similar arrangements have been available to private parking lots for even longer. "In the old days," Ron Perl says, New Jersey "municipal prosecutors refused to handle pooper-scooper violations on private spaces; now they do."

Taken together, these moves represent a qualitative, though little noted, expansion of public law enforcement into the realm of private space. Is there anything wrong with this? The best way of answering that question is to observe how these new arrangements often fail to "take." It is as if private space is covered with an invisible coating that causes the domain of public law to slip and slide over its surface, never quite snugly adhering to it. Consider Panther Valley, a gated community near Hackettstown, New Jersey, which invited the police onto its private roads to enforce public traffic ordinances. Because its roads were private, Panther Valley also wanted to reserve the right to set and enforce its own private traffic rules *even as* the public police would be enforcing public traffic ordinances on the exact same space. In January 1998 a state superior court shot down that idea. If a private community invites the public police to enforce public traffic laws on its private spaces, the court reasoned, it cannot also enforce a separate system of private rules. It is just too confusing (not to mention dangerous) to post two sets of speed limits on the same roads.

But what Panther Valley could not manage to pull off in New Jersey has already been accomplished—indeed done one better—by a homeowners association in the village of Northfield, Illinois. Imagine yourself driving along Northfield's Happ Road, which is a public street. As long as you observe the village's thirty-five-mile-an-hour speed limit, the police won't ticket you. Now, turn off Happ onto Woodley Road, a privately owned and maintained avenue, whose twenty-mile-an-hour speed limit is set not by the village, but by the Woodley Road homeowners association. Still going thirty-five, you could be pulled over and given a real-live speeding ticket by a Northfield police officer.

Northfield is not just enforcing public traffic laws on private roads. The village has in effect delegated the lawmaking power itself—the determination of what rules the public police will enforce on those private spaces—to a private party, the homeowners association.[25] Across the lake in Michigan, cops, if requested, now directly enforce private parking rules on private parking lots. If you park in the law firm's space, the lot owner will swear in an affidavit that your car is "an unauthorized user of this particular parking stall," and the cops will tow you. "They do not tow you for trespassing; in fact you've violated no ordinance," says Michigan criminologist Brian Johnson.[26] The same practices exist in Denver and Kansas City. Precisely because there is something unnatural in private space yielding over its most intimate governance to public authorities, ambiguities like these are to be expected whenever the attempt is made.

The use of public power to enforce public (let alone private) speeding or parking laws on private spaces is still uncommon. While "some city attorneys are willing to be innovative," notes Atlanta private community attorney Wayne Hyatt, "most are quite conservative, saying 'We won't touch private roads.'"[27] But what is happening in California, Florida, Illinois, and New Jersey transgresses a principle that was once deemed universally applicable across America. "Where is the public interest or welfare being served?" asks Anchorage's David Brennan. "You need that for the use of police powers to enforce law on private property."

PUBLIC PAYMENTS, PRIVATE POLICE

The next turn in the public-private policing debate may well come when private communities and businesses begin to seek tax rebates from the local municipality for policing services they purchase privately. This sort of subsidy is familiar enough when it goes in the other direction. During every home game, for example, the Philadelphia Eagles management has traditionally paid for one hundred extra police officers to patrol Veterans' Stadium—and now Lincoln Financial Field—above and beyond the number the city police department would normally provide. These extra police, like the regulars with whom they work, enforce public laws only. They perform no private security role; and in witness of this fact the Eagles send their payments directly to the department, which then pays the officers at a fixed rate.

Such practices are common across the United States. It seems fair, after all, to ask anyone who is deliberately creating their own extra need for police—whether an NFL team, a jewelry store owner, or a director shooting a scene on a public street—to pay for the additional coverage. There are certain risks involved: public police must enforce the law, but their employers may not want them to enforce it too zealously. "Businesses don't want the cops they hire to make arrests," Richard Zappelli, the Philadelphia deputy police commissioner, says. "It's bad publicity."[28] But while underzealousness can sometimes be a problem, the norms are clear. We know what privately paid public police officers are obligated to do, and, assuming we have all the facts at hand, we know it when they fall short. Here again, the problems arise when we reverse the private-public arrow, for this raises the specter of publicly paid private police—police who are underwritten by the government but who are privately directed and controlled.

In some areas of the country, as discussed in chapter 1, residents of private communities are now seeking rebates of the property taxes they pay for trash collection, street cleaning, sewer maintenance, road repair, and the like. Their argument? They purchase those services privately through their homeowners association dues, so the local municipality is still taxing them for those amenities but not actually providing them. In 1990 New Jersey passed the Municipal Services Act, under which counties and towns, at an estimated cost of more than $100 million annually, are rebating to residents of private communities the property taxes they pay to support public trash collection, snow removal, and street-lighting services.

Can the logic of rebates apply to policing as well? Can the approximately 25,000 private communities that pay for their own private security patrols argue successfully that they should not have to pay to support the public police system because they are policing themselves? "I think they can," says San Diego attorney Jon Epsten. "It's ripe for class action; it's just that private communities don't want to spend the attorney's fees."[29] "Clearly the rebate argument could be made to apply to policing," agrees Florida State University economist Bruce Benson, an expert on private security. "Some large private communities have their own security forces and don't call in the public police."[30]

The majority of the private community lawyers and lobbyists with whom I've spoken agree that the logic of rebates should apply to policing. A few, however, express concerns that seeking such rebates may seem like a politically unpalatable overreach on the part of private community residents. They insist that their goal is to obtain rebates only for services that the public system explicitly refuses to furnish to private communities. Trash collection, street lighting, snow removal, and street cleaning clearly fall into this category, because municipalities, as part of their original deals with private community developers, deliberately relieved themselves of the responsibility to provide them. Policing "is more like education," says Phyllis Matthey of the Coalition of Associations for Political Action, a New Jersey private community group. "The public police, much like the public schools, are there for you even if you live in a private community," she says, "but if you decide to hire private security—just as when you opt to send your kid to a private school—that's your choice, not something that government's withdrawal has forced onto you."[31]

Such an analogy might seem like a potent barrier against rebates for policing if it were not for the fact that the educational voucher movement has already attacked the logic of public education on just the same grounds and with a good deal of success. In fact the advocates of policing rebates might be able to make comparable arguments with even greater plausibility. Unlike public schools, which must accept all children within a given geographical area, police have far greater discretion over how to allocate services. In many private communities the police have withdrawn an array of services that they normally provide to the rest of the public. Mike Walker, security director of PGA West, a golf-centered gated enclave in Palm Springs, California, says he knows of private communities where the local public police say, "You've got private security, we won't respond to that call." If "somebody shoots your window with a BB gun," Walker says, "normally the cops come out, but here, the police say, in a private community we don't take criminal mischief calls"—a response that Walker, a former cop, finds "appalling."[32]

Experts in other states agree. With more and more "belt tightening by local police," says William Cunningham, a nationally celebrated private security consultant, "people will start saying, 'Hey, wait a minute—when we pay for our own private security and for the public police, that could be construed as double taxation.'" Businesses could make the same argument, Cunningham says; he recalls hearing of "a Fortune 500 CEO saying to his head of security, 'Why in hell are we paying property taxes for cops when we're paying $120 million a year for our own private security system?'" A policing rebate movement "makes sense," Cunningham argues, adding, "I would be glad to lead it."[33]

No town or municipality has yet staged a full-scale debate over policing rebates, and even Cunningham believes that any such controversy lies at least some years away. But the stirrings are evident. Mike Woo, a Democrat who ran for mayor of Los Angeles in 1993, says he knows rich Angelenos "who wonder, 'How come we have to pay for public police?'"[34] Mike Gambrill, former police chief of Baltimore County, heard the same thing while he was in office.[35] One hitch that might derail a policing rebate movement is the fact that, as Phyllis Matthey puts it, "private security provides only peripheral policing services. . . . Private patrols can chase kids off vacant lots or ticket cars, but they cannot follow in hot pursuit or wrestle suspects to the ground." They cannot, in other words, offer the kinds of core arrest, investigative, or deterrent services the real police provide. Thus the range of services that could be legitimately rebated would likely be limited to the narrow periphery of private security services that most private communities and businesses now obtain.

But there is a problem with that argument. In education, unlike policing, it is *private* providers that boast a greater array of offerings than their public counterparts. No one, accordingly, expects any publicly funded education voucher scheme to cover the "extras" private schools offer; the amount of any proposed voucher will always hit a natural ceiling at the core public minimum. The more a private school expands its menu beyond the core curriculum to the extracurricular—from math to macramé—the more it moves those offerings toward the realm of pure market goods, a realm where the state has long since taken leave and has no general obligation to help parents out. But as private security forces expand their offerings, they will travel in precisely the opposite direction, from the peripheral (traffic control) to the core (arrests)—hence moving ever closer to the realm of central state responsibilities. Precisely because the public policing system is so much more powerful than the private, it provides no breaking point at which to terminate any push for rebates. The more private communities arm themselves, says Florida attorney Charles Morgenstein (who himself looks askance at the prospect), the "more the rebate argument should stick."[36]

A small but growing number of private communities and businesses have, in fact, managed to get their private security forces installed with full police powers. In South Carolina's Sea Pines and Hilton Head Plantation; in Virginia's Aquia Harbor, Oregon's Sun River, and Tennessee's Fairfield Glade; in a cluster of private communities in the Poconos; and even in Cunningham's own home community of Amelia Plantation in Florida, the homeowners association security force remains privately controlled, paid, and attired but is court sworn with the full capacity to arrest, search, and seize. Their members can follow in hot pursuit, just as they can wrestle suspects to the ground. In the Poconos private communities had their security patrols deputized under Pennsylvania's dormant 1895 so-called "night watchman act"—originally adopted to enable coal companies to create their own union-busting police. Sun River and Fairfield Glade got special legislation passed permitting their security personnel to obtain training and accreditation at their states' police academies. In Michigan similar legislation recently vested private security at certain malls and hospitals with total police power. Frenchman's Creek, a wealthy gated enclave in Florida's Palm Beach Gardens, boasts its own five-man Special Tactical Operation Patrol (STOP), which does not have full police powers but is equipped with camouflage clothing, night vision scopes, infrared heat detectors, high-speed vehicles, and specially trained dogs. As these private police expand their scope from private rules to public laws, so they move beyond private to acquire public enforcement techniques. Why then, private communities are beginning to ask, should these private security forces not also be publicly paid?

LAWS, RULES, FORCE, AND SPACE

All three of these movements, in a traditional view, would seem to represent creeping privatization: incursions of the private realm into the public. In the first, private rules and not just public laws are getting themselves enforced by uniformed public police. In the second, private spaces and not just public spaces are getting themselves covered by public-space-related laws. In the third, privately controlled police, not just public police, would be getting a share of the public budget.

But there is another way to look at these political movements, in which they appear not as efforts to maximize the private realm's bite out of the public but as attempts to combine public and private—public and private enforcement, public and private laws—in new modes. When, as with Lieutenant Lewis of Jacksonville, a public police officer moonlights for a private golf course or restaurant, he is being employed to enforce private laws. But the method of enforcement he is using is mezzo-mezzo: a combination of the private with the public. He won't hand out tickets or follow in hot pursuit; however he will wear a Jacksonville police uniform and drive an official police car.

Conversely, when, as with Sergeant Jones of Boston, a public police officer tickets a car on a private parking lot for something that arguably violates the public law against trespassing but actually violates a private rule against parking in a reserved space, he is using full public enforcement measures. But what he is enforcing in such a robust public fashion are laws that, in their most accurate description, are mezzo-mezzo: a combination of public and private: public laws that simply redescribe or rubber-stamp private rules.

Policing is unlike any of the other policy domains I discuss. It's not that it is the most central state obligation or even that it involves the use of coercive power. Some would say that the provision of education rivals policing as a public duty or that welfare services can, in their own way, be coercively supplied. Instead, what is unique about policing is the fashion in which what is public or private can take the form of either the most concrete physical entities—force, spaces—or else the most abstract social constructions: laws, rules.

In most of the other debates that this book examines, it is economic resources—money, as with payments for health insurance, or vouchers, as with state aid for parochial schools, or food stamps in the domain of welfare—that raise questions about the public-private border. Or else the tussle is over the extent to which policies or programs should be infused with publicly versus privately set social goals: the extent to which parochial schools should fulfill publicly established curricular purposes, for example, or private health insurers should be executing public mandates concerning the coverage of particular medical conditions, or welfare aid should be in kind, rather than in cash, to embody the public's preferences that poor children not be malnourished.

Against this background, what makes policing unique becomes apparent. Public and private versions of physical entities, or public and private versions of legal regimes, are simply harder to combine—especially when they are being asked to coexist in the exact same place—than public and private versions of economic resources or of social goals. That's because physical force and space are far more concrete, far less fungible, than economic resources. And laws and rules are far more formalized or set in stone, far less malleable, than social goals.

Yet attempts to forge such public-private combinations are precisely what underlie some of the newer policing gambits being launched by communities and businesses in America. The problem is that it is not physically possible, for example, for a moonlighting police officer to wear two kinds of uniforms representing two types of force—public enforcement and private enforcement—at the same time, even if she is enforcing two different sets of laws. Inevitably the enforcement will come to be seen as one or the other: more specifically, public, as the Supreme Court saw it in *Griffin* v. *Maryland*. Nor is it possible for two different sets of laws to govern the same physical space—a set of roads, for example—even if both a public government and a private government have jurisdiction over it. Inevitably, the law will come to be only public or private; more particularly, if the experience of Northfield, Illinois, is indicative, it will become private.

As a consequence of policing's unique reach into the domains of the physical and the legal, the associated debates offer a variation on this book's theme of two competing sides, each relying coequally on the same public and private values. It is only one side in these policing debates, the side that would traditionally be understood as seeking to expand the private realm, that relies on combining norms of public and private—in particular, norms that have to do with physical force and space, or legal constructions and rules—in ways that are ultimately untenable. And so, finally, one can remain rightly alarmed about the prospect of police who, while maintaining full public enforcement powers over fully public laws, at the same time attempt to retain their status as private police, privately enforcing private rules. That, of course, is the project on which Sun River, Fairfield Glade, Hilton Head, and many of America's wealthiest private communities have begun to embark.[37]

3

SPACES, REAL AND VIRTUAL

To talk of public spaces in early twenty-first century America is to speak in terms both real—the real estate of plazas, courtyards, civic centers, museums, universities—and virtual—the Internet, and specifically blogs, YouTube, and Facebook-type sites open to the view of all. But the deepest dynamics in each domain, virtual or real, are moving in opposite directions. Virtual public spaces are encroaching on traditional private realms, lending ever-increasing publicity to aspects of life—the most mundane and the most intimate—that traditionally have remained private. Real public spaces, by contrast, are being encroached upon by the private realm, allowing themselves to be privatized through the contemporary penchant for naming their various bits and pieces—a building, a bench, even a brick—after private individuals in return for a donation.

Despite these opposing dynamics, what is happening with both virtual and real public spaces is ultimately rooted in the same phenomenon: the desire for some semblance of immortality. Not literal immortality, of course, or the biological immortality that results from perpetuating our genes through procreation but the lesser immortality that comes from leaving at least some mark for generations to come that says, "I was here, and this is who I was." Both the privatization of real public spaces and the virtual publicity being lent to private lives are in fact means of democratizing immortality—of affording ordinary men and women the kind of immortality that was formerly reserved only for the greats.

For much of human history, for example, only an eminent artist or thinker could have hoped to have his mind, along with its visual or verbal fruits, live on. Now, many are coming to believe, the Internet has democratized such immortality. Thanks to the web, claims D. Raj Reddy, a professor of computer science and robotics at Carnegie-Mellon, the possibility of "virtual immortality" is now available to everyone. Anyone can post material on the World Wide Web, and because the web is impervious to the degradation that time inflicts on printed records, whatever it contains carries the capacity to exist indefinitely in some form. True, websites currently disappear with alarming frequency, and so Professor Reddy might be overstating matters when he says that "we can feel confident" that our web postings will "not be forgotten, but [rather] preserved as a thread in a multimedia quilt that keeps a permanent record of the human race."[1]

But even if this is not true of every single website at this early moment in the web's history, it is certainly true that, in principle and for the first time, the Internet offers the technological means whereby anyone can keep his or her work universally accessible indefinitely. That is why bloggers—those who on a regular basis post their autobiographical narratives, political musings, photos, and poetry online—so often express the inchoate hope that the Internet will allow them, as blogger Radley Balko puts it, to "leave [their] mark on the world" and achieve a kind of immortality (Balko, a thirty-something "writer, editor, and wonk living in Alexandria, Virginia," gets a respectable 8,000 visits a day on his blogsite).[2] Indiana blogger Joshua Claybourn, whose web address appears as a link on numerous other websites, makes no bones about the matter: "I admit to considering the blog's impact on my immortality."[3] What appears on many such blogs, of course, are streams of consciousness—what the blogger did and thought at any given moment—that hitherto would have remained private; what typically appears on YouTube or other web videos are large tracts of daily life that would otherwise have remained cosseted away in the realm of privacy.

In addition to the incipient promise of virtual immortality through the Internet, there is a second phenomenon that promises, so it would seem, to bring a formerly restricted type of immortality within reach of us all. In days gone by, individuals whose names lived on after them affixed to buildings— museums, schools, universities, hospitals, and the like—were usually figures of some note: politicians, military heroes, or major industrialists. Now, with the burgeoning need for public and nonprofit organizations to raise private funds, anyone can have his or her name placed on an institutional structure—for a price. This might seem more like the plutocratizing than the democratizing of immortality but for the fact that "naming opportunities" are available to people of all income levels. Those of more modest means can, for lesser sums, have their names placed on a classroom, a bench, or even an individual brick. And they often admit to seeking what Tasha Thomas, a fundraiser at Grant Medical Center in Columbus, calls "a little bit of the immortality that used to be available just to famous people."[4] "Call it an answer to the yearning for immortality," says the *New York Times*. "For a price, universities will carve the name of a generous benefactor in limestone or on an imposing building."[5] Or on a brick.

Are we really living at the dawn of immortality's democratization, thanks to the privatization of real public space and the extension of virtual public space into private realms? Or does the kind of immortality they proffer to ordinary would-be immortals differ from that which traditionally has descended on the extraordinary individuals who have monopolized immortality up until now? More the latter than the former. For as we shall see, both kinds of ordinary immortality—that sought through virtual spaces and that pursued through real space—rely on combinations of public and private sphere values in ways that jar.

Consider first some problems with the quest for immortality in cyberspace. With the globalization wrought by the Internet, as author James Gleick says, "traditional namespaces are overlapping and melting together."[6] This poses no problem for a popular icon like Bill Wyman of the Rolling Stones who, even though *Bill Wyman* is not his real name (he was born William Perks), is so identified with that appellation that he felt justified in trying to force Atlanta music critic Bill Wyman to add to his byline the phrase "not of the Rolling Stones." Of course, just for that reason—just because Bill Wyman of the Stones is the mother of all Bill Wymans—few are likely to have attributed his accomplishments to Bill Wyman the critic; most of us have a sufficient sense of the rock star Bill Wyman that we would be able to distinguish him from all the others.

Confusion, however, begins to emerge when it is ordinary individuals, and in particular those of us with ordinary names, who seek to immortalize themselves on the web. Blogger Megan McArdle remarks that she has "had people who once knew someone named . . . Megan McArdle ask me if I was that person."[7] A certain Michael Wood, one of many people to post comments on a site for people with the name *Michael Wood*, complains that "someone else's [view will be] mistakenly attributed to me."[8] The Internet allowed Dave Gorman, who calls himself a "documentary comedian," to discover fifty-four other people who share his name. "Before I did this," he writes, "the words *Dave Gorman* used to define me; now they don't."[9] As Ellen Rony, author of *The Domain Name Handbook*, says, there already "are far too many Internet users, and too many coexisting and legitimate uses for identical words, to justify [any] presumption" about what a web surfer "can expect to find at [a given] name."[10]

Of course, if you discover that your name is already being used by others in cyberspace, you can always, as innumerable bloggers now do, pick a singular pseudonym to distinguish yourself. But that merely makes the problem worse. If a person posts material online under a pseudonym, how will its everlasting preservation immortalize him?

We ordinary mortals, it seems, are not given enough unique names to differentiate all the distinct websites we will want to establish. The reverse difficulty confronts those who seek immortality by attaching their names to buildings, rooms, walls, and bricks: there are too many competing names for the suitable physical sites that institutions can or will establish. Even now, institutions increasingly face the need to tear down an old structure named for John Doe—a lab that is obsolete, an auditorium that is too small—to construct a new one, courtesy of a generous donation from Richard Roe. Institutions' limited spaces dictate that, sooner or later, the name on an old structure will have to be folded into a differently named new one. That is why at Northwestern University athletes play on Ryan Field at Dyche Stadium. Some libraries sell naming rights to bookcases and then to the individual shelves they contain.[11] When New York University tore down a named building to replace it with one funded by a new benefactor, development officer David Koehler says, the institution kept the old donor's name alive by attaching it to a couple of floors in the new edifice.[12] And there is, of course, the growing practice of having one's name engraved—for a small price—on a brick in a walkway or a wall, which itself may well be named for somebody else.

Yet this kind of cramping and overlapping of spaces can go on for only so long. Institutions are already beginning to place plaques commemorating old donors on central walls of honor, such as Hackensack University's Margery S. and Charles J. Rothschild Jr. Recognition Gallery (a wall of honor itself offers an additional naming opportunity).[13] Even on walls of honor, though, space is finite. There are already so many candidates for the new wall of honor for Jefferson County, Missouri, that it consists simply of four television screens displaying, over the course of the viewing day, names and faces drawn at random from a large database. Donors to institutions can always avoid these issues by giving anonymously, of course, but giving anonymously no more immortalizes the donor than posting pseudonymously does the blogger.

The discontents of having to share confined physical spaces with other names do not, in nearly the same way, confront the truly eminent in their quest for immortality. Statues of Civil War generals will always preside over Gettysburg without having to make room on their pedestals for anyone else. It is true that in 1996 Thomas Jefferson High School in Richmond closed to make way for Maggie Walker High. But there are scores of other Jefferson High Schools in America, let alone innumerable further memorials to the third president.

Ordinary would-be immortals face a further set of difficulties. Consider a donor to a university or a hospital, and let us assume that his name will remain embossed indefinitely on some kind of physical marker within the institution, even if transferred from pillar to post to plaque over time. In what sense would people fifty, a hundred, or a thousand years from now, noting John Doe's name, think of John Doe and thereby contribute to his immortality? All that will pass through their consciousnesses is a name, with no accompanying narrative, no biographical information about the person attached to the name.

In fact, after a time the name will cease to signify a person and identify simply the memorial itself. In 2005, more than three decades after the closing of Emmett Scott High, the town of Rock Hill, South Carolina, opened a brand new secondary school. Many who had attended Emmett Scott decades previously, coalescing into a group called "The Friends of Emmett Scott," wanted the new institution to bear the old one's name. Although school board policy had come to prohibit naming Rock Hill schools after people, it is clear that the Friends' aim, in seeking to have the new school named "Emmett Scott High," was to memorialize not Emmett Scott the person, who was a nineteenth-century black cabinet member, but Emmett Scott the place, the old Emmett Scott High School.

In a letter to the *Rock Hill Herald*, local resident Larry Carter said, "I would bet 99 percent of persons below age eighteen of all races could not tell you who Emmett Scott was or what he accomplished."[14] Carter's point was that precisely because the person Emmett Scott is unmemorable, he does not deserve to be memorialized. But then if Emmett Scott the person is so unmemorable, the chances are that Rock Hill residents—seeing the name "Emmett Scott" on a new school building—would be thinking precisely of a place, the old Emmett Scott High, and not of a person. And in that case, naming the new school "Emmett Scott High" would not have violated the board's policy against naming schools after people; the new school, if it were named Emmett Scott, would simply have been a memorial to a previous memorial. As Friends supporter Meredith E. Bynum put it in a letter to the *Herald*, the new edifice should have been named Emmett Scott because "Emmett Scott was an outstanding school."[15]

If a place is meant to keep alive the name of an ordinary man or woman, there will inevitably come a point at which viewers will not only fail to think of the particular person whose name it was, they will fail to think of a person at all, but only of a place. Froebel High School in Gary, Indiana, was built in 1912 and named for turn-of-the-century local educator Friedrich Froebel. In 2006, "long past the time when the locals still remember who Friedrich Froebel was," as state representative Vernon Smith says, the building was slated to be torn down with the idea of selling off the building's bricks individually, as mementoes, to former students.[16] Originally, when the school was built, the bricks were meant to publicly memorialize Froebel the person. Now, all they can do is privately memorialize Froebel the place. "When people said, `I'll meet you at Froebel,'" Gary Community Schools Corporation spokesperson Chelsea Stalling says, "the thought of a person never crossed their mind, only a place."[17]

The problem of an ordinary person's name migrating from the person to the place commemorating him gets underlined in the cases of individuals, and this includes a great many of us, whose names sound like a place. Jim Camanger, a communications specialist with Zeeland Public Schools in Michigan, notes that the locals believe that Woodbridge School is named after a wooden bridge that, so they mistakenly assume, must have existed nearby; the school's logo is even a wood bridge. In fact, Woodbridge school is meant to memorialize a forgotten governor of territorial Michigan, William Woodbridge.[18] And then there is the case of Cornelius Cole, an obscure nineteenth-century California politician, who established a ranch in what is now downtown Hollywood; the area currently is known as "Colegrove." When Hollywooders hear the name, do they think of a person or a place—of Cole, or of the grove? Actually, neither would be correct, since the area is named after Cole's wife, the former Olive Colegrove.[19]

The irony is that for a memorial to evoke someone's memory, that person needs to be memorable independently of the memorial. A disease named for a famous patient, such as Lou Gehrig, makes us think of that person; so does a law named after a famous victim—James Brady, for example. But if the person is not memorable apart from the memorial, then it will not remind us of him. A reference to Parkinson's disease or the Glass-Steagall Act does not bring to mind either Parkinson, or Glass, or Steagall.

True, institutions sometimes try to inscribe a few biographical words on a plaque along with the name, but there is no more room for a real biographical narrative on a plaque than there is for an epitaph on a grave. As the

Richmond Times Dispatch reported some years ago, "Because of space limita-tions, the inscriptions on the brass plates" hanging on the city's municipal wall of honor were being capped at "forty letters and spaces."[20] At best, there is room on plaques, as on gravestones, for the recitation of a few vague and generic virtues, such as "generous benefactor" or "institutional pioneer": a *virtue-al* narrative, so to speak. But this hardly recounts a life, or memorializes it. The immortality-seeking institutional donor thus seems caught in an unfor-tunate space-time warp. The available spaces are too few for the names to be accommodated, and the span of time to be memorialized—the span occupied by the person's life—is too large to ever be commemorated adequately by the inevitably skimpy accompanying narrative.

Those who pursue immortality in cyberspace face a different challenge when it comes to biographical information. The Internet imposes no limits on the material bloggers can post, allowing them to record the most mundane or tangential details of their lives with a stream-of-consciousness flow. The blog-ger Dave Walker boasts the title of the "Dullest Blog in the World," offering as he does items such as "I had a towel in my hands. It was a bit damp. It hung over the banister so that it would dry off 27/06/2003 2:18 PM," or "I took off one of my shoes and placed it on the floor near the front door. I then took off the other shoe and placed it adjacent to the first one. I left the two shoes there until such time as I needed them again 2/06/2003 11:59 PM."[21] Walker is hardly alone. The blogger Craig Taylor says he faces a "challenge [in] refusing to let the promise of endless space act as an excuse to write about the size of my finger-nail."[22] The blogger Justin Hall's "unofficial biography," on his website, runs to 4,800 pages.[23] It is "the job of a blogger," so it seems to the commentator Andrew Ferguson, "to record his every neural discharge faithfully and minutely, leaving no thought unpublished."[24]

So unlike the virtue-al narratives on institutional real estate that barely begin to fill the broad expanse—a lifetime—being memorialized, the real-time narratives on blogs' virtual spaces often actually overflow the sliver-sized time periods (2:18 PM, 11:59 PM) indicated. The phenomenon calls to mind John Updike's remark that it often takes more time to read a history doctoral dissertation than it did for the event it discusses to happen. Yet it is unclear that overly loquacious narratives—especially when they are con-sumed with the sorts of mundane activities we all share—memorialize a person any more effectively than do overly curt ones. As Samuel Johnson said, referring to the biographers of his day, they "imagine themselves writing a life when they exhibit a chronological series of actions [even though] more knowledge may be gained of a man's real character by a short conversation with one of his servants, than from a . . . narrative begun with his pedigree and ended with his funeral."[25]

True, the majority of blogs do not begin at birth and end at death. "Over 132,000 blogs are abandoned after a year of constant updating," *PC Magazine* reported a few years ago; others are discontinued after a few months or weeks of intense postings.[26] But that only makes their narratives, however chock full, even less representative of the life to be commemorated; for the purposes of immortalization, fewer entries over a longer period would be better. It would seem, then, that those who seek immortality online encounter their own kind of space-time warp: they share too few names to distinguish all the cyber-spaces on the Web, and they post far too much narrative for the time periods being memorialized.

All of this provokes a question: Even if we assume that what is posted in cyberspace and inscribed in physical space will remain in perpetuity, is earthly immortality in fact available only to the extraordinary among us? Is the democ-ratization of immortality an illusion? And what does the answer reveal about the understandings of public and private that underpin the privatization of real public space, and the extension of virtual public space far into private life?

Consider how immortality descends on great people, a process analyzed by Hannah Arendt in *The Human Condition*. Arendt speaks of two kinds of great immortals. There are extraordinary men of action such as Lincoln or Churchill; they are remembered through historians who narrate their lives in biographies or by sculptors who do so in monuments. And there are extraor-dinary artists or thinkers, such as Rembrandt or Flaubert, who are remembered not for their life narratives but for the works they create, for a *Night Watch* or a *Madame Bovary*. "The essential truth," biographer Michael Holroyd says, "is simple: Flaubert was born, Flaubert wrote his novel, Flaubert died. It is his work which is unique, that matters, not the ordinary experience which he shared with so many others."[27] Faulkner said that a writer's obituary should read, "He wrote books, then he died."

In effect, great men of action get remembered, their lives become visible, *through* various media of various works—biographies and monuments that recount their acts—while great artists or thinkers get remembered *for* various works, for having created this painting or that novel.

Ordinary would-be immortals are forced to reverse these roles. Ordinary "men of action"—managers, lawyers, merchants—are not going to be immor-talized by biographers or sculptors. Instead, the ordinary man of action has to create his own monument to himself: by donating to an institution, for instance, and having anything from a building to a brick bear his name. But this mechanism does not allow him to be remembered through the work—the building, the bench, the brick—in the way great men of action are remembered through a work of biography or a monument. Buildings, benches, and bricks hold no narrative. The individual whose name is on one of them may have been anything from an adept fly fisher to an arms salesman. At most, he will be remembered simply *for* the work—for being the name responsible for the building, bench, or brick.

Now consider bloggers or amateur web-video auteurs. All of them, blogger Eric S. Raymond says, are at some level "artists seeking an audience,"[28] not "all that different," in the words of psychologist David Greenfield, "from . . . other artists who create and hope their work will be accepted."[29] But the vast majority of blogs are not great works of art or thought for which their creators will be remembered. At best, individual bloggers or videographers can be remembered only *through* the work, which is essentially autobiography and self-portrait, giving a sense, however choppy and unwieldy, of who they were and what they did.

For the ordinary artist or thinker, then, what lives on after him is essentially a narrative of his life on line; for the ordinary man of action, it is a work, a building or a bench, that carries his name into the future. This seems considerably less satisfactory than what survives a great man of action—a narrative of his life in song and story—and a great artist or thinker—a work of art or thought carrying his name into the future.

So the quest to democratize immortality seems ill-fated. But in terms of public and private, what is going on here? On a traditional understanding—and at the most apparent level—donors are seeking to privatize portions of public physical space, while bloggers are virtually publicizing vast tracts of the private sphere. Although donors and bloggers vary the theme of this book insofar as they are not engaged in a debate with each other, they do represent two dominant forces, flowing in contrary directions, in the realm of contemporary space in America, one privatizing and the other publicizing. And yet, here as elsewhere, each force ultimately draws equally on values of the public and the private spheres, while applying them in mutually inverse ways.

Let's return to the way in which Hannah Arendt uses the terms *public* and *private* in *The Human Condition*. Arendt equates the public sphere with the realm of action, in which great "public men"—men in the public sphere, such as Lincoln or Churchill, who *do* things—acquire immortality through an appropriately public mode: a mode best suited for public men, namely, biography and monuments, through which the narrative of their deeds and acts will be set down for posterity. "[A]cting . . . men need the help of . . .

monument-builders or writers," Arendt argues, "because without them the only product of their activity, the story they enact and tell, would not survive at all."[30] Great men of action become known *through* such stories.

What of the great men who remain in the private sphere, having chosen not to act out the narrative of their lives on the public stage, preferring the *vita contemplativa* to the *vita activa*? If they seek to be remembered, they generally do so in the only way in which men who live a private life—men like Faulkner or Flaubert—can: for a work of art or thought. They don't do things; they create things. For such a person, Arendt writes, his "creations [will] survive him eventually"; and for all great artists and writers "their worst product is likely to be better"—and better known—"than they are themselves."[31] Great artists thus become known *for* their work.

Now, apply Arendt's concepts to the world created by the privatization of real public space and the encroachment by virtual public space into the realm of private life. First, consider the ordinary men of action—lawyers, businesspeople, local politicians, and community activists—who donate to public institutions and get their names recorded on a wall or a brick. Their lives are spent in the public sphere as Arendt understood it, the sphere of action. But they can be known only for, not through, the rooms, walls, and bricks their donations provide. Containing no narrative, those rooms, walls, or bricks are incapable of perpetuating the life "stories" of those who donated them; hence those stories, in Arendt's words, "cannot survive at all." In effect, those who have led these ordinary public lives find themselves seeking recognition in a mode more suited, ultimately, to those who have led private lives: those whose lives disappear behind the works they have created.

Now consider ordinary men and women leading private lives: bloggers and digital creators, ensconced at home in the domestic sphere in front of their computers. They are far more likely to be known through, rather than for, the blogs or videos they create, which are less great works of art or thought than narratives of their lives. Hence, it turns out that those who lead these ordinary private lives are seeking recognition in a way that ultimately is more suited to public men and women, to those who have led lives of action that more aptly lend themselves to narrative.

Donors push in the direction of increased privatization in real space, bloggers in the direction of increased publicity in virtual space. But at a deeper level, each side mixes modes, embracing traditions and values drawn from both the public and private realms. Donors live their lives in the public realm while necessarily seeking a mode of recognition appropriate for those who live their lives in the private sphere. Bloggers live in the private sphere but are compelled to seek a mode of recognition more suitable for public lives. Each side contains a flaw—how tragic a flaw depends on how much sympathy it evokes—born of the attempt to combine values that are mutually ill at ease, values concerning the kind of life worth leading, and the kind of recognition worth seeking, drawn in awkward hybrids from both the public and the private realms.

EDUCATION

4

WHAT'S WRONG WITH PRIVATE FUNDING FOR PUBLIC SCHOOLS?

In 1998 Diane Mancus was principal of Houston's Ser Niños Elementary School, located in a poor neighborhood a few miles from Rice School, a K-8 institution smack in the center of one of the city's wealthiest enclaves. Mancus remembers the day in March when both schools staged fundraisers. Rice held an auction, at which one parent bid $20,000 for a reserved parking space in front of the school so that he could drop his child off at the last minute. Others bid large sums to enable their sons and daughters to spend a day with the principal or to go on a weekend camping trip with the school's teachers. Ser Niños, by contrast, opted for a garage sale that raised $44. Unfortunately, Mancus recalls, the event ended on a sour note when "several parents who worked the sale complained that others were taking some of the items home with them."[1]

The contrast between Rice and Ser Niños is evocative for many reasons—not the least being the way in which Ser Niños's garage sale turned into a form of personal charity for the poverty-stricken parents, not just for the school itself, while Rice auctioned off parts of the school itself—teachers' time, principal's time—and not just, as is often the case, football tickets or computers donated by wealthy parents. But at the heart of Mancus's recollection is a story that is repeating itself across America: the growing willingness and capacity of parents to contribute private funds to their children's public school, thus introducing a new magnitude of inequality into the public system. As the title of a

Time magazine article on the subject suggested, and as the amounts raised at the Rice auction confirm, we have moved "Beyond Bake Sales."[2] Or, as Lydia Moss, principal of the District of Columbia's Clark Elementary, puts it, when wealthy parents contribute private funds to top up the public school budget, they are "getting a private school education for their kids on the public nickel."[3]

That description, "a private school education on the public nickel," almost makes it sound as if we are talking about vouchers. But in fact the idea behind vouchers is the opposite. With vouchers, parents use public funds to purchase services from the private schools their children attend. What Mancus describes is the reverse: parents using private resources to purchase services for the public schools their children attend. Although this practice has received much less national attention than vouchers, it provokes fierce equity debates at the local level across the country.

In a larger sense, though, the growing tendency for parents to fund public schools privately and the movement to get government to fund private schools publicly are of a piece. It is no accident that act60.org—a Vermont website devoted to advancing the cause of private funding for public schools—also contains several links to sites that promote public funding for private schools. Both are part and parcel of a two-decades-old political movement toward privatizing what have typically been public functions.

Defenders of parental fundraising have several ways of deflecting concern from the inequities that private money can introduce into the public school system. They note, for example, that far more substantial inequalities exist in public funding for public schools. This is true, but it is also beside the point. Public inequities exist between school districts, with wealthy districts in many states continuing to fund their schools at levels impossible for poorer districts. "Within districts"—as Kathy Christie of the Education Commission for the States notes—"boards and superintendents do not favor one school over another when allotting public funds."[4] And it is precisely this long-standing intradistrict level playing field that parents, who naturally favor their own child's school over others, disturb when they inject their own money into the system. It is exactly because "public money is being spent equally within districts," says Wayne Sampson of the Illinois Association of School Boards, that "parental inequality in private funding becomes a real problem."[5]

Even so, defenders of parental fundraising point out, the wealthiest parents can raise only a fraction—though sometimes as much as 10 percent—of the amounts their schools get in public funds. The inequities, they claim, are not all that significant. But this is reductionist: people's beliefs about whether they are being treated justly do not display a one-to-one correspondence with economic measures of inequality. Tocqueville noted long ago that as the most egregious social inequities diminish, the smaller ones grow vexatious and disruptive beyond their size; massive political discontent can fix on relatively small discrepancies. If one school "can hire a half-time art teacher with parental money, that becomes a real problem for that local community," says Sampson. "It raises all kinds of moral and ethical issues."

And, of course, it's not always just another half-time art teacher. Parental money now pays for auditoriums, science labs, extra first-grade teachers to reduce class sizes, and much more. True, there has always been some parental fundraising for public schools, and no one proposes to get rid of it outright.[6] But the question now confronting school boards across the country is this: Assuming the inevitability and desirability of at least some parental funding of public schools, where—on the spectrum from playground equipment to computers to teachers' aides to half-time art or language teachers to full-time grade-level teachers—should we draw the line as to what private money should be allowed to fund? Does anything go as long as parents can pay for it? When does the inequality become egregious? As it turns out, communities across the country have, willy-nilly, come up with a near universally shared if universally unspoken answer to this question. The problem is that it is not a very good answer.

WHICH INEQUALITIES?

To understand the answer and why it's not a good one, let's examine the anatomy of a particular parental fundraising controversy. In the late summer of 1997 parents at Greenwich Village's P.S. 41 organized to pay the salary of a fourth-grade teacher who would otherwise have been yanked from the school because student numbers no longer justified her presence. The then-chancellor of New York City schools, Rudy Crew, squelched the parental bid, and he did so on equity grounds, arguing, according to the *New York Times*, that it was "unfair for affluent parents to be able to reduce class size in this way while poor parents could not."[7]

Defenders of the parental bid were quick to point out that there was a problem with Crew's refusal. The chancellor had allowed New York parents to pay for playground equipment, computers, French teachers, art teachers, teachers' aides: everything short of grade-level teachers. Why was he drawing the line there? Indeed, several months after he clamped down on the P.S. 41 proposal, Crew warmly welcomed an alumni gift of $10 million to Brooklyn Technical High School, money intended to fund new computers, an aerospace-quality wind tunnel, and an electron microscope, each costing hundreds of thousands of dollars. Not surprisingly, as the *Times* reported, "word of the gift [to Brooklyn Technical] once again raised questions about . . . a potential double standard."[8]

Does allowing parents to spend money on some items for the public schools imply allowing them to spend on all? That's what the P.S. 41 parents seem to have been saying, thereby forcing Crew to come up with a rationale for his decision. Although he had no quarrel with "efforts by individuals . . . to finance fringe items—like computers or enhanced teacher training," Crew told the *Times*, it was vital that private money not skew "basic educational services" such as grade-level teachers.[9] As Steve Conn of Manhattan's Center for Education Innovation pointedly asks, however, "What is the difference, in this day and age, between computers and teachers?"[10] And even if you believe that grade-level teachers are more vital than computers, there will necessarily come a patch on the spectrum somewhere in between—say, the patch separating teachers' aides from French teachers—where the issues cease to be so clear-cut. "Funding an extra aide is maybe more inequitable than an extra French teacher," hazards Jim Terrell of Montgomery County Public Schools in Maryland, "but maybe not. . . . Where do you draw the line?"[11]

So Crew's attempt to carve out and protect some school services as more basic than others on pedagogical grounds founders. And yet, perhaps without saying so publicly, Crew was drawing another kind of line, not a pedagogical but a political one. Pat Lawrence, a former P.S. 41 PTA president, notes that a privately paid grade-level teacher—unlike a computer or a French teacher—would have created not just interschool but intraschool inequity. In contrast to a computer or a language teacher or even an electron microscope, all of which serve the entire student body or at least a large proportion of it, P.S. 41's proposed grade-four teacher would have served only students in the fourth grade. Instead of wanting to "help the school as a whole," Lawrence says, the fourth-grade parents were "earmarking their money to benefit their own children."[12] For many years, Lawrence points out, P.S. 41 had had a "dance teacher, paid for by the parents, and there was no squawk. But with a fourth-grade teacher, parents of first-graders were saying, 'Why is that important?'" Indeed, according to another former PTA president, Rebecca Daniels, P.S. 41 itself had an established rule on the books that said, "No raising money for your own class." There is thus, she says, a "policy of intraschool equity at P.S. 41," and "the hiring of the grade-four teacher"—which Daniels supported—was concededly "not consistent with it." The problem is that "it happened so fast and got so out of hand . . . parents were raising money in a matter of hours and that money . . . had to be embraced"; accordingly, it was ratified by the school PTA.[13]

So Crew did have available a rationale for saying no to P.S. 41's teacher (while saying yes to Brooklyn Tech's computers), but one that really had to do with intraschool, not interschool equity. Indeed, though Crew never said so, Pat Lawrence believes it was intraschool inequity that "really bothered the chancellor." She notes that shortly after the controversy, Crew began enforcing an old rule that forbids parents to give anything worth more than $50 to their own child's classroom—although parents can give a thousand times that to their own child's school. Anne Bryant, executive director of the National Schools Boards Association, offers a similar assessment: Crew "felt it's better for parents, if they're going to raise private money, to fund stuff that will enhance all the school's students."[14]

Further confirmation comes from Richard Goldstein, assistant principal at P.S. 321 in Brooklyn. Around the time that Crew denied P.S. 41's fourth-grade parents their wish to raise $46,000 for an extra fourth-grade teacher, parents at P.S. 321 raised $100,000—without running afoul of the chancellor—to pay the salaries of an art and a music teacher. If Crew had really been worried about interschool inequity, his denial of P.S. 41 and his nod of approval to P.S. 321 would have been inconsistent. But if his guiding principle was in fact "no intraschool inequality," then his two decisions were "easily reconciled," Goldstein says: "A fourth-grade teacher is more troubling than an art teacher, because its benefits to the school are less general."[15]

But if anything was testimony to the chancellor's focus on intraschool equity, it was the way in which he finally resolved the P.S. 41 affair. After prohibiting the grade-four parents from paying for their children's teacher, Crew turned around and directed the district superintendent to find public funding for the position. According to Lawrence, the money "came from a professional development fund that would have benefited all the teachers in the district." Ironically, the denouement in the P.S. 41 case was that the chancellor, though he avoided intraschool inequity in private funding, introduced a new measure of interschool inequity in public funding. To uphold the principle that all classes within a school must benefit from private parental support, Crew mollified the angry parents by raiding a public fund that would otherwise have benefited all schools within the district.

It is far from a singular case. Paul Vance, former superintendent of schools in Montgomery County, Maryland, recalls a group of parents in an east Silver Spring school seeking to pay privately for a special computer-lab teacher for advanced students. The board said no; the parents were upset, and "what ended the debate," Vance says, "was that the superintendent hired the teacher himself on the public payroll."[16] All of which goes to show how very sacred is the rule that requires private funding to be distributed equitably within the school. Officials are willing to distribute public funds inequitably across schools in order to uphold it.

In a sense, it is not surprising that intraschool inequity should emerge as such a powerful sub rosa criterion in debates over parental funding. It has a least-common-denominator quality: when politicians know that a particular expenditure raises equity concerns not only for other school communities but even for some parents at the particular school in question, they have enough cover to say no. The problem, however, is that intraschool equity is a very poor proxy for interschool equity; the two frequently diverge. Indeed, the universal fastidiousness with which the taboo against intraschool inequity is observed, in a nation where far more substantial amounts of interschool inequity are routinely tolerated, is remarkable.

Consider some examples. When it comes to funding field trips—at costs of $200 or so each—Brooklyn's Goldstein, whose school otherwise raises money in the six figures that he would never put into a districtwide pot, insists that parents put their contributions into a schoolwide fund. "They cannot go ahead," Goldstein says, "and raise money for a particular grade's outing." Likewise with Sam Skootsky, head of the booster club at Westwood School in Los Angeles, which raises $240,000 in parental money annually. "Fundraising," he says, "must benefit the whole school communally; you can't fundraise just for kindergarten. . . . We have turned down contributions earmarked for particular classes." Yet Skootsky dismisses the idea of parents giving their money to a districtwide fund, one that would benefit all schools in the area, precisely because that would be "too communal."[17]

Even in cases where individual classes are allowed to raise limited funds—as they still are, for example, under the old rule Chancellor Crew revived in New York—the intraschool equity norm cabins the practice within tight constraints. "For a long time," says Nancy Wainman, head of the well-heeled booster club at L.A.'s Warner Avenue Elementary, which contributes mightily to interschool inequity by raising $200,000 annually, "individual classes at Warner raised money for various projects and then kept the surpluses; we put a stop to that. Now, the surpluses must go into the general school kitty, to be spent by the [school's] leadership council."[18]

This principle of intraschool equity should not be confused with the very different principle courts have applied in cases concerning individual parental fee-paying. Courts tend to permit such fees precisely when only some students within the school will benefit—asking sixth-grade parents to pay individually for their child's field trip, say, is okay—but not when the fees are meant to benefit the whole school, in which case they are considered an illegitimate tax.[19] But while intraschool equity might not govern when parental monies flow into the school through fees, it does rule when they come in through fundraising. The problem is that although intraschool equity provided Chancellor Crew with a rationale with which to prohibit privately paid grade-level teachers, it does not, as Nancy Wainman and Sam Skootsky attest, seem to preclude much else in the way of interschool inequity.

And, in fact, the intraschool-equity norm does not even protect this last redoubt of grade-level teachers. Consider the case of Portland, Oregon. Unlike in New York—where parents may privately pay the salaries of French teachers but are forbidden to pay for grade-level teachers—in Portland, parents are allowed to pay the salaries of grade-level teachers, while a parent group at one local school was denied permission to underwrite the salary of a German teacher. It turns out, however, that the principle of intraschool equity was at play in Portland too; it just generated a different conclusion. One of the conditions that attaches to the hiring of an extra grade-level teacher in Portland is that the whole school, or at least a large proportion of it, benefits. Grade-level teachers can be made fungible, and in Portland an extra one is generally used to lower student-teacher ratios not just in the grade itself but throughout the school. Or, as Portland middle-school director Peter Hamilton puts it, "When you privately fund one more grade-one teacher, it can help [the] kid in grade four because of how the splits work out."[20] The problem with the proposed German teacher at Portland's Lincoln High, by contrast, was that German was of interest only to the kids of the few parents pushing it. When the council said "no German teacher," the interested parents declined to make a comparable contribution to the school as a whole—just as most of the P.S. 41 parents did in New York, when their plans for the grade-four teacher were turned down.

WHAT'S WRONG?

From superintendents to school boards, and from principals to parents, intraschool equity is the abiding norm across America, the mother rule to which parental fundraising for schools must adhere. But it is useless as a standard for drawing distinctions between more or less egregious kinds of interschool inequity. So it seems we come down to a stark question: Given the difficulties that exist in drawing a coherent line between acceptable and unacceptable interschool inequity, should we allow parents to raise funds for their own child's school? And if not, is there an alternative? The answers are no, we should not (perhaps beyond a certain de minimis level) allow parents to raise funds for their own child's school. And yes, there is an alternative: they can raise parental money for a fund that would distribute it, on fair criteria, to all schools in the district.

Consider the first question first: Why should we prohibit parents from contributing money to their own child's school? Actually, the argument of parent fundraisers provides the best answer. They insist that money be given communally at the school level, not parochially to the classroom. But on what consistent principle can they then require it to stay parochially at the school level, instead of going communally to the district—to be allocated on some equitable basis to all community schools? I asked several parent fundraisers this question; their answers were best articulated by Nancy Wainman of Warner Elementary's booster club. Ultimately, though, Wainman's attempt to square intraschool equity with interschool inequity fails.

Wainman begins by defending parental giving that confines itself to a child's school instead of flowing to the district as a whole. "Charity begins at home," she says, and "the local school is a part of you. It's like your extended family, and so you have the same obligation [to it as] you do to your family to help out." People, Wainman concludes, "just don't have the same feeling about the district." Wainman's argument here is reminiscent of the philosophical position taken by the moral theorist Bernard Williams, who believed that we bear special obligations to meet the needs of those closest to us, even if those needs are not as significant as those of strangers. It's permissible, in other words, to give your own child a bicycle, even when another child is starving in a village half way around the world. And this is exactly what Wainman urges, when she says that parents bear an obligation to care for those near and dear in the local school, before attending to the needs of those more distant in the rest of the district.

There's just one problem, though. The very claims of proximity that Wainman uses to defend the school against the district as a whole are also available to parents who would prefer to give to their own child's classroom rather than to the school as a whole. According to Neal Rosenberg, an attorney who represented the P.S. 41 grade-four parents, many of them—precisely because they, too, believe that charity begins at home—thought that "their primary obligation was to see that their own child's class was well-provided for first, and then they'd concern themselves with the school."[21] In other words, the argument that Wainman uses to oppose interschool equity undercuts her defense of intraschool equity.

But Wainman has a comeback to parental opponents of intraschool equity: there is something selfish about their position. When you "give to your own child's classroom," Wainman says, "it's like giving a gift to a member of your own family; it's not truly communal giving since your own child disproportionately benefits. . . . [P]arents who simply want to funnel money back to their own child's classroom don't always show enough community spirit."[22] When, on the other hand, "you give to the school, you are engaging in a more public-spirited act." In this case, the recipients are sufficiently distant from your own immediate circle of private interests—or, at least, your own child's interest remains sufficiently diluted within the relatively vaster student body—that there is a truly selfless, hence commendable, aspect to what you are doing. Here, Wainman's argument is redolent of the claims made by the philosopher Peter Singer, who criticizes people for donating to medical research in the hope that they will thereby benefit an ill relative. "That's not charity," Singer says; "it's self-interest."[23] By contrast, giving to starving villagers halfway round the world—which is what Singer counsels us to do—is clearly altruistic, since there is no way that you benefit.

But this very same Singeresque argument that Wainman uses to defend the claims of the school as a whole against the classroom is also available to those who would defend the claims of the district against the school. Beth Dilley, who raises private money for a districtwide fund in Grand Rapids, puts it this way: "Come on, let's not kid ourselves; giving to the district as a whole is a generous and community-minded act in a way in which giving to your own child's school simply is not, no matter how you dress it up."[24] In other words, the very argument Wainman uses to defend intraschool equity undercuts her opposition to interschool equity.

None of this is to find fault with Nancy Wainman or other fundraisers, nor is it to diminish the good she and others are doing for their schools. She is doing it, however, in a context that requires her to fight a war about obligation on two fronts, defending the claims of the school against those of the larger district on the one hand and against those of the smaller classroom on the other. If Bernard Williams says that charity begins at home, and Peter Singer maintains that when we get too close to home it ceases to be charity, Wainman has to take both positions, thereby handing each opponent the weapon she wields against the other.

In fact not only are parental fundraisers like Wainman fighting on two fronts, they are also—unlike Williams and Singer, whose competing claimants are a family member in the next room and a starving villager ten thousand miles away—doing so at very close range. The alternative recipients for Wainman's funds reside in another district school only six blocks away, or in a particular school classroom maybe a mere six yards away. To see why this creates uniquely serious moral problems for parental fundraisers, imagine a war about obligation being fought on two fronts, but where the alternative recipients are operating at far greater range. Because of the longer distances involved, for example, it seems plausible to say that giving to the United Way is indeed charitable by comparison with giving a bike to your son, along the lines advanced by Peter Singer. But it is still sufficiently close to home, by comparison with the stranger several continents away, to fulfill a legitimate prior obligation of the sort that Bernard Williams emphasized.

Certainly, that is more plausible than what parent fundraisers have to say: namely, that by comparison with your own child's classroom, your own child's school is somehow so significantly more removed from your circle of interests that giving to it would be demonstrably more altruistic. Not only that, but by comparison with schools as close as two or three miles away, the immediately local school is somehow so much closer to home that you have a greater obligation to it than you do to your own district as a whole.

There is thus a troubling inconsistency in the arguments that parent fundraisers make in defense of their activity. Once they have conceded that it is selfish to give to your own child's classroom instead of to the entire school, they have disarmed themselves against those who say it is selfish to give to your own child's school instead of to the entire district. Wainman reveals the strain in her argument by explicitly likening the local school to one's own "family"—so that you have a greater obligation to give to it than to the district—but then explicitly distinguishing the local school from one's "own family"— so that giving to it is distinctly less self-serving than giving to your own child's classroom. But it can't work both ways.

ALTRUISM, SELF-INTEREST, AND THE ESTATE TAX: A DIGRESSION

Wainman's sense of the school as both like and unlike one's family—so that giving to it falls within the bounds, by turns, of legitimate self-concern and admirable altruism—finds an echo in other contemporary American political debates. Consider, by way of a short digression, the battle over repealing the federal estate tax (a tax of up to 55 percent of a deceased person's bequest provided that it is larger than $1 million).

Those who favor repeal argue that the tax has the unwelcome effect of inducing wealthy individuals to spend their money on themselves—as opposed to leaving it for their heirs—because everything they spend on themselves eludes the tax. In this way, the tax unattractively favors "those who live lives of luxury," as University of Southern California law professor Ed McCaffery told a Senate committee, encouraging them to "leave smaller taxable estates" to their heirs.[25] Those opposing repeal argue that the tax actually has the welcome effect of inducing wealthy individuals to give charitably to the broader community—again, as opposed to leaving it for their heirs—since everything they donate to nonfamily members also remains exempt from the tax. The Brookings Institution has estimated that repeal would reduce charitable donations in America by between 22 and 37 percent, to the benefit of family members.[26]

In other words, those opposing the tax argue that once it is off the books, wealthy individuals will become more altruistic; they will spend less on themselves personally and leave more for their families. Those supporting the tax counter that if it is repealed, wealthy individuals will become more selfish, spending less on the community and leaving more to their own families. In the estate tax debate, the exact same act—supporting one's family—is seen as criticizably selfish by tax supporters and commendably altruistic by tax opponents. In that way, the estate tax debate runs into its own version of the complexities that beset the position taken by Nancy Wainman in the debate over private funding for public schools. There, the exact same act—giving to the school—is seen as both legitimately self-concerned, like giving to one's own family, but also as *not* like giving to one's own family, and thus commendably altruistic.[27]

WHAT IS GOING ON IN THE DEBATE OVER PARENTAL FUNDING FOR PUBLIC SCHOOLS?

On a traditional understanding, parental fundraisers represent a straightforward encroachment of the private realm—private money—into a formerly much more pristine public sphere of education. But underlying their movement is an unstable argument that relies equally—and awkwardly—on both public sphere and private realm values, the values of looking out for others and of caring for one's own.

Accordingly, opponents of parental fundraising—those who come at the matter from the community-wide level, such as Beth Dilley—cite those very public sphere values to eviscerate fundraisers' claims to be engaging in a legitimately self-interested act. Fundraisers, after all, insist that money go to the school as a whole, not to the individual classroom, so why not take that to the next level and insist that money go to the community as a whole instead of to the individual school? Simultaneously, opponents who come at matters from the other direction—parents seeking to support their own child's specific class-room, such as those Neal Rosenberg represented—cite school fundraisers' rhetoric about legitimate self-interest to diminish fundraisers' claims to be engaging in a respectably public act: fundraisers are, after all, raising money for the school and not the community as a whole. So why shouldn't parents be able to give to their own child's classroom instead of to the school as a whole?

If confining parental giving to the school level rests on a shaky political foundation, even on the principles held by its practitioners, what is the alternative? The PTA—which has always had an uneasy relationship with booster clubs like Wainman's—takes the position that individual schools face a choice: Either they should not raise money at all, or they should raise it for a districtwide fund, knowing, as Illinois PTA president Brenda Diehl puts it, that the fund "could then very well decide to use what they donate at a different building."[28]

Surely, of the two, it is better that parents raise money for the district than not at all. And indeed, about 30 percent of the country's school districts have such funds, which are generally established and governed by volunteers operating at arm's-length from the school board, distributing the money they raise according to criteria for which all district schools are eligible. Currently, however, they raise most of their money not from parents (with whom they often find themselves in frustrating competition) but from local corporations and foundations, which generally have no problem with interschool equity. Perhaps because they have no personal stake in a particular child's class, though, they are less constrained to observe intraschool equity and so frequently take a classroom-specific focus, as Amoco does, for example, when it concentrates its support on grade-five math classes.

But some parent fundraisers—and this is their ultimate fallback position—point out that whatever the moral niceties, the raw reality is that parents simply won't raise money if it is not going to their child's school. True, this isn't necessarily the case. A recent *Washington Post* report noted that the D.C. school board, in responding to parents who proposed to pay for stadium lights at select public schools, "insisted that lights be installed at every high school, not just those with deep-pocketed parents. The donors agreed, and the school system began raising private funds."[29]

But in other cities, when it comes to parental giving, the best answer has been to move from intraschool to interschool equity by degrees. Portland, Oregon, where parents are allowed to pay even for extra grade-level teachers, has piloted an interesting initiative. "Parents can pay for teachers at their kids' school," says Cynthia Guyer of the Portland Public Schools Foundation—a districtwide fund devoted to raising private money for Portland's schools—

"but they must give 33 percent back to the district fund, and we take that money and pool it for high-poverty schools through a competitive grant process." This one-third rule is a "marriage of tensions," Guyer acknowledges; "equity folks say it's too little; some parents say it's too much."[30] But so far, it's working.[31]

The greatest hope of reconciling psychological reality—parents often want to give only to their own child's school—with the moral context that undermines their justification for so doing, is to split the difference in this way. Districtwide funds and PTAs should accept that parents prefer to give to their own child's school and harness that preference by piggybacking on their fundraising, not hampering it. But in return, booster clubs and parent fundraisers should give more thought to the moral structure of their situation and allow that if they are going to deny the claim of the classroom just down the hallway, in the name of the school's greater good, they cannot then deny the claim of the school just down the highway, made in the name of the district's even greater good.

5

WHAT'S WRONG WITH STATE AID TO PAROCHIAL SCHOOLS?

At the core of American debate over public support for private schools lies the Establishment Clause of the First Amendment: "Congress shall make no law respecting an establishment of religion." Although state aid programs are invariably directed to all private schools, parochial or not, in every jurisdiction where a controversy has arisen, parochial schools constitute the "vast majority of private schools."[1] And although considerable debate surrounds nonconstitutional issues, ranging from the educational proficiency of parochial schools to their impact on the civic culture, the constitutional issues are central. Hence, I will focus on constitutional discourse over state aid to parochial schools.[2]

Nowhere is that discourse richer, of course, than in court cases, briefs, and legal commentary—the legal arguments advanced by opponents and supporters of local programs and by deciding judges—and so they will be my sources here. This discourse is very much centered on the most basic of grass-roots issues, issues having to do with parents, children, and their schools, but it is conducted centrally in the forum of the courts.[3] At the heart of this discourse, albeit in a number of different versions, lies the so-called "primary effects" test, articulated by the Supreme Court in 1971's *Lemon* v. *Kurtzman*: If the state aid in question—assistance to parochial schools for anything from bus transportation to textbooks, test administration to remedial instruction, vouchers to tuition tax credits—has the effect of advancing religion, then it violates the Constitution.[4]

My goal here is not to account for or critique the evolution of constitutional doctrine in the area of state aid to parochial schools, nor is it to explain and analyze the current state of the law, which is anything but settled. Cases on the subject have been decided by slim majorities, judges themselves have shifted their own individual positions over time, and lower courts continue to produce conflicting decisions. In fact, the only thing that remains stable is the rhetoric, the argumentation, that each side invariably advances no matter what kind of aid is at issue. I am interested here in following one strand of that argumentation, but it is a central one: the twisting strand in which either side—those judges or litigants upholding a particular program of aid to parochial schools and those opposing it—deploys the concepts of public and private. My goal is to puzzle through a particular contradiction that, in mirror-image form, lies at the heart of each camp's argumentation.

Aid opponents must (and indeed they invariably do) portray the program in question—whatever it is, from state-subsidized field trips to tuition tax credits—as one that illegitimately channels *public* money into *private* purposes—in particular, the parochial purposes of religious schools.[5] If the aid program can be so described, then the foundation for establishing its unconstitutionality has been laid. In countering, aid defenders reverse that portrayal. For them, the money in question is private, not public, while the purposes it serves are public, not private or parochial. And, after all, there can be nothing unconstitutional about the disposition of private money, whether it serves public or private purposes. Nor can there be any constitutional violation whenever public purposes receive money, regardless of whether that money itself is better understood as public or private.

How do aid proponents mount such an argument? First, they depict the aid money—notwithstanding its origins in the public treasury—as private money, on the ground that it flows to any given parochial school in the first place only because of the private choices parents make to send their children there. As Justice William H. Rehnquist wrote for the Supreme Court in 1983's *Mueller* v. *Allen*, "Where aid to parochial schools is available only as a result of decisions of individual parents"—where private individuals, not the state, control its ultimate disposition—then, on this argument, "no 'imprimatur of state approval' can be deemed to have been conferred on any particular religion, or on religion generally."[6] And as UCLA law professor Eugene Volokh vividly puts it, "No one cares whether government employees or Social Security recipients donate parts of their checks to religious organizations [or whether] college students . . . spend G.I. Bill funds or Pell grants or government subsidized student loans to attend college at Notre Dame or Georgetown or even to study theology."[7] With state aid to parochial schools, the parental intermediary—as does the recipient intermediary with Social Security or the student intermediary with Pell grants—"break[s] the circuit," as Justice David Souter said, between "the government and the ultimate religious beneficiary."[8] Such circuit-breaking thereby converts what would otherwise be constitutionally regulated public money into freely disposable private money.

With some programs, money flows to parochial schools literally through the hands of parents, as when the state gives them vouchers that they can then use at any school they choose for their child. In other cases, the state sends the money to the school directly—as with money for the administration of exams—but even here the aid still goes to any given school per capita: only to the extent that parents choose to send their children there. And "although the presence of private choice is easier to see when aid literally passes through the hands of individuals, there is no reason why the Establishment Clause requires such a form."[9] Any per capita benefit that goes to a religious school—that which flows literally through parental hands and that which does not—flows there, aid proponents conclude, "only as a result of the intermediating" and "genuinely independent and private choices of individuals."[10] For this reason, aid proponents claim, state money that goes to parochial schools via everything from programs of assistance for counseling and test administration to vouchers is actually better understood as private, not public, in character. Hence constitutional concerns do not apply.

Second, proponents of state aid to parochial schools argue that the aid money, which they depict as not public but private, in any case serves purposes that are not private—not parochial—but public. What presumption underlies these claims? Far from "carry[ing] out . . . private purposes," the Supreme Court declared in 1947's *Everson* busing-aid case, "the New Jersey legislature has decided that a public purpose will be served by using tax-raised funds to pay the bus fares of all school children, including those who attend parochial schools."[11] The "transportation of children to school," as one commentator elaborated this argument, amounts to "general welfare legislation similar to providing police and fire protection."[12] And the same with aid for textbooks: publicly provided textbooks for parochial schools are like "public provision of police and fire protection, sewage facilities, and streets and sidewalks," which we do not deny to churches or other parochial institutions.[13] That's because a legitimate public purpose—educating children in the case of busing and textbooks, providing for public health and safety in the case of policing and fire protection—is being advanced.[14] The "public welfare . . . require[s] that state and local communities give assistance to [parochial school] education programs," as the Supreme Court has said, because a well-educated citizenry is as "important [as] national defense [to] the general welfare of the state."[15]

So, when they argue that aid for parochial schools is going for a public, not a parochial, purpose, aid defenders conceive it as "analogous to the provision of services such as police and fire protection."[16] In the same way, when they are trying to urge that the money in question really is no longer the public's but rests in private control, aid defenders liken it to Social Security checks or Pell grants, money that may originate in the state treasury but whose expenditure we clearly think of as private.[17]

There is a large element of plausibility to both claims—so large that, though it by no means has ended heated debate over state aid to parochial schools, it has shifted the arena of disagreement. Almost all money that flows from the state to parochial schools indeed does so, as aid defenders claim, through the private choice of parents; in other words, it takes per capita form. And all such aid goes directly to public purposes, in that it is always confined to the secular component of the parochial school's activities, supporting such items as busing, English textbooks, or science field trips. Never does it go to parochial purposes such as prayer books or religious instruction; even vouchers are generally set so that they pay for only a portion of a parochial school curriculum: that portion that can reasonably be called secular.[18] True, there are aid opponents who continue to insist that any and all money that originates in the public treasury is ipso facto public money, whether its disposition is controlled by private individuals or not. And there are those who steadfastly maintain that all instruction undertaken by parochial schools, no matter how ostensibly secular, is susceptible to being subverted to parochial ends—that a parochial message can always creep into the interpretation of a textbook in an English course, or a discussion of evolutionary biology in science.

But the main debate lies elsewhere. Even if aid flows only on a per capita basis—that is, only because parents choose to send their children to a particular school—that does not mean, aid opponents say, that parents are making such decisions free of any and all interference by the state, in the way that aid defenders say. The structure of the aid monies might still be such that the government is, in effect, pulling strings or nudging parents in some indirect way, giving them a new incentive to choose parochial school. And if so—if the state is exerting this kind of influence over the money's disposition, even if not outright control—then the money must be deemed to be public. By the same token, even if the purposes to which the money flows are purely public ones— even if no parochial messages seep into the secular remedial instruction or the textbooks that the aid supports—the aid might still indirectly free up school funds that the parochial school could then devote to parochial purposes: worship services and sectarian instruction. Because money is fungible, that would be tantamount to state funds flowing to parochial purposes.

This is the current arena of debate over whether state aid for parochial schools amounts to public money for private purposes, as opponents say, or private money for public purposes, as defenders insist. But in advancing their arguments, each side makes claims for how to understand the public-private nature of "money" that undermine its arguments regarding the private-public nature of "purpose"—and vice versa.

MONEY: PUBLIC OR PRIVATE?

The argument over whether the money can best be understood as public or private comes down to this question: How much control over its disposition do private individuals—parents—actually have? For an individual's choice to be "truly voluntary and autonomous of government," the "state may not attempt to influence that choice."[19] But when "the state create[s]. . . incentives for students to select sectarian schools"—as aid opponents believe most aid programs do, per capita though they may be—the state in fact plays a "role in the decision-making process that ultimately determine[s] where the funds would be spent." And so religious institutions cannot be said to "receive . . . assistance only as a result of the genuinely independent and private choices of aid recipients."[20]

By definition most aid programs embody such an incentive, aid opponents argue, a state thumb on the scale of parental choice. After all, any proposed program that would direct some new aid to private schools—even though comparable aid (whether free transportation, textbooks, or busing) is already available to public schools—provides a new incentive for parents to patronize private schools. It disturbs an immediately preexisting—what I call an "existential"—baseline. Compared with the status quo ante, at least some parents will now, as a result of the aid program, have a greater incentive than they previously had to send their children to private school.[21] Compared with yesterday, such aid—directed as it would be toward private schools—"clearly increases the financial incentive to choose religious schools by lowering their price," as one commentator has argued, thus "significantly chang[ing] the price structure of the available options. [It makes] religious education . . . significantly cheaper than it is at present."[22] Here, the words *change* and *at present* are key. What the aid program does is to change the present, the immediately existing status quo, creating a new publicly provided incentive for parents to send their children to parochial school.[23]

Even if another near-identical program exists for public school students and their parents, that is insufficient—for aid opponents—to eliminate the incentive effect. The proper baseline is not some historical or theoretical plane of prior equality, such that, if the state then at one point provided (say) free transportation for public school students and later offered a comparable private-school program, no skewing incentive either way would be deemed to have been created. Rather, the proper baseline is whatever immediately preceded the introduction of the privately oriented program, even if what existed previously included comparable or (for that matter) more significant aid to the public system. As Justice Lewis F. Powell Jr. said in *Nyquist*, a 1973 case that struck down New York's package of tuition tax benefits for parents of private school children:

> We do not agree with the suggestion . . . that tuition grants are . . . analogous [to] comparable benefits to . . . public . . . schools. The grants to parents of private school children are given in addition to the right that they have to send their children to public schools "totally at state expense."[24]

Aid opponents, then, take what I will call an "existential" approach in determining whether the aid money—by representing an "addition," as Justice Powell said, to whatever existed previously—shifts the playing field in favor of parochial education. They look at the immediately preexisting status quo, however much, by some normative measure, that status quo already favors public schools. And they view any inducement to depart from it as a choice-influencing nudge by the state, one that "by necessity creates [an] impermissible financial incentive for students to undertake sectarian education,"[25] "induc[ing] attendance at those schools."[26] That incentive or inducement takes the aid's disposition out of the unfettered discretion of private parties—parents—and places it in the hands of the state. For when a program "creates [a] financial incentive for parents to choose a sectarian school," what we really have is an instance of "state decisionmaking."[27] Because the state is still controlling the money, that money remains public—subject to constitutional strictures—and not private.[28]

Aid proponents, by contrast, adopt a normative approach, on which the baseline is not the happenstance of whatever the immediately preexisting empirical state of the world might have been. Instead, it is some theoretical or prior historical state, one in which the state is or was providing no aid to any schools, public or private. Against that kind of baseline, aid defenders claim, a new aid program—even if it focuses exclusively on private schools—comes with no incentives that might influence private, that is, parental choice. After all, it is matched (and then some) by a more long-standing and generally more generous program of comparable state aid to public schools. Hence the money, free of any skewing effect, remains wholly privately controlled. As Joseph P. Viteritti says, "Even if [a new program] had paid the full tuition, it only would have equalized the financial burden that exists between the public and non-public school populations. That alone is not an incentive."[29]

In criticizing Justice Powell's decision in *Nyquist*, a *Harvard Law Review* commentary complained that Powell had looked only at the "newly provided benefits to the private schools." He had looked at the "effect of the program in isolation," and "[f]rom this perspective it naturally appeared as an 'incentive' to religious education."[30] A more appropriate focus, the commentary argued, would have required stepping back from the existential present and viewing the new program instead from a theoretical or historical baseline: what the constitutional scholar Jesse Choper calls "both a traditional and normative one,"[31] from which "overall government programs in aid of [public and private] education would be weighted against one another."[32] Such a baseline would, as one legal scholar put it, take into account that while "[s]ome of the statutes presented to the Court have involved aid to private schools alone, [they] have often been direct counterparts of provisions for public schools," and "it is immaterial whether the aid was made available to all schools through one statute or two."[33]

In his appearance before a 1981 Senate committee, then-professor Antonin Scalia offered one of the most explicitly normative, antiexistential understandings of incentive on record. The "'broadness' or 'narrowness' of benefit coverage," Scalia said,

> should be determined by the total scope of a logically and conceptually unitary program, and not by the scope of [the actual program itself]. For the 'broadness' or 'narrowness' factor speaks to the presence or absence of preferential purpose and effect, and it can hardly be called preferential to add to an existing program a group that could logically have been included in the first place.[34]

Scalia here strips away what existed immediately prior, rejecting the idea that any mere addition "to an existing program" renders the aid narrowly focused on whatever beneficiaries have been newly added. Instead, he reaches further back to a theoretically grounded or historically significant—a "logical or conceptual"—baseline. Only then can one ask whether, when taken together with any support that exists for public schools beyond that baseline, the proposed aid to private education will skew parental choice in favor of the latter. And he concludes that any such aid simply evens out the advantage previously given to public schools against a theoretical or historical baseline of no state assistance to any schools, public or private.[35]

What follows, then, if on the appropriate normative baseline, the aid money comes absent any state-fashioned incentives or skewing mechanisms? In other words, what follows if, as Scalia argues, any aid to private schools is canceled out by previously bestowed aid to public schools? The answer is that its expenditure in parochial schools is entirely at the discretion of the parents. It ceases to be public money and becomes private. "When the government offers [aid] that 'is in no way skewed towards religion'"—aid that "creates no financial incentive for parents to choose a sectarian school"—then its disposition "cannot be attributed to state decisionmaking" and it "does not offend the Establishment Clause."[36] It reaches the parochial school only through "private choice" and is "completely devoid of state intervention or direction."[37]

MONEY: A SUMMARY

In sum, the debate over incentive—over whether a particular aid package creates an inducement to choose private over public schools—comes down to this. On the one hand are aid opponents, who take the immediately preexisting status quo, whatever it is, as the baseline. For them, "judgments about the state of the world must be brought to bear."[38] After all, the "state of the world" is a real and definable baseline, they urge, whereas a "background norm"— such as the "principle of [utter] neutrality" between public and private—"by itself is insufficient to define the baseline" because it gives "free rein to our political preferences and prejudices."[39] A normative baseline can be located in any one of a number of places depending on the beliefs of the person advancing it. And because aid programs invariably create some new reason, by comparison with any immediately preexisting baseline, for parents to go private, they fall afoul of the incentive test. The parents are not deciding wholly for themselves, but rather are being subjected to a new influence, created by the state and skewing them toward parochial schools. The money remains public, not private.

On the other hand are aid defenders, who urge a more normative baseline, one that theoretically abstracts from or is historically antecedent to the existential state of the world, whatever that happens to be. Or, as Justice Clarence Thomas put it in his concurring opinion in *Rosenberger*, "The constitutional demands of the Establishment Clause may be judged against . . . a baseline of 'neutrality'" or some other theoretically defended or historically significant baseline. "But," whatever it is, "the appropriate baseline surely cannot depend on the fortuitous circumstances," the existential state of the world, "surrounding the form of aid."[40] On the kind of theoretical or historical baseline that Justice Thomas prefers, one that abstracts from or exists prior to state support for public schools, any assistance for private schools simply (and only partially) counterbalances that support. Far from embodying a state-fashioned incentive to go private, the aid makes the matter at best a wash, throwing all decisions back to unfettered parental discretion. The money becomes private, no longer public. And private money, of course, can constitutionally serve private, even parochial, purposes.

The remaining question, however, is whether those purposes really are private-parochial, or instead are public. Here, as we shall see, it is opponents of aid, in claiming that its purposes are ultimately private, that is, parochial, who adopt a resolutely normative baseline in assessing the issues. And it is proponents of aid, in arguing that its purposes are really public, who use a relentlessly existential baseline: just the opposite of the positions each side occupies in the debate over whether the money is public or private.

PURPOSES: PRIVATE OR PUBLIC?

Even aid that flows (as all aid does) to purely secular purposes—English textbooks or administration overhead, busing or remedial math—can further a school's parochial purposes. For if it was the school's responsibility to supply those textbooks or remedial math instructors, however secular they might be, then any state aid for those purposes relieves that responsibility. It allows the school to free up funds that it can then devote to religious purposes. As Justice William O. Douglas put it in his *Lemon* concurrence, the "school is an organism living on one budget. What the taxpayers give for salaries of those who teach only the humanities or science without any trace of proselytizing enables the school to use all of its own finds for religious training."[41] They "relieve the sectarian school of costs it otherwise would have borne in educating its students."[42]

Consequently, where courts have deemed a contested aid program to be furthering purposes that the school would otherwise have had to underwrite, no matter how secular, they have struck it down. In *Ball*, where the aid at issue—salary support for teachers—"in effect subsidize[d] the religious functions of the parochial schools by taking over a substantial portion of their responsibility for teaching secular subjects,"[43] the programs were stricken.[44] On the flip side, where courts have determined that aid goes to purposes supplemental to anything the parochial school bore an obligation to provide—as the *Mitchell* Court did with aid for instructional equipment—they have held the program constitutional. After all, it would not be relieving schools of any financial responsibility that they would otherwise be shouldering, freeing up funds for sectarian purposes.[45]

But of course, the question of what constitutes a school's responsibility is by no means incontestable. Consider first the argumentation of aid proponents. In *Zobrest* v. *Catalina*, an appeals court struck down public provision of an interpreter for James Zobrest, a deaf student attending Salpointe parochial school (a decision the Supreme Court later reversed). The dissent, in arguing for the constitutionality of the state's aid to Zobrest, pointed out that the "provision of an interpreter . . . would not relieve Salpointe of any *preexisting* financial or educational obligation."[46] The key word *preexisting* literally reveals an existential criterion, a concern with the immediate state of the world. And the existential reality is that the school had not, in fact, been providing the service in question. Hence, the dissent insisted, the aid would have freed up no school funds—funds that otherwise would have been spent on an interpreter—that the school could then have used for religious purposes.

In *Everson* and *Allen*, where the aid consisted of busing and textbooks, defenders likewise observed that neither good fell under an immediately preexisting obligation of the school, meaning that no parochial school funds that might otherwise have been spent on them would have been freed up. As the *DiCenso* court noted in reviewing these cases, "prior to enactment [of the aid package], parents bore the costs" of the bus fares at issue in *Everson* and the textbooks in question in *Allen*.[47] The phrase *prior to* is key. It is an existential term, one that directs our attention to what, in fact, schools had (or more to the point, had not) been doing.[48] Similarly, in *Ball*, defenders of a program that placed public school teachers in religious schools to teach certain secular classes "argue[d] that [the] 'subsidy' effect is not significant . . . because the . . . program . . . supplemented the [parochial school] curriculum with courses *not previously* offered."[49] Again, whatever the situation was existentially "previous" to the initiation of the program is controlling. And if parochial schools were not in fact providing the service at that stage, then a new state program that offered it would free up no parochial school funds to be used for religious purposes.[50]

So aid defenders, taking the preexisting situation as the baseline, note that none of the programs contested in the major court cases would—as a matter of existential fact—have underwritten services that parochial schools were otherwise offering. No school funds would have been freed up by the aid. State support, then, remained confined to whatever public, secular purposes—books, English teachers, test administration—the program was meant to boost and thus did not abet parochial purposes even indirectly, let alone directly.

Aid opponents, consequently, must and do appeal to a normative baseline of school obligations. They argue that the services in question, secular though they may be and lying as they may well outside the school's existing baseline responsibilities, nevertheless fall within its baseline responsibilities understood according to the proper theoretical or historical standard. Thus, for the state to help defray the service is indeed tantamount to its supporting the school's sectarian activities. Any such support frees up funds that the school would otherwise have had a normatively construed obligation to spend on equipment or busing or remedial education or whatever the aid in question happens to support, whether or not it was *actually* fulfilling that responsibility at the existing moment. On this interpretation, the purposes the aid furthers can very easily become private—parochial—instead of assuredly remaining public.

So, for example, in *Everson*, which upheld aid for school busing—something that had not as a matter of fact fallen within parochial schools' existing responsibilities—Justice Wiley B. Rutledge, in dissent, took a normative approach. "Transportation," he opined,

> where it is needed, is as essential to education as any other element . . . No less essential is it, or the payment of its cost, than the very teaching in the classroom or payment of the teacher's sustenance. . . . For me . . . payment for transportation is no more, nor is it any the less, essential to education, whether religious or secular, than payment for tuitions, for teachers' salaries, for buildings, equipment and necessary materials. . . . No rational line can be drawn between payment for such larger, but not more necessary, items and payment for transportation.[51]

Justice Rutledge's repeated use of the word *essential* is key here. It echoes a venerable terminological opposition in modern philosophy between the *essential* and the *existential*. The first defines the nature of a thing by its essence—by a normative notion of what it should do—and the second by its existential qualities, by the happenstance of what it actually is or does do.[52] In these and other cases, aid opponents argue that "where the state has supplied [parochial] schoolchildren with transportation and books, sectarian educational enterprises are indirectly aided by being relieved of a financial burden which they might otherwise feel obligated to bear."[53] Not that they actually happen to bear, but that they "might otherwise feel obligated to bear": a normatively, not existentially, drawn baseline.[54]

What of cases like *Ball* and *Meek*, involving programs of state support for instructional materials and teachers of secular subjects at parochial schools? Recall that aid defenders "argue that [these programs] supplement the curriculum with courses not previously offered in the religious schools."[55] But aid opponents remain unmoved by what might immediately "previously" have been the existential case. "[W]e do not," they say,

> find that this feature of the program is controlling. . . . The distinction between courses that "supplement" and those that "supplant" the regular curriculum is therefore not nearly as clear as petitioners allege. [And] although the precise courses offered in these programs may have been new to the participating religious schools, their general subject matter— reading, mathematics, etc.—was surely a part of the curriculum in the past, and the concerns of the Establishment Clause may thus be triggered despite the "supplemental" nature of these courses.[56]

Here, we see both a theoretically based claim—the "distinction between courses that 'supplement' and those that 'supplant'" is not clear—and a historical one— "surely" these supplementary programs were "a part of the curriculum in the past." These claims get put up against the admitted fact that, by comparison with the immediately preceding existent state, the courses supported here were indeed "new" to the schools in question. What matters, though, is that state-funded instructional materials or secular teaching frees up money that parochial schools should have to spend (even if they aren't actually doing so) on those purposes: money that they can then devote to sectarian ends.

What of the only major case where the teaching services that the state sought to support were *in fact*, and not just on a particular norm, part of the parochial school's mandate? What, in other words, of the only major case where, as an existential matter, the school was actually already providing the service in question? That case was *Lemon* itself, where the state sought to assist parochial schools in paying the salaries of instructors teaching core secular subjects. But even here, although aid opponents could have appropriated the existential argument—claiming that as a matter of fact the services were indeed previously being funded by the school, so that the aid would in fact free up funds for possible sectarian purposes—they chose instead to argue on normative grounds. They opted to claim that the English and math teaching services being assisted were, as a normative matter, part and parcel of a school's responsibility. Or, to use the old distinction, they argued on essentialist, not existentialist, criteria, looking at the essence of what a school should be rather than the existent fact of what it actually does. "Quality teaching in secular subjects is an integral part of the religious [school] enterprise," Justice William J. Brennan Jr. declared in his *Lemon* concurrence, and "[g]ood secular teaching is as essential to the religious mission of the parochial schools as a roof for the school or desks for the classroom."[57]

PURPOSES: A SUMMARY

In almost all school aid cases, then, the service in question—from busing to textbook provision, from remedial to interpretive services—is, as a matter of existential fact, not one that the private school had been supplying previously. Aid defenders seize on this fact, arguing that it means the aid in no way relieves the school of a burden it would otherwise have been bearing. It thus in no way frees up any of the school's resources for private religious purposes. And so the purposes that the aid does underwrite—busing, textbooks, interpretive services, remedial instruction—remain, defenders conclude, purely public. But in so conceiving baseline school educational responsibilities, aid defenders rely on precisely the kind of "fortuitous" existential criterion they critique, in the debate over the public-private nature of aid money, for determining baseline government educational responsibilities.

Aid opponents, by contrast—here eschewing whatever fortuitous circumstances happen to surround the aid as a thin reed on which to base definitions of school responsibility—advance their own normative view. They make the case that regardless of what the immediately preexisting situation might have been, the aid supports a service that, on some set of theoretical grounds, would be considered part of a parochial school's mission. Or else historically, at some time before the immediate present, it might have fallen under the parochial school's responsibility.[58] Thus, to publicly subsidize that service is indeed to assist the school. It is to free up funds that—were the school operating not as it is, but as it would under the appropriate "social norm" or "historical baseline"[59]—the school would otherwise have been obligated to spend on whatever it is that the aid now supports. Those funds, then, are in effect being made available for private, parochial purposes. Here, the objection that aid opponents register against normative baselines in debates over the public-private status of money—that such baselines can be plucked out of the theoretical or historical air to support any position—seems to have evaporated.[60]

CONTRADICTIONS

On a traditional understanding, the debate over state aid to parochial schools gets characterized as a battle between defenders of the public sphere and partisans of the private realm. Supporters of the public school system are seen to be locked in combat with those who would enable private schools, most of them parochial, to capture for themselves a large chunk of that public terrain.

And at one level that is certainly an apt description. But at another level, one more focused on their argumentation, what divides the two sides is how to apply two different kinds of baselines on which they each rely equally. One of those baselines, an existential one, leads to a public framing of whatever it is deployed to conceptualize, whether money or purposes. The other, a normative one, leads to a private framing.

So it is that aid opponents use an existential baseline for determining *governmental* responsibilities in the realm of secular education. Against an existential baseline—a baseline derived from whatever the government had been doing immediately before the aid program—the government, in initiating the program, is providing a new incentive to choose parochial school. The aid money thus remains controlled or directed by the state, hence public and subject to constitutional strictures. Meanwhile, their antagonists—aid proponents—use an existential baseline for determining *parochial school* responsibilities in the realm of secular education. Against an existential baseline—a baseline derived from whatever parochial schools had been doing immediately before the aid program, which generally would not have included the new services the program funds—the aid would be freeing up no parochial school monies that could then be used for sectarian purposes. The aid's purposes would remain public, hence constitutionally unproblematic.

If an existential baseline leads to a public framing, whether of aid money (for opponents) or of its purposes (for proponents), a normative baseline leads to a private framing. Thus, it is to a normative baseline that aid proponents appeal in determining governmental responsibilities in the realm of secular education. After all, against an appropriate normative baseline—a baseline derived from a theoretical or historical notion of government neutrality between public and private education—the government, in initiating the aid, is providing no overall nudging incentive to choose parochial school; rather, it is just countering the advantage that, over time, public schools have come to enjoy. The aid money thus falls entirely within the realm of private discretion and hence lies beyond constitutional concern. Aid opponents, for their part, recur to a normative baseline in determining parochial school responsibilities in the realm of secular education. After all, against an appropriate normative baseline—a baseline derived from a historical or theoretical notion of the kinds of services parochial schools should be providing—school responsibilities are being relieved, and school funds therefore are being freed up for parochial activities. The purposes that the aid supports are thus, properly understood, private-parochial. Hence, constitutional concerns are quite legitimate.

In constitutional discourse there is a primordial incompatibility between existential and normative approaches to baselines, one well illustrated in Cass R. Sunstein's *Partial Constitution*. For Sunstein, the conflict between those who take "existing arrangements," "existing practices," or "the status quo as the baseline" for analyzing the constitutional effect of law and policy—and those who "abandon the status quo as a baseline and instead rel[y] on ... principle" or "historical context"—is a fundamental fault line in American constitutional jurisprudence.[61] Yet what separates pro- and anti- forces in debates over state aid to parochial schools is not that one side takes an existential view and the other a normative perspective, as is the case in the interpretations Sunstein offers of the constitutional debates he analyzes, such as those over pornography, abortion, or campaign finance. Rather, in American discourse over state aid to parochial schools, each side adopts both an existential and a normative perspective, by turns, the one leading to a public and the other to a private framing of whatever is being described. The difference is that for aid proponents, what is private is the money and what is public are its purposes, while for defenders, it is the other way around.

And so a question remains for each side to grapple with. To aid opponents: If government's baseline responsibilities are to be determined by looking simply at the existing status quo, why not so determine the school's? And to aid proponents: If the government's baseline responsibilities are to be ascertained by adopting some normative or historical perspective, why not so define the school's? Currently neither side has an answer to these questions. Each is thus equally afflicted by a central tension in its position.[62]

6

COMMERCIALISM IN
THE PUBLIC SCHOOLS

Los Angeles–based Tooned-In Menu Team, Inc., prints four million menus each month for school cafeterias around the country, each one laden with ads for products such as Pillsbury cookies or Pokemon. The deal is this: in exchange for getting their menus done up for free, participating schools provide Tooned-In with a ready market for its advertisers. It is just one of a proliferating number of arrangements forged each year between schools (or school boards) and companies. Consider McDonald's All-American Reading Challenge, in which McDonald's gives hamburger coupons to elementary school students in exchange for their reading a certain number of books. Or Piggly Wiggly's offer to donate money to a school in return for sales receipts from the school community indicating proof of purchase at the store. Or the American Egg Board's "Incredible Journey from Hen to Home" curricular material, which is provided to schools for free while also promoting egg consumption. Or ZapMe!, which furnishes schools with free computer labs in return for the opportunity to run kid-oriented banner ads on the installed browsers and collect aggregate demographic information on students' web-surfing habits.

In each case, the school gets something—money, equipment, incentives for students to learn, curricular material—at a time of shrinking public education budgets. And the companies also get something: access to a lucrative market, enabling them to build brand loyalty in a new generation of consumers. That is why the term *commercialism in the schools*, with its controversial connotations, never gets applied to the sorts of universally praised deals—such as company-sponsored scholarship, internship, or training programs—in which companies treat students not as future consumers but as future employees.

And indeed commercialism in the schools is controversial; it attracts fierce criticism. National organizations such as the Yonkers-based Consumers Union or Oakland's Center for Commercial-Free Public Education—as well as numerous ad hoc parental movements at the local level—have taken up arms against commercial deals, battling companies in school board hearings and courtrooms. Their concerns: that commercial deals cede control of the education agenda to nonteachers, that they prey upon a captive audience, that they distort kids' and families' consumer choices, that they foster materialistic values, and that they bombard schoolchildren with biased, commercially motivated messages in a place where the information disseminated is expected to be objective and confined to pedagogical purposes. The debate has become shrill and polarized. "I was speaking to one of my critics not long ago," says Tooned-In's director of school relations, Frank Kohler. "She doesn't own a car because she's opposed to the use of fossil fuels. She doesn't go to the movies because she resents the commercials. I said to her, 'Lady, you don't represent America!'"[1]

Yet there is a big problem with both commercialism's critics and its defenders. Neither side adequately distinguishes—among the many kinds of deals out there—between those that are genuinely troubling and those that are not; both paint with a broad brush. In the eyes of Ernest Fleishman, senior vice president for education at Scholastic, Inc., a New York–based company that sells books and posters through the schools, many of his antagonists "tend to use shotguns" in their attacks. "They draw no distinctions," Fleishman complains, between the "very, very different kinds of deals schools strike with companies."[2] But certainly, defenders of commercialism in the public schools are themselves not always prone to drawing boundaries and ceding some ground to the opposition. Paul Folkemer, spokesman for the controversial "Channel One"—which beams a twelve-minute newscast including two minutes of paid advertising into 8,000 schools daily—justifies his company's business this way: "Commercialism has always existed in the schools; think of the local drugstore that used to advertise in the high school yearbook."[3] But is there no pertinent way of distinguishing Channel One from the high school yearbook?

If we were going to draw lines between the various kinds of commercialism so understood, the best way to begin would be to distinguish two basic types of commercial deal, types well exemplified by the contrary arrangements that Pizza Hut and Domino's have struck with American schools. On the one hand,

Pizza Hut rewards children who read a certain number of books in a particular period of time with free pizza. On the other, Domino's rewards kids who buy pizza—or more exactly their school, which sends the receipts in to the local franchise—with free books. The dynamics of these two programs precisely reverse one another. In the Pizza Hut deal, students perform an act that is supposedly part of their role in the public schools: They read. In return, what the company offers is a private market commodity: pizza. With the Domino's arrangement, kids slip outside of their public school roles and perform a private market act by buying pizza. In return, the company furnishes schools with the wherewithal to buy public goods—goods that are of value to the teaching role of the public schools, such as books.

As it turns out, the Pizza Hut and Domino's programs aptly symbolize the two basic kinds of arrangements companies invariably make with schools; almost every instance of commercialism falls into one or the other category. Either, as in the Pizza Hut deal, the school offers a public good—students' reading time, or classroom space, or curricular access—and the company reciprocates with whatever private market commodity it happens to sell, whether pizza, coupons for orange juice, or samples of spaghetti sauce, sometimes dressed up as curricular material. Or, as with the Domino's deal, the school offers the company something of private market value—namely, its own students as consumers—and the company offers the school matériel or monies of public value: books, equipment, computers, or outright cash gifts that have no connection with whatever it is the company sells. The first kind of deal can be troubling, but not for the reason most critics believe. The second, however, is simply far less disturbing than critics allow.

SCHOOLS PROVIDE PUBLIC GOODS; COMPANIES PROVIDE PRIVATE MARKET COMMODITIES

Begin by considering a few examples of the first kind of deal, the Pizza Hut type. Minute Maid, for instance, has staged its own version of the Pizza Hut arrangement: Students read—that is, they do something that is part of their role in the public schools—and in return they receive book covers advertising Minute Maid's private market commodity, orange juice, or rebates on purchases. A few years ago, in a similar vein, schools across the country struck an agreement with General Mills, according to which they would devote classroom time—a public good—to a science experiment in which students would pop free samples of Fruit Gushers (the company's new private market commodity) into their mouths, making comparisons between the resulting sensation and the dynamics of volcanic eruptions. A prominent Campbell's Soup deal, which offered schools a science experiment purporting to show that Campbell's Prego spaghetti sauce is thicker than Unilever's Ragu, falls into the same category. So too does a sixth-grade math textbook, published by McGraw-Hill and introduced into public curricula around the country, which featured a passel of references to brand-name private market commodities such as Nike and Gatorade.

In all of these cases, the school offered something in its public capacity— its own classroom time and space—and the company reciprocated with whatever it happened to sell on the private market—orange juice, spaghetti sauce—wrapped in some form of curricular material. The typical deal struck by Channel One, the 800-pound bête noire of commercialism critics, falls into the same category. What the school turns over to Channel One is the public good of classroom time: The typical Channel One deal calls for 90 percent of a school's students to watch the show, beamed daily by satellite, on 90 percent of school days. In return, what Channel One furnishes is its own private market commodity—namely, two minutes daily of advertising for other private commodities such as Reebok or Nintendo—wrapped in the ten minutes daily of current events curricular coverage that its programs provide

It is true that Channel One also gives each subscribing school approximately $17,000 worth of wholly public goods, in the form of free televisions for each classroom and satellite dish equipment. Yet interestingly, both Channel One and its critics deny that these public goods are of much value to schools. Noting that "a couple of hundred schools haven't even asked for [the equipment]," Channel One's Folkemer says that "if the deal was just to get the equipment, schools wouldn't continue it. Equipment is not that significant." Channel One's opponents, such as Alex Molnar, previously of the University of Wisconsin at Milwaukee and now at Arizona State's Education and the Public Interest Center, agree, denying that the equipment Channel One offers is "valuable to the school[s even] in the most crass commercial terms."[4]

Of course, the two sides have different motives for dismissing the utility of Channel One's gifts of videos and satellite equipment. Channel One does so to allay any charge that schools are taking its programs because of the free equipment rather than the educational merits of the programming; critics, for their part, want to argue that Channel One is exploiting schools, getting valuable advertising access to children's minds in exchange for virtually nothing. But the bottom line is this: If indeed the public good of free equipment means so little, as both Channel One and its critics seem to agree, then the Channel One deal remains essentially identical to the Pizza Hut, Minute Maid, and

Fruit Gusher arrangements. What the school turns over is public curricular space and classroom time, and what the company provides in return is essentially a private market commodity—in this case, advertising—fashioned in a curricular package that inserts itself into the public time and space made available.

What is so wrong with these kinds of deals? Critics have a full quiver, but the most prominent salvo misses. On it, the problem with Channel One—or Minute Maid's book covers, or Campbell's curricular material—is that, installed as they are inside the classroom, their promotional efforts prey upon a captive audience. If the company's pitch were removed even to the cafeteria, as with Tooned-In's menus, that would be a different story: students don't have to eat lunch there. Better still that the ads should move onto the school roof: there is little to say against the two suburban Dallas school rooftops that feature Dr. Pepper ads for overflying planes. But as the public space that the school makes available to a private commodity's promotional material moves from the outer perimeters of the building to the inner sanctum of the classroom, the audience grows more captive; the private market advertisements, consequently, more allegedly harmful. In a 1995 memo concerning Channel One, the New York State Department of Education put it this way: "It's [sic] mission is to . . . deliver up a large, captive . . . audience to advertisers."[5] And this, presumably, is a bad thing.

But is it? Captivity is double-edged. If a captive audience means that Channel One's ads might carry more suasive clout than otherwise—because students can't avoid them—it also means that the content of the surrounding news material might be of greater quality than otherwise. It is harder to accuse Channel One, as some accuse PBS, of feeling under pressure to water down the quality of its programming to attract the audiences that corporate sponsors desire, precisely because Channel One's viewers can't go anywhere.

Accordingly, some critics of Channel One backpedal. Far from berating Channel One for exploiting a captive audience, they instead adopt an assault based on denying that its audience is all that captive. Students, they say, actually have a tendency to mentally wander, do homework, gossip, or simply space out during the Channel One broadcast; and this, they worry, means that Channel One faces an enormous incentive to dilute its news content, rendering it ever more glitzy and gimmicky, in order to attract student attention. Channel One's news broadcasts, the media critic Mark Crispin Miller has written, rely on "brilliant, zippy graphics," a "young and pretty . . . team of anchors," and content that is "compressed and superficial" to compel the attention of students—precisely because they tend to "zone out," as Miller puts it, during broadcasts.[6] "The content of Channel One News," says William Hoynes, a Vassar sociologist who has studied the company's programming, "suggests the difficulties of holding the attention of even captive audiences;" it is clear, Hoynes writes, "that Channel One has consequently tailored a [news] product that is, first and foremost, about inducing students to pay attention, with a relentlessly hip style and . . . gimmicks."[7]

If, however, students' attention can and does wander, is it not misconceived to describe those students as constituting a "captive" audience? Either the audience is captive, in which case the ads are potent but the news programming encounters less of a need to be diluted—or else students' minds are free to roam, in which case programmers might be tempted to water down the news content but the ads likely have less impact. It's true that one study has shown that students tend to remember more about Channel One's ads than about the news content; but because they are equally captive (or noncaptive) in either case, captivity per se is not the issue. The captivity critique is not quite ready for prime time.

There is, however, a critique of the Channel One deal—and, by extension, the McGraw-Hill or Minute Maid arrangements—that has some merit. In a much-cited 1993 study, Michael Morgan, a professor of communications at the University of Massachusetts at Amherst, reported that "Channel One is most often found in schools . . . that have the least amount of money to spend on conventional educational resources."[8] Among poorer schools—where total spending per student was, at the time of the study, $2,599 per year or less—about six in ten were taking Channel One. But among wealthier schools—those that were spending at least $6,000—only about one in ten subscribed. Morgan's conclusion: For those schools that cannot even afford books and maps, the free ten minutes of news content itself—forget the TV sets and the satellite dishes—may, by filling a curricular void, prove sufficient to overcome any reservations that teachers may harbor about Channel One's content.

As the Center for Commercial-Free Public Education puts it, in "schools where text books are old or there is no money for supplemental materials," Channel One—or Campbell's Soup or General Mills curricular material—"can be a popular way for teachers to brighten a subject up."[9] David Shenk, a fellow at the Freedom Forum Media Studies Center, agrees: "Poorly funded school districts are the most likely [to take Channel One or Campbell's or Minute Maid curricular products] because prefabricated lesson plans save preparation time and provide relief for overburdened teachers."[10] A *Wall Street Journal* article a few years back reported on the case of Laurie Bjoriykke, a third grade teacher in Gaithersburg, Maryland, who "says she has no textbooks for her history and science classes" and so "shows two corporate tapes a month to supplement her resources."[11]

What all of this means, says the Consumers Union's Charlotte Baecher, is that schools taking Channel One have put themselves into a kind of "conflict of interest."[12] As with all public officials, teachers should make their official decisions, including their decisions about how to allocate curricular time and classroom space, on the merits, according to the public interest, and not on the basis of their need for private support.[13] Of course, the kind of deal represented by Channel One is not the most serious kind of conflict of interest imaginable: that's the kind where an official has the capacity to use her public role to benefit a private company in return for a personal payment. Instead, the Channel One arrangement resembles the milder form of conflict (but one still statutorily regulated at the federal level) in which officials take something of value from a private company not for themselves personally but to help serve the purposes of their cash-strapped public agency. The rule is that the public agenda should never be skewed by an agency's need for private assistance, let alone the official's personal desire for private gain. As Senator Richard Shelby, Republican of Alabama, recently put it, "I want [school] decision makers to be able to decide for themselves rather than have to settle for a 'deal.'"[14] According to education scholar Gerald Jude Kowal, the main concern of the teachers and administrators he surveyed about these kinds of deals is that they "may interfere with learning" or "may influence the curriculum."[15]

The fact that Channel One makes its way preponderantly into poorer schools, however, confronts not only those schools but the company itself with a problem. Jim Metrock, a former steel industry executive who came to head an Alabama-based anti–Channel One organization called Obligation, notes that because Channel One "is going into school systems where kids may not be able to pay for the product, Channel One's advertisers" might not be "getting the audience they paid for . . . probably the demographics are different."[16] Kevin Gordon of the California School Boards Association agrees: "Their hope was that they'd be in all sorts of markets," Gordon says, "but that hasn't happened."[17] William Hoynes adds that Channel One wanted to "be seen to reach the youth market, not the poor youth market."

Ironically, then, while the Channel One–type deal might skew the curricular path taken by poorer schools, it also, in a way, threatens to skew the marketing path taken by the company. Just as schools risk making public decisions based not on the public interest merits but on extraneous private inducements, companies like Channel One risk making their private market decisions—their decisions as to where to prospect for consumers—based not on which schools afford the most lucrative private markets but on the extraneous consideration as to which are most publicly needy. Channel One's former president for programming, Andy Hill, acknowledges that if the company "went to advertisers and said, 'Poorer kids watch our programs,' that would be insane." Yet he maintains that he "hasn't seen a demographic breakdown" of Channel One's audience and concedes that "all other things being equal, a wealthier school is less likely to be enticed" by the curricular material Channel One offers. Indeed, Hill says, if the "far left-wing Democrats who oppose Channel One instead devoted their energy to electing politicians who would raise funding for public schools, Channel One would be gone quickly."[18]

The typical Channel One deal, then, perverts the company's purposes, leading it to prospect for markets not where the private capacity to pay for the products it advertises is highest but where the public needs for its curricular material are greatest. In the same way, it is likely that Channel One diverts some schools from their purposes, causing them to make decisions on how to allocate public space and time not on the basis of the public interest—the pedagogical merits—but according to the blandishments offered by a private enterprise. In this sense, this first type of commercialism arrangement—where what the school offers is its own public space and time, and what the company supplies are its own private market commodities or advertising for them—can rankle on both sides.

SCHOOLS BUY PRIVATE MARKET COMMODITIES; COMPANIES PROVIDE PUBLIC GOODS

In the second form of school commercialism, the school does not offer the company its students in their public role as students, or public curricular time, or public classroom space. Rather, what it offers centers exclusively on students and parents in their private market role as active purchasers of commodities. And what the company offers the school is a public good, pure and simple—such as equipment, computers, or a cash bequest—purged of any association with the company's own private market commodity. In the Domino's deal, students buy pizza; the school gets books. Or take another example: parents in many states purchase products from their local Wal-Mart and return the receipts to the neighborhood school, which then sends the receipts back to Wal-Mart, which in turn rewards the school with free computer lessons for its students. Apple's "Apples for Students Program" does much the same with Apple computers: students and their families purchase produce from a local grocery store that then, in a deal with Apple, provides the school with free or reduced-price computers once a certain threshold of purchases has been reached. Hershey and Orville Redenbacher, likewise, will give a school cash for every candy wrapper or popcorn label its parents and children send in.

Brita Butler-Wall, who led an ultimately unsuccessful fight to keep advertising out of Seattle's schools, calls such arrangements "travesties."[19] She and other critics indict them both because of what they mean for the students and because of what they imply about the companies. As far as the students are concerned, Consumers Union complains, deals such as Apple's or Wal-Mart's teach them "to choose products or stores for all the wrong reasons"—not on the basis of the private market criteria of price and quality, which is what they should be learning to use, but rather on the hope of gaining some form of public benefit for the school.[20] As for the companies providing cash or equipment to schools in exchange, Consumers Union argues, they are not doing so for purely altruistic reasons but are engaging in "self-serving philanthropy,"[21] giving because they expect to reap a return in goodwill. Companies' gifts of public goods such as books, equipment, or the cash to buy them—which should be made purely on the public-spirited criteria of generosity and benevolence—are instead given in the hope of gaining some private benefit.

But the critics say too much. In such arrangements, both the school and the company are no longer compromising their principal roles, having stepped outside of them. The school is no longer a public forum but a private market; the company no longer a private enterprise but a public philanthropist. As far as the school is concerned, there is thus no turning over of any kind of public space, let alone the sanctum of the classroom, to the service of private ends. Rather, the school community's private market decisions are being diverted to serve public ends. And this is no more troubling than, say, someone's holding in his wallet a Sierra Club or Multiple Sclerosis Society affinity credit card, where his determination as to whether to buy a particular private market commodity can be colored, at the margins, by his knowledge that in paying for it he'll benefit a favored public cause.

As for the company—say Wal-Mart or Apple—it does not (as does Channel One) find itself directing a promotional campaign to markets where the public needs for curricular filler may be large but the private capacity to buy its products is meager. Instead, in these arrangements, the company steps entirely outside of its profit-making role and enters a philanthropic one. And in distributing its public largesse, it simply does what many a company does, namely, allow itself to be guided by the possibility of, at the same time, cultivating a private market. This is no more troubling than what happens when a company sponsors a charity sporting event.

But there is a further wrinkle here. Even with deals of this relatively benign sort—in which the school offers a private market and the company a public good—there lurks, critics say, an insidious danger. There is a tendency, they argue, for the private market in question to move from outside the school to inside. During the 1997–98 school year, South Fork High School in Florida's Marlin County executed a deal with Pepsi in which, instead of students buying Pepsi at local stores in return for a corporate gift to the school, Pepsi got the exclusive right to sell drinks to students within the school itself, in return for which the school got $155,000 cash. A year later, the Colorado Springs school district awarded Coke a similar privilege in return for $8 million over ten years.

More and more such arrangements are cropping up.

And here, critics say, an added problem emerges. Unlike the Wal-Mart or Apple deals, where students and parents buy products outside the school—and where they retain the option of shopping at Sears or buying from IBM should they prefer—when the market moves inside the school, such choices often evaporate. When Coke won its contract with Colorado Springs, fifty-three schools had to jettison their Pepsi machines as part of the arrangement. "Exclusivity," says Brita Butler-Wall, "is against free enterprise; it means a lack of consumer choice."[22]

The Consumers Union's Charlotte Baecher agrees. "Look at the great diversity of beverages you and I had when we were kids after a school football game," Baecher says; "today, with exclusive pouring arrangements, kids don't have the same broad range of choice."[23] Echoing this concern, the Berkeley school board tried to make an in-school marketing deal with Pepsi more palatable by requiring the company to offer a variety of drink alternatives in its school vending machines.

It is, though, a little hard to take this "exclusivity" complaint seriously. Critics of commercialism in the schools are (or at least should be) coming from a perspective in which there is too much consumerism—too much commodity choice—in the schools, not too little. A critic of commercialism in the schools who complains that a particular deal is "against free enterprise," or that it fails to offer students a range of soft-drink alternatives, needs to do a little more work on her argument. It was, after all, the city of Berkeley that forty years ago gave prominence to the leftist philosopher Herbert Marcuse. Choices such as the one between Coke and Pepsi, Marcuse famously declared, are a form of "repressive tolerance," a false dichotomy staged by capitalists to distract people from the real, more fundamental choice between "wage slavery" and socialism. Odd that Berkeley should now be passing laws designed to preserve such small-beer choices in the school, as if the presence of Coke but not Pepsi were some form of deprivation. It is true that some critics zero in on Coke or Pepsi deals because the drinks are so lacking in nutritional value. "Calcium intake among active girls who have switched from milk to soft drinks," declares Maryland anticommercialism activist Michael Tabor, "has decreased bone density."[24] This attack, however, would have more credibility if the Consumers Union publication *Captive Kids* had not also scrutinized the Dairy Council of Wisconsin's "Delicious Decisions" curricular material for signs of "bias toward milk products."[25]

What concerns over captivity are to the first kind of deal—where what the school offers is its public space—concerns about exclusivity are to the second kind of deal, where what the school offers is a private market. Both worries are red herrings. In witness whereof, it is worth noting that corporate practitioners of the first kind of deal—such as Channel One vice president Jeff Ballabon—defend themselves in a backhanded way by assailing the second kind of deal, the Coke or Pepsi arrangements, precisely for their exclusivity. "The deals schools make with vendors to feature only their products in the schools," Ballabon says: "that smacks to me of commercialism."[26] Returning the compliment, practitioners of the second kind of deal—such as Dan DeRose, whose DD Marketing helps forge Coke and Pepsi arrangements—take aim at the first kind of deal, the Channel One sort, for preying on a captive audience. "Personally," DeRose told a 1998 symposium, "we feel that [commercialism] should stay out of the classroom."[27]

Frank Kohler's fretfulness notwithstanding, when it comes to commercialism in the schools, it is possible to draw lines. When a school gives over classroom space to a company like Channel One in return for curricular material advertising perfume or running shoes, each party hazards the perversion of its principal role: its role as a public entity in the case of the school; its role as a private profit-making entity in the case of the company. The school risks suborning public space to private purposes, not public criteria. And the company risks aiming its promotions at student bodies that are the most publicly needy, not necessarily the most privately lucrative.

On the other hand, when a school steps out of its public role to create a private market for a department store's products—and when in turn the store steps out of its private profit-making role and contributes something of public value, such as computers, to the school—what happens is relatively benign. It should be difficult to find fault with students whose private market purchases are guided by their hope of winning some public goods for their school. Likewise with businesses whose public philanthropy is affected by their desire for some private gain.

Let me reformulate this in a way that brings out the book's larger theme. Each kind of deal, in its own way, can be seen to honor both a recognizable public sphere value and a recognizable private market value. The public sphere value is that decisionmaking meant to be based on public sphere norms should never be perverted by private market commercial considerations. The private market norm is that decisionmaking meant to be based on private market commercial criteria should remain unclouded by larger imperatives concerning the public interest.[28]

What separates the two kinds of deals is the way in which each applies these two values, one derived from the public sphere and the other from the private market. Deals like the ones that Domino's or Wal-Mart offer manage to honor the two values insofar as the public school and the company operate in their principal roles. Such deals avoid subverting the public school's capacity to make public decisions, decisions about its curriculum. And they avoid subverting the private company when it makes private market commercial decisions, decisions about where to promote and sell its product.

In contrast, deals like the ones Pizza Hut and Channel One offer avoid transgressing the two values only to the extent that public schools and private companies operate outside of their principal roles. Such deals avoid holding the private market consumption decisions of public school student bodies hostage to their concerns about the public interest: about the need to help their school. And such deals also avoid skewing private companies' public-spirited decisions, that is, their philanthropic decisions, with private market concerns about how to gain the best marketing bang for the buck.

On a traditional understanding, debate over commercialism in the public schools represents just what the term suggests: the encroachment of the private market realm into the public sphere. Yet at a deeper level, there are two forms of commercialism, the Domino's and the Pizza Hut types, and they each recommend themselves on the basis of the diametrically inverse ways in which they manage to avoid the transgression of public sphere and private market values. As for those who criticize all commercialism—defenders of a strong public education system, such as Consumers Union, say, or the Center for Commercial-Free Public Education—they rely on both combinations of public and private sphere norms to impeach both kinds of deals. And yet, when these deals are viewed on the interpretation being advanced here, as inverse ways of honoring (or transgressing) public sphere and private market values—instead of simply as privatizing incursions into the public school—one kind, the Domino's type, emerges as less objectionable than the other, the Pizza Hut sort.

Of course, just because it is possible to draw lines between the two types of deals doesn't mean they never get blurred. General Mills once had an arrangement whereby children would collect box tops from its cereal products—acting in their private market roles as consumers, not their public roles as students—yet what they got in return were not public goods such as books, equipment or cash, but school visits by cartoon characters featured on General Mills cereal boxes, who would urge them to consume more of the company's private market commodities.

It is hard not to raise one's eyebrows at such a deal. But beyond this kind of line blurring, most commercialism arrangements fall into either one class or the other, resembling either the Pizza Hut or the Domino's deal. The problem with commercialism's critics is that they tend to place the two on a par—finding fault equally with both arrangements. And they are joined in their criticism of Domino's-style arrangements by proponents of Pizza Hut–type deals such as Jeff Ballabon, and in their assaults on Pizza Hut–style arrangements by supporters of Domino's-type deals like Dan DeRose. All these parties, however, paint with too broad a brush, with the result that every deal from Minute Maid orange juice coupons to Apple computers risks being placed on the same plane. Yet when it comes to commercialism in the schools, as in so many other areas of life, it's important not to mix apples with oranges.

HEALTH CARE

7

THIN THE SOUP OR
SHORTEN THE LINE?

Barring a major revolution in the politics of health care in America, one question will continue to lie at the core of the ongoing debate over how to configure public health insurance for nonelderly Americans. It is a question that arises every time legislators consider budgets for their state's Medicaid and Children's Health Insurance Program (CHIP). The same question looms whenever a state that sponsors its own homegrown public insurance program has to wrestle with financing issues.

In good budgetary times, the question takes this form: Is it better to use newly available dollars to expand eligibility for public insurance—going up to, say, 150 to 250 percent of the poverty level in the case of parents, or 250 to 350 percent in the case of children—while keeping benefits tightly focused on core medical needs such as diabetes and cancer care? Or is it better, instead, to expand benefits beyond core medical necessities—to include, for example, orthodontia, weight-loss treatment, or Viagra—while keeping eligibility tightly focused on the poorest children and families?

In tight budgetary times, the eligibility-versus-benefits question takes the reverse form. What should be cut first? Should it be the benefits that are less needed, to protect eligibility for children or adults even at higher income levels? Or should eligibility for children and adults at higher income levels be cut to preserve the fullest possible range of benefits for those in the direst financial straits? In other words, is it the poorest or those with the most significant medical needs who lay greatest claim to public health insurance resources? Even a new national health insurance program, should it come to pass, will perpetually be faced with the question of how far up the income ladder to go in subsidizing the purchase of insurance and how far out the spectrum of health conditions to go in extending coverage. So the structure of comparable state-level debates carries ongoing implications for any national program.

THE TRADE-OFF

Before examining this debate over the boundaries of public health insurance, it is important to put it in broader perspective and to understand the uniqueness of public health insurance. No other public program—whether welfare, municipal services, or education—involves such a trade-off between the claims of the poor and the claims of those who, independent of any issue of poverty or wealth, need the services that particular domain offers. In welfare, for example, there is no difference between the poor and those who need food stamps or public housing; by definition, the two are the same. In public municipal services—policing and sanitation, for instance—those who make the greatest per capita claims are not only the poorest neighborhoods, where property faces greater risks of degradation, but also the wealthiest neighborhoods, where property is of greater size or value. And debates over public education resources typically become four-way tugs of war, not only between poor and wealthy communities but between parents of challenged and gifted children as well.

In public health insurance, the sick, regardless of wealth, and—as a legacy of the close link between the funding of public health insurance and welfare in America—the poor, regardless of their health needs, place the greatest claims on public health insurance resources. And so Americans are faced with a unique dilemma. "Every legislative session," says state senator Leonard Teitelbaum of Maryland, "we're into a debate between [covering] the sick—even if they're not entirely poor—or the poor, even for less serious sicknesses."[1] Or, as Ginny Hamilton of Washington State's Basic Health Plan puts it, "When you have limited funds you either thin the soup or shorten the line, and we continually wrestle with this trade-off."[2]

So which side, on balance, has the better model of public health insurance? It's a question worth pondering because, though different states stage their debates around different income eligibility and benefit starting points, the arguments made are everywhere the same.

As it happens, there is a symmetry to the claims made on each side. Those who prefer to expand eligibility up the income ladder mount both an argument drawn from private market norms and one rooted in values derived from the public sphere. According to the private market argument, by expanding eligibility to higher income levels, public insurance will bring within its ambit families—those at 250 or 300 percent of poverty—who are working hard in the private market but are not receiving a living wage, that is, they are not able to purchase the health insurance they deserve to be able to buy, given the work effort they are expending. At this income level, the argument is a private market one, based on notions of appropriate reward and the fact that such families pay to support public health insurance and so should enjoy its benefits. It is an argument based neither on redistributive norms nor on the notion that public health insurance is a form of welfare.

But public sphere values, too, are marshaled to argue for expanding public health insurance up the income ladder as much as possible. By going up the income ladder, public insurance will gain the vital civic support of the newly eligible, making it that much more difficult for opponents of public health insurance to contemplate retrenchment. Public insurance will become—by degrees—a unifying civic institution for more and more of the public, who will rally to sustain it with their political will.

For their part, those who prefer to expand benefits further out the spectrum of conditions—to cover less serious ailments such as crooked teeth or mild neurosis—also make both a private market and a public sphere argument. According to the private market argument, expanding benefits to cover more conditions can actually help the public health insurance system get value for the money it expends, because less serious conditions, if untreated, often become more serious and more costly. And once they become more serious, public insurance will be obligated to deal with them. According to the public sphere argument, expanding benefits to cover more conditions will lend vital civic validation to those suffering from these conditions—such as infertility, obesity, or occupational defiance disorder—thereby assuring them that, compared with those suffering from cancer, heart disease, or diabetes, they are not second-class citizens.

COVER MORE PEOPLE

To see whether one side has the better case, we must consider these arguments in a little more detail, beginning with the claims made by those who would prefer to expand eligibility for public health insurance further up the income ladder, rather than offering benefits to cover every last medical condition.

Proponents of this approach often advance the private market argument that even a family at 250 percent or 300 percent of the poverty level, though working, is not earning a living wage—not earning enough, more specifically, to be able to purchase insurance. In doing so, they in effect—and in their argumentation—expand the definition of what it means to be poor, to not be able to pay for basic needs, in America. "Even if you're earning 200 percent or 300 percent of the federal poverty level," says Virginia state legislator Karen Darner, "you're really still part of the working poor" and so deserve access to public health insurance. The argument here is based on the "deservingness," as demonstrated by their involvement in the labor market, "of those who work yet remain poor": those who merit health insurance for their families as part of the legitimate compensation, the quid pro quo, for their work efforts.[3] They earn it.

The second argument that eligibility-expansion advocates make is a public sphere one: Expanding public health insurance up the income ladder gives a new set of families a vital stake in preserving public health insurance as an entitlement of citizenship. And yet, in one respect, the public sphere argument sits uneasily with the private-market claim. For in making the public sphere claim, these advocates are motivated to describe those earning 250 percent or 300 percent of the federal poverty level as middle class, not poor. Indeed, it is precisely because they are part of the broad American middle class that they should be brought into coverage.

Consider the argument made by Vermont Medicaid director Paul Wallace-Brodeur. "We're now at 300 percent for CHIP—that's $52,000—and many people think that families at this level should be able to afford [private] coverage" for their children. But Wallace-Brodeur, whose gubernatorial boss at the time was Howard Dean, says, "My governor's view is that we should create a middle-class entitlement" out of public health insurance. Such an entitlement "would gain the validation of middle-income" Vermonters for the program, so that "it would be politically impossible to dismantle in bad fiscal times."[4]

Wallace-Brodeur's argument jibes with the position occupied most prominently in academic debate by Harvard government professor Theda Skocpol. According to Skocpol, "While middle-class . . . Americans are typically reluctant to see public monies spent for the poor through welfare programs, they have repeatedly been willing to support politically" those social programs that are universal in their eligibility—Social Security, for example—which benefit "worthy citizens such as themselves."[5] Says Jane Chiles, an activist with Kentuckians for Health Care Reform, "Once you get middle-class families in, it's tough to go back, because it creates a powerful political constituency for public health insurance."[6] The public sphere argument here is that, by going up the income ladder, ever more Americans will become linked in a common right of citizenship.

COVER MORE CONDITIONS

The arguments mounted by those who would prefer instead to limit public insurance to the very poorest, while expanding benefits to cover conditions that are not quite so medically serious, are also rooted in both public sphere and private market values. In a reversal of the public sphere argument for expanding eligibility up the income ladder—by which public health insurance would draw civic validation from those newly insured—the public sphere argument for covering more health conditions contends that the newly insured will gain vital civic validation from public insurance. Indiana state representative Win Moses, among others, has used precisely that language to defend expanding benefit coverage to include fertility treatment, podiatry, and orthodontia. To extend benefits to those who suffer is to confer civic recognition on their ailments; to fail to do so, Representative Moses says, "is to treat those who need podiatry or fertility treatment as political invisibles or second-class citizens." We don't, he continues, "want to say that some won the lottery and some didn't because they have the right diseases."[7] In a similar vein, Janet Varon, director of Northwest Health Care Advocates in Washington state, expresses her dismay with proposals to cut back dental benefits. "It's discrimination based on the fact that it's a medical problem that has to do with your mouth instead of another part of your body," Varon says.[8]

Proponents of expanding benefits to cover more health conditions also mount an argument rooted in private market values, one that sits uneasily with their public sphere claim. In wielding this argument, proponents in effect concede that podiatry or orthodontia might not, in fact, address medical conditions as serious as does cancer care or hip replacement. They must do so in order to argue that, even if those conditions aren't serious today, if untreated they could become serious, and the public insurance system would then be obligated to pay for them. As Colorado legislative aide Alexis Senger says, "You might think it's pushing matters to get public insurance to pay for pedicures for poverty-stricken old ladies, but an improperly cut toenail can lead to serious infection, which public insurance does cover, and that can be very expensive."[9]

The private market–based argument for expanding eligibility up the income ladder, recall, claims that public insurance will thereby be helping to provide due recompense for the work effort expended by working families. The private market argument for expanding benefits, by contrast, claims that public health insurance will thereby be getting due value for the money that it spends.[10] Even infertility, if uncovered, can in many cases lead to serious emotional or mental problems, which the public system is obligated to cover. Likewise erectile dysfunction. When patients seek treatments for impotence, says Steve Cooper, a New York attorney who in 1999 sued the insurance industry to gain coverage for Viagra, they frequently discover underlying illnesses such as diabetes or vascular disease that could grow far more serious (and hence costly) if untreated.[11]

If we pull all of this together, a symmetry emerges. Each side premises its arguments on the combination of a recognizable public sphere value—the value of civic support and validation—and a private market norm, the quid pro quo of appropriate return for effort or expenditure. It's just that those who seek to expand public health insurance up the income ladder want to make the public health insurance system itself the beneficiary of the public sphere value of civic validation. And they want to make hard-working individuals at previously uncovered income levels the beneficiaries of the private market value of an appropriate return for their work effort in the labor market. Those who want to expand public health insurance out the spectrum of medical conditions, by contrast, want to make poor individuals with previously uncovered conditions the beneficiaries of the public sphere value of civic validation. And they want to make public health insurance the beneficiary of the private market value of an appropriate return for its expenditures in the medical services market.

At one level, the level on which a traditional understanding would settle, these are debates over how to configure the border between public insurance and the private market, in which families must rely on their own resources to purchase health care. When state budgets are flush, such debates focus on how to expand public health insurance into the realm of the private market; when state budgets are shrinking, they center on what ground public health insurance should cede to the market. But at another level, both sides in these debates rely equally on public sphere values—the values of strengthening bonds between public institutions and citizens—and private market norms, the norms of appropriate return for expenditures of effort or money, in making their cases. They simply do so in inverse ways.[12]

RECONFIGURING THE DEBATE

As we have seen, however, each side embraces arguments—about whether newly eligible families are poor or middle-class, or whether potentially coverable conditions are more or less serious—that ultimately sit uneasily with one another. Given its internal tensions, the debate over public health insurance seems misconceived. Suppose, then, that we reconceived it so that the fault line runs instead between those who base their case wholly on private market criteria of an appropriate return for effort or expenditure—regardless of whether they are arguing for going up the income ladder or out the spectrum of conditions—and those who believe that public sphere considerations of civic validation and support should exclusively dominate. Such a shift would make clear what is ultimately at stake in these debates over public health insurance.

The side that emphasized private market criteria would argue that we should expand eligibility up to families on the next step of the income ladder to the extent that, in doing so, we will help ensure that those families earn a due monetary reward for the value of the work effort they expend. And we should expand benefits to cover more health conditions to the extent that, in doing so, we can promise that—by catching potentially more serious illnesses when they are less serious—public health insurance will reap due value for the amount of money it expends. By contrast, the party that held public sphere criteria supreme would argue that we should expand eligibility up the income ladder to the extent that public health insurance would gain pivotal citizen validation as a middle-class entitlement. And we should expand benefits to cover more health conditions to the extent that, in doing so, we are able to offer the stamp of basic civic validation to people suffering from those conditions.

In this kind of debate, between those advancing private market and those marshaling public sphere values, which side would have the better argument? Those advancing private market values would. That's because to make adjustments purely on private market criteria—ensuring an appropriate return for the work effort expended by individuals or for the money expended by the system—offers a way of pursuing the more public sphere, civic aims as well.

According to those more concerned with public sphere values of civic validation, expanding eligibility up the income ladder will win support for public health insurance from middle-class citizens in their role as newly eligible beneficiaries. But by instead expanding benefits to cover more health conditions—in pursuit of the private market value of gaining a suitable return for public health insurance's outlays—the public health system could win the support of middle-class citizens in their role as taxpayers. By heading off less serious conditions before they become more serious, public health insurance could claim to be run at maximum efficiency and minimum cost. It might require adroit politicians to communicate such gains. Nevertheless, as Tim Berthold of the California nonprofit organization Health Access says, even if much of the middle class were not eligible for public health insurance, its members nevertheless "would be more willing to support the system" if they "saw it as being efficiently run and [as] keeping expenses as low as is reasonably possible."[13]

Now consider the public sphere argument for expanding benefits to cover more health conditions: that doing so will extend civic validation to those among the very poor who suffer from less serious ailments, ensuring that their conditions will not consign them to second-class citizen status. The same very poor families and individuals, however, could also be helped by expanding eligibility up the income ladder in pursuit of the private market value of ensuring a decent return for one's work efforts. They would of course not necessarily be helped as current beneficiaries but rather as potential workers with aspirations to reach a higher income level. Expanding eligibility up the income ladder would ensure that public health insurance will be there for them as they get better jobs and work their way up to incomes at 200 or 300 percent of the poverty level. As New Jersey assemblyman Sam Thompson says, "Someone below the poverty level might well accept that his ingrown toenails or crooked teeth remain uninsured if the trade-off would be to have the economic burden of insurance lifted for his more serious conditions as he moves up in the workplace."[14]

To apply the private market criterion to the public health insurance system itself—to insist that when it spends, it should get proper value—is, then, to appeal to the middle class as taxpayers. And to apply the private market criterion to individuals and families—to insist that when they work, they should get a proper reward—is to appeal to poor heads-of-household as workers. It is thus to appeal to both groups as people who contribute to, not merely take from, society. By contrast, to use public sphere criteria is to appeal to the middle class as beneficiaries—who will then lend validation to the public health insurance system—and the poor as recipients, whose medical conditions will all get validation from the system. To the extent that Americans should (and do) think of themselves as taxpayers and workers, and not simply as beneficiaries and recipients, private market criteria should prevail in shaping the contours of Medicaid or any national public health insurance system.

And so, thinking in these terms, how should public health insurance be structured? In expanding public insurance up the income ladder to ensure that hard-working families are getting an appropriate return for their efforts, we must ask ourselves: At what point, as a family climbs the income ladder, is it earning a sufficient amount that private health insurance—whether through the workplace or otherwise—becomes affordable? As states have expanded Medicaid and particularly CHIP up the income ladder, they have had to bear in mind that the higher they go, the more likely it is that they will be offering public health insurance to families that are already managing to pay for insurance privately. In Michigan a very rough estimate drawn from a recent *Population Survey* indicates that at 250 percent of the poverty level, 83 percent of nonelderly individuals have private insurance, while 12 percent remain uninsured, and 5 percent have some form of special public insurance.[15] These figures almost certainly have changed along with the economic climate, but I use them here merely to illustrate a principle.

If Michigan decided to make public insurance available for all families up to 250 percent of the poverty level, the 83 percent who were already privately insured would face a tremendous (and perverse) incentive to drop their private coverage. In the face of this possibility, legislators in some states have relied on so-called anti-crowd-out rules to prevent those who have been privately paying for insurance from dropping that coverage and going on the public nickel. Such rules allow only those families that have not been privately insured for some specified period, often six months, immediate access to public insurance.

And yet anti-crowd-out conditions have flaws of their own. Illinois state senator Steve Rauschenberger captures the problem thusly: "Imagine two factory workers earning the same income, John and Bill, except John gave up a new car so that he could put his family on private insurance but Bill didn't. Now say public insurance expands to their income level. Government shouldn't provide benefits to Bill while saying to John, 'Since you did the right thing, we're not going to help you.'"[16]

Often in public debate, those concerned with rewarding responsibility and those concerned with achieving equality are at odds; in this case, though, both concerns argue against crowding-out provisions. But if anti-crowd-out rules are untenable, then so is expanding public insurance up the income ladder to points where 80 or 90 percent of families are buying insurance. Instead, if a state aims to use the private market criterion of ensuring an appropriate return for effort to determine an income cutoff for eligibility, then it should locate that cutoff at the income level where around half of (nonelderly) families are privately purchasing health insurance. At such a level, enough families are purchasing insurance privately to suggest that for a family that makes it a priority—and especially where insurance is offered through work—private insurance is not out of reach. But not so many families are purchasing insurance as to suggest that, hardworking and deserving though they may be, they are receiving a living wage. Those who are scrimping to buy it at that level can reasonably be rewarded for doing so by being given public insurance, not punished through anti-crowd-out prohibitions.

Nothing in such a proposal is inconsistent with the idea of states tapering families off public insurance—for example, requiring increasing copayments as incomes rise above this middle-range level—rather than abruptly cutting them off. Nor is it inconsistent for states to continue to provide "high-risk" pools, through which individuals whose insurance burdens are substantially larger than normal because of their particular health conditions could get further assistance above this middle-range level. In any event, whatever taper-off levels are implied by this approach, they lie well below the level suggested by the public sphere rationale for extending insurance to include the middle class, which justifies eligibility levels as high as 300 percent of poverty and beyond.

Suppose that a state has satisfied the private market criterion for expanding public health insurance to the level where it helps provide an appropriate return for the workplace efforts of working families, that is, the point where they can reasonably be expected to begin shouldering the burden of paying for private insurance. If more funds then become available, instead of going even higher up the income ladder, private market values would suggest that public health insurance turn to the spectrum of health conditions covered. Private market logic demands that we devote any extra funds to extending coverage for those less serious conditions that risk becoming more serious and hence could more cost-effectively be dealt with earlier, thus providing public health insurance with a more appropriate return for its outlays. In practical terms, this would imply that public insurance should cover a "less serious" condition whenever a physician believes in good faith that the condition will become more serious if it remains untreated.

Of course, not all orthodontic problems will lead to abscesses and not all cases of infertility will lead to psychological problems. But only the physician on the ground can make the determination as to whether less serious conditions of these sorts will grow worse. Yes, this will be a judgment call. The process will be subject to moral hazard, which is the tendency for medical providers to supply more health care than necessary, simply because it is not they—nor the patient—but the insurer who will have to pay for it. A doctor might claim that a patient's athlete's foot will develop into something worse, even when this is unlikely, simply to obtain coverage for that patient.

Yet as it is, the risk of moral hazard is ever present. Right now, physicians associated with health maintenance organizations face an incentive to claim that a patient's condition continues to remain serious when it has in fact improved, so that insurance will continue paying for treatment. To curb this kind of abuse, nearly every state has established external appeals committees (discussed in chapter 8) composed of independent physicians. These committees could expand their purview to embrace public health insurance and to consider disagreements over whether a patient's current condition is likely to become more serious. In any event, the private market criterion for covering "less serious" conditions—the principle that such conditions should be covered only when they will grow more serious and hence more costly—should not extend benefits as far as would the public sphere criterion, which can be used to argue that any and all conditions deserve equal recognition and coverage.

The basic structure of the debate over expansion or contraction of public health insurance, and its consequences for the extent to which families should have to rely on their own private resources to meet their health care needs, replays itself in every state. It will emerge, too, in any federal-level debate over a national public insurance program. That basic debate pits those who wish to see public health insurance cover the sickest, even if not the poorest, against those who would like to see insurance cover the poorest, even in circumstances where they are not the sickest. And each side draws equally—albeit in inverse ways—on public sphere values of civic validation, and private market values of a fair return for effort and expenditure, to make its case.

A defensible consensus between these two sides can be reached, though, by appealing to only one of those two commonly held sets of values—the private market values—and combining each side's interpretation of them. So whether legislators are expanding or contracting the public health insurance system, they should set eligibility levels to furnish working individuals with an appropriate return for their efforts, not to buy their civic support. And they should cover less serious conditions to provide the public health insurance system with an appropriate return for its outlays, not to extend civic validation to poor individuals suffering from those conditions. These private market criteria will, in the foreseeable future, be demanding enough for strained public budgets. When faced with a difficult choice of shortening the line or thinning the soup, we should at least choose for the right reasons.

8

TOURING THE BOUNDARY
OF MEDICAL NECESSITY

Deborah Fuller was proud of her "long, brown ringlets" when she was a child. But as an adult she suffers from alopecia areata, an ailment that causes substantial, often total, hair loss from the scalp. Testifying before a state legislative committee in New Hampshire in 1992, Fuller asked whether she might remove her wig: "If it would not upset anyone," she said, "I would like to demonstrate what it looks like to have alopecia." The committee was considering whether the state should mandate—require—private health insurers to pay for wigs for such patients. The question in New Hampshire and other states has been: Are wigs in such cases a "medical necessity"?

Yes, they are, Fuller argued. "There are people who consider suicide because of [alopecia]. I didn't because I am a strong person, but I will tell you that this," and she pointed to her wig, "replaces a shrink in a minute."[1] The problem is that a proper wig can cost up to $3,000, and many patients cannot afford one without help from their insurance companies. Yet it could cost as much as $6 billion to provide wigs for the estimated two million to three million women in the United States who suffer from the disease.

No one, including spokespersons for the insurance industry, would deny that cancer care or hip replacements are medical necessities and warrant insurance coverage—unlike, say, a visit to a spa to relieve stress. But between the poles of the clearly necessary and the plainly not, the terrain grows ever more contested, with patients arguing for medical necessity where insurers see none.

Indeed, what used to be a cold war has recently turned hot. During the past couple of decades, legislatures in every state have considered bills that would mandate private insurers to cover everything from wigs for alopecia patients to Viagra to abortion. The amounts of money involved can be substantial. Viagra, which came on the market in 1998, now racks up over $1.6 billion in sales annually. Infertility afflicts around 6 million American women and their partners; the cost of treatment ranges anywhere between $10,000 and $40,000, depending on the number of rounds needed. And in addition to legislative hearings, forty states in the past few years have established external appeals panels: rosters of independent physicians who arbitrate disputes between patients and their health insurers, including health maintenance organizations, making decisions—thousands of them annually—about what is medically necessary in particularly hard cases.

Insurers sometimes claim to be agnostic about the medical necessity of the contested procedures. Their real concern, they say, is that each new covered service drives up the price of insurance. But if cost were the only issue, they would be covering contraceptives, which they don't, but not cancer care, which they do. In fact, insurers employ an arsenal of arguments in their struggle with patients in order to draw the boundary of medical necessity to exclude or include various conditions. One of their weapons of choice is analogy: insurers will liken a proposed procedure to one that anyone would concede lies beyond the realm of medical necessity. If insurers were required to cover wigs for alopecia sufferers, what would be next? Would they have to cover wigs for male pattern baldness? Or long-sleeved shirts for eczema sufferers? Patients counter with analogies of their own: because insurers cover ointments for alopecia, they have in effect acknowledged that alopecia—unlike male pattern baldness—is a real medical condition. And because insurers cover wigs for chemotherapy patients, they have acknowledged that wigs—unlike long-sleeved shirts—are a genuine medical treatment. So how can insurers deny wigs for alopecia?

Another favorite tactic of both sides is to call attention to inconsistencies. Insurers will pay for a psychotherapist to deal with the suicidal thoughts that alopecia provokes but not for a wig to deal with the physical hair loss. They'll cover the costs of depression associated with infertility, but not the costs of in vitro fertilization to remedy the infertility itself. Yet the same insurers who want to cover only the mental consequences of certain physical conditions also want to cover only the physical aspects of mental conditions such as bipolar disorder and attention deficit disorder. Insurers have fought hard, at the state level, to be required to cover mental conditions only to the extent that they have an immediate biological cause, something that doctors can attack with drugs rather than with talk therapy, which is generally more expensive. But if the insurance industry pays for mental conditions only insofar as they are really physical, and physical conditions only insofar as they are mental, doesn't its position risk collapsing under the weight of the irony?

Debate over the extent to which the state should compel private insurance coverage of certain services, while allowing the market free rein to determine the coverage of others, is every bit as much a question of the public-private border as it would be if the state were covering those items itself. As Jacob S. Hacker has observed, "[t]he point is not that direct spending or provision is unimportant. It is merely that these familiar policy instruments do not exhaust the available strategies for intervention. Governments may provide a good directly, or they may regulate its private provision. . . . But the difference is not that one counts as government intervention and the other does not."[2] So the principles on which Americans argue such public-private borders—including the border between what kind of coverage the public should mandate as medically necessary and what it should leave individuals to pay for privately—bear exploring.

As it turns out, state legislators approach this question by focusing on whether a particular service is a necessity, not on whether it qualifies as medical. After all, legislators are not doctors but politicians, who are used to having to distinguish between genuine needs and mere desires. In contrast, appeals panels, because they are composed of physicians, tend to be uniformly sympathetic to what they view as a sea of undifferentiated need and to make their distinctions by focusing on whether the service at issue qualifies as genuinely medical. The battle over medical necessity—over the boundary up to which the state can legitimately compel private insurance coverage—thus has two theaters: one that focuses on the meaning of *necessity*, the other on the meaning of *medical*. And to understand what's at stake, we must spend time in each of them.

THE MEANING OF *NECESSITY*

Much of the recent debate in state legislatures has been over whether it should be mandatory for insurers to cover three particular treatments: prescription contraception for fertile couples, in vitro fertilization for infertile couples, and wigs for alopecia patients. This is the current no-man's-land into which patients' groups are encouraging the state to enter, with private insurers and businesses trying to fend them off. But these debates inevitably lead those involved to consider the relative medical necessity of three other treatments: Viagra, abortion, and breast reconstruction after a mastectomy.

Why? Because in most states, insurers generally do not have to pay for contraception, but they have been mandated to pay for Viagra. And so, as Wendy Royalty of Maryland's Planned Parenthood observes, there would seem to be "a kind of irony here." After all, insurance companies "are covering something that embraces a man's capacity to control his sexuality, but not a woman's."[3]

Likewise, insurers are steadfastly resisting covering in vitro fertilization for infertile couples who want to conceive, but a substantial majority of them cover nontherapeutic abortion for women who do not want a child. The *Los Angeles Times* reported in 1998 that about "70 percent of health plans will pay for abortion, but only 17 percent will pay for in vitro," and there is no reason to think the figures have changed dramatically since.[4] No wonder that people like Tracy Barnes, spokeswoman for the Houston chapter of the national infertility group Resolve, marvel at the irony that "insurance companies will pay to end life but, for some reason, not to begin it."[5]

Finally, insurers generally have not been mandated to pay for wigs for alopecia sufferers. But they have been mandated, in every state, to pay for breast reconstruction after a mastectomy. The seeming disparity prompted this response from alopecia activist Judy Horton of Nashua, New Hampshire, at a legislative hearing: "I hope this is not a cheap shot, but let's pretend . . . that each one of us women in this room has one breast and is wearing a breast prosthesis as well as a scalp prosthesis. Given a choice that you had to remove one and walk down Main Street today, which would you rather remove?"[6] By Horton's measure, insurers appear to have their priorities backward.

Is there a common principle at play in the patients' complaints—that if Viagra, abortion, and breast reconstruction are covered, then contraception, in vitro, and wigs certainly should be? Consider the criterion that Norman Daniels, a philosopher at the Harvard School of Public Health, offers in his 1985 book *Just Health Care*, the first—and still the most influential— philosophical treatment of these questions. Daniels defines our "important [medical] needs" as whatever is "necessary for maintaining [the] normal functioning" of human beings viewed "as members of a natural species."[7] An equivalent way of putting it, Daniels argues, would be that a "necessity" is whatever medical treatment "it is reasonable for persons to choose in a given society"—that is to say, it is what most of us would choose if we found ourselves faced with a certain health condition.

Daniels' natural-functioning criterion would overturn current private insurance practice on the grounds that it has indeed gotten things exactly backward. Consider in vitro, which insurance generally does not cover, versus elective abortion, which insurance generally does cover. Daniels has said that his principle would require insurance coverage of infertility treatment, because bearing children is part of our natural functioning. But it would not require coverage of abortion, because "unwanted pregnancy is not a disease" and miscarrying is not part of the natural functioning of our species.

When it comes to Viagra, which insurers widely cover, and contraceptives, which they do not, one might expect Daniels's natural-functioning approach to uphold the status quo. After all, Viagra aids the natural procreative functioning of the male, while contraception thwarts the natural procreative functioning of the female. But suppose we view "natural" sexuality in recreational, not procreative, terms. Because "most Viagra users are men aged 50–75, hardly peak biological years for procreation," as a writer in the Seattle *Post-Intelligencer* has pointed out, "the specter of 'recreational' use is hard to ignore."[8] Viagra users, it would seem, are not fulfilling their natural functioning so much as thumbing their noses at it. After all, as Robert Scheer wrote in the *Los Angeles Times*, "Isn't sexual impotence God's gentle way of saying to a 75-year-old man, 'You've had enough'?"[9] Contraception, by contrast, enables a woman "to enjoy sex," Paige Shipman of Wisconsin Planned Parenthood told me, precisely by "eliminating a direct threat to her natural functioning: the ravages on her body that would result from having to bear twelve to fifteen children."[10]

So if sex is understood in procreative terms, Viagra promotes natural functioning while contraception thwarts it. If it's understood in recreational terms, Viagra frequently mocks natural functioning while contraception protects it.

Recall that Daniels suggests another principle—a majoritarian principle—for establishing the meaning of natural functioning: Observe what most members of our species would choose to do when faced with a particular condition. It turns out that only 15 percent of American men over age fifty who suffer from impotence choose to seek treatment, while fully 90 percent of sexually active couples in their fertile years choose one of the five major reversible contraceptives. According to the natural-functioning approach, then, the status quo, in which insurers cover Viagra far more often than they do contraception, assigns precisely the wrong priority.

Daniels's natural-functioning criterion would also favor wigs for alopecia patients—which insurance generally does not cover—over breast reconstruction for mastectomy patients, which insurance does cover. Wigs serve a physiological function, in that hair and hair prostheses protect against loss of body heat from the head. But a reconstructed breast does not serve its natural function. And, according to Jay Mahler, an alopecia activist from Ann Arbor, Michigan, almost all women with total scalp hair loss would choose to wear wigs if they could afford them.[11] By contrast, the proportion of women who choose breast reconstruction after a mastectomy is estimated at between 15 and 40 percent.

Daniels's natural-functioning–majoritarian criterion suggests something fundamentally perverse about the way the boundary of necessity—the public-private boundary between what is state-mandated and what isn't—is located under current practice. There is, however, another principle, every bit as appealing as Daniels's, that could explain why the line is drawn where it is. This principle considers not how many people eligible for a particular procedure would choose to have it, as Daniels does, but how many choices an eligible person would have without it. The principle assumes that necessity emerges as choice diminishes and that a person can be said to need something because he or she has no alternatives to it.

The couple who need—but lack—access to Viagra have fewer choices in the pursuit of sexual gratification than the couple without access to prescription contraception. The Viagra-less couple, says Tom Bruckman of the American Urologic Foundation, are "barred from engaging in a wide variety of mutually satisfying sexual activities." The couple without prescription contraception, by contrast, are barred "from only one kind of sexual activity—intercourse without the risk of conception," and even then, the risk can be controlled by nonprescription methods of contraception. Since "sex is impossible in the absence of virility, but not in the presence of fertility," Bruckman observes, there is a "significant ethical and moral difference" between the use of Viagra and the use of contraception.[12]

Oddly enough, Bruckman's point has been made effectively, if unwittingly, by some advocates of contraceptive coverage. During hearings on a contraceptive mandate bill in New Hampshire in 1999, legislator Martha Fuller Clark, one of the bill's proponents, declared that it was "about choice," as did her colleague, Candace White Bouchard.[13] In describing contraception as a choice, Fuller Clark and White Bouchard used language very close to the rhetoric wielded by their main opponent, Blue Cross/Blue Shield of New Hampshire, whose spokesperson at the hearings dismissed contraception as a "lifestyle choice," unlike something that's clearly a necessity, such as insulin.[14]

The legislators' comments were an acknowledgment, and a revealing one because unintended, that sex without prescription contraception eliminates but one of a number of choices for sexual expression or gratification that remain available to a couple. Sex without Viagra, however, is in a real way impossible—hence its provision is a necessity, not a choice. It is tough to find anyone who argues for insurance coverage of Viagra on the grounds that it would help fulfill "a man's right to choose."

True, insurers cover abortion, and abortion is famously described as the fulfillment of "a woman's right to choose." But that happens in debates about abortion's legality, not in discussions of its subsidization through health insurance. Indeed, as Rickie Solinger points out in her 2001 book *Beggars and Choosers*, before *Roe v. Wade* in 1973, advocates of access to abortion rarely spoke of it in terms of choice; they spoke rather in terms of rights.[15] If necessity is the opposite of choice, then there is an argument for the public-private border status quo: for insurers being mandated to cover Viagra, which is more of a necessity for sexual expression, even if they aren't required to cover contraception, which is less of one.

Is it possible to justify mandates for insurers to cover abortion without extending them to in vitro fertilization? If we define a procedure as a necessity when those eligible for it enjoy few if any alternatives, it might seem that in vitro fertilization is actually more of a medical necessity than abortion. After all, one of the principal alternatives to in vitro—adoption—is usually not preferred to having a child of one's own through the fertilization process. By contrast, when a pregnant woman who does not want a child considers her alternatives, putting the baby up for adoption would seem a more worthy choice than having an abortion.

But it is also a tougher thing to do, as opponents of abortion are the first to acknowledge. Ed Rivet of Right to Life Michigan says that "women indeed find it more emotionally wrenching to give up a child through adoption than undergo an abortion" because "they will have bonded with it and there's a real physical presence."[16]

When it comes to infertility, conversely, adoption can actually be a more emotionally accessible alternative to in vitro fertilization. Jennifer Gosselin, spokeswoman for the Maine chapter of the national infertility rights group Resolve, told me that she is glad that her in vitro was unsuccessful because the little girl she then adopted "was what was meant to be."[17] In fact, many state bills mandating in vitro fertilization would require insurers to cover adoption expenses if in vitro failed—testimony to the relative ease with which adoption can be contemplated as an alternative to in vitro.[18]

To say this, of course, is to say nothing about whether abortion represents the taking of life. But as long as the procedure is legal, an argument can be made that abortion is a greater necessity for women who do not want a child than in vitro fertilization is for women or couples who do.

Can one make an argument that breast reconstruction for mastectomy patients, which insurers cover, is more of a necessity than wigs are for those afflicted with alopecia? And, hence, that states need not feel compelled to broaden the reach of their mandates into the private marketplace to require wig coverage? It is hard to dispute that most women would rather appear in public without a breast reconstruction than without a wig. In public situations, the sense of sight is dominant, and whereas the torso is clothed, the head is visible; hence, a wig becomes more of a necessity than a reconstructed breast. There may be alternatives to wigs—hats, scarves—but they are neither as numerous nor as effective as the sartorial alternatives to a reconstructed breast.

But what about private situations, where the sense of touch becomes as important as the sense of sight? Susan Scherr of the National Coalition for Cancer Survivors, whose members often suffer both loss of a breast from cancer and loss of their hair from chemotherapy treatments, says that "in the privacy of a person's home, the first thing that comes off at the end of the day is the wig. In the intimacy of your own bedroom, having a normal body image is more important than hair on your head."[19] When you touch a reconstructed breast in intimate situations, you touch a woman; when you touch a wig, you do not. In private settings, there is no alternative to the reconstructed breast, while the wig is no alternative at all to real hair.

We have found two possible criteria, then, for defining the meaning of necessity—and hence the border between public regulation and private market—in tough cases. One criterion looks to natural functioning; as the philosopher Norman Daniels argues, a procedure is a necessity to the extent that most people—members of our species—eligible for it would choose to undergo it. The second criterion rests on the idea that a procedure is a necessity to the extent that people eligible for it would have fewer choices without it.

The natural-functioning principle, certainly, holds great appeal as an argument for extending mandates to include the procedures currently in contention: contraception, which nearly all eligible couples at one time or another choose and which protects the natural functioning of a woman's body from the "ravages" of serial pregnancy; in vitro fertilization, which a substantial percentage of infertile couples pursue and which serves the purposes of the natural reproductive function; and wigs for alopecia sufferers, which nearly all eligible women would choose and which fulfill the natural function of retaining body heat. And yet, natural functioning doesn't manage to encompass all that we commonly understand by necessity. For if necessity is viewed instead as arising when a person eligible for a particular procedure would have no other choices without it, then it does indeed confine itself to those procedures whose coverage is already mandated: abortion, the use of Viagra, and breast reconstruction after a mastectomy. The fact is that each principle contributes something important to our understanding of necessity in the border zone.

Here is another way to conceive these two principles—the one on which a procedure is a necessity to the degree that those eligible would choose to have it, the other on which it is a necessity to the degree that those eligible would have no choice without it. The first is a public sphere norm. It asks us to take our cues as to what insurance should cover from what substantial majorities of the publics involved, by reason of the natural biological functionings they all share, would choose. Such a public or majoritarian norm would more easily justify coverage of prescription contraception, in vitro, and wigs—which majorities of those eligible, in the quest to fulfill basic human biological functioning, choose—than Viagra, abortion, or breast reconstruction. Only minorities of those eligible choose these latter, which in any case are less integral to our species' natural functioning.

The second is a norm that stresses, by comparison with the first, the importance of fulfilling the most personal—indeed, private—needs of individuals; and in that sense it is a private sphere norm. On this norm, necessity is the simple absence of any other choices in very private and personal matters: no other way of expressing oneself sexually, as with Viagra; no other way of being in an intimate situation, as with breast reconstruction following a mastectomy; no other emotionally accessible way of handling an unwanted pregnancy, as with abortion. When, however, it comes to prescription contraception, in vitro, and wigs, this norm suggests that because other options exist, their lack of provision by insurance does not pose, by comparison, as great an impairment on the personal, domestic, and intimate autonomy of private individuals. Individuals can, more easily, enjoy a private life without them.

On a traditional understanding, the debate over the meaning of necessity pits patient groups, each of which seeks a public mandate requiring insurers to cover its particular condition, against insurers and businesses, which fight to preserve maximal authority for the private market. To press their case for state intervention, however, patient groups have had to rely on both public values of majority choice and private values of intimate personal need. They have had to apply public sphere principles of majority will to justify coverage of treatments that a majority of those eligible would choose—contraception, in vitro, and wigs—even if other options exist to fulfill the private or intimate desires involved. And they have had to apply private sphere principles of personal and intimate need, to require insurance to fill a niche—Viagra, abortion, and breast reconstruction—where individuals find they have no other choices in pursuing their private lives and even if majorities of those eligible seem uninterested in such procedures.

For businesses or insurers fighting the expansion of state mandates, the reverse obtains. On the one hand, an appeal to public values is useful for arguing against mandated coverage of Viagra, abortion, or breast reconstruction. After all, while no other emotionally accessible option may exist for meeting the personal needs involved, what matters is that majorities of those eligible don't choose them. And an appeal to private realm values, on the other hand, is useful in arguing against mandated coverage of prescription contraception, in vitro, and wigs. While majorities of those eligible may choose them, what matters is that the private needs involved can be met in other ways.

Both sides—those pushing for the expansion of state mandates into the marketplace, and those resisting—thus need to recur equally to public sphere and private realm values in defining *necessity*. And yet, it would seem as if any public-private tension is more serious for the side resisting mandates than for the side pushing in favor. For in citing public sphere values as definitive of necessity when majorities do not choose the procedures involved, insurers legitimize the use of those values to require mandates when majorities would so choose. And in citing private realm values to define *necessity* when other options exist for fulfilling private and intimate needs, insurers legitimize the use of those values to impose mandates when such options do not exist.

THE MEANING OF *MEDICAL*

The critical term *medical necessity* consists of two words, not one. What about *medical*? After all, we can concede that breast reconstruction belongs in the category of necessity and still ask whether it is a medical necessity or rather merely a cosmetic one. As it happens, the question of what constitutes a medical procedure gets debated most ferociously in the other theater of battle: independent physician appeals panels that render decisions when patients challenge an insurer's denial of coverage for a particular procedure. Each time a panel rules in favor of a patient, it amounts to the state imposing an outcome that private insurers have been resisting: a public-private border battle.

A relatively small number of conditions figure prominently in the cases these panels hear: scars, the disfiguring birthmarks known as port-wine stains, the shape and size of breasts, the apron of abdominal skin known as the panniculus that develops after gastric bypass surgery for obesity. In each case, insurers try to push the condition from the domain of the medical into the domain of the cosmetic.

In rendering judgment, external physician reviewers are likely to invoke the criterion of natural functioning. If, in other words, these surface imperfections are impeding natural functioning—port-wine stains, for example, can be associated with abnormal blood vessel development—appeals boards will deem their correction a medical matter and force insurers to cover it. But if such conditions "impair no functioning" or "constitute [no] functional deficit" (to quote some recent decisions), then treating them is deemed not a medical but a cosmetic matter, and the patient's claims are denied.[20]

Two recent cases involving this "natural functioning" approach, however, induce a sense of unease. In May 2001 a Massachusetts boy who had suffered severe lacerations on the left side of his face in a skiing accident appealed his insurer's refusal to pay for the necessary scar-revision surgery on the grounds that it would not be a medical procedure. "In the absence of any functional deficit," the physician-reviewer declared, "the insurer's decision to deny coverage is upheld."[21] In July 2001 the physician-reviewer turned down a Massachusetts girl's request for laser surgery to deal with a large port-wine stain that extended from her left arm to her upper chest. The insurer had defined the surgery as cosmetic, designed to "improve appearance, not to restore bodily function," and the physician-reviewer agreed, noting that the stain posed no "functional impairment."[22] Both judgments force us to ask whether natural functioning may be too dogmatic a criterion. And if it is, what other might be available to sustain the claims of this boy and girl?

The boy's facial scars were the result of a trauma visited upon him. His skiing accident diverted him from a personal state of normality, which means that we know what it would take to restore him to his old self. A port-wine stain, on the other hand, is congenital. It would not have diverted the girl from some previous state of personal normality; instead, it is her state of normality. The girl can offer no notion of what she, as an individual, would have been like without the stain. There is no personal norm in this case, but there is a social norm to which she can refer—the norm of what most people are like—on the basis of which she can ask for a medical correction.

If our intuitions lead us to sympathize with the boy and the girl, it is because we have been influenced by certain moral principles. When someone suffers a disease or trauma—in the boy's case, facial lacerations—that deflects him from a state of personal normality, we want to restore him to that state. When someone is deprived congenitally or developmentally from achieving the social norm—in the girl's case, by the port-wine stain—we want that norm to be hers. Unlike the external reviewers, most of us would consider these cases to fall properly within the realm of legitimate medical need.

Embracing these two principles would still exclude from the domain of the medical a good many procedures on the surface of the body. In particular, it would mean a thumbs-down on procedures that mix modes. Consider, for example, a case involving a fifty-year-old Connecticut woman who underwent gastric bypass surgery for obesity, a procedure that removes or closes off part of the stomach. Her insurer paid for the operation because obesity, by heightening the risk of cardiac disease or diabetes, directly threatens natural functioning. The woman lost 125 pounds but was left as a consequence with a fold of loose abdominal skin, as is often the case after major weight loss. There was no impairment to natural functioning, no health-threatening abdominal-wall strain, and no rash. The woman, however, very much wanted to have the skin removed.[23]

The requisite procedure is called a panniculectomy or, more colloquially, a "tummy tuck." In this particular patient's case, the procedure would have mixed modes. Even if her obesity was congenital, the bothersome tummy was not. It resulted from a trauma inflicted on her—the invasion of her body by a scalpel—that diverted her from a previous state of personal normality, just as the Massachusetts boy's lacerations resulted from a trauma that diverted him from a previous state of personal normality. But unlike the boy, the woman seeking a tummy tuck was not asking to be restored to her own personal state of normalcy. She wanted, rather, to have her abdomen fashioned according to the social norm. As Sacramento plastic surgeon Jack Bruner says, the "kid with lacerations is trying to be restored to what he was before," while the tummy tuck is a "cosmetic case; she would have been obese to start with."[24]

Now consider mode mixing of another kind. A woman, for congenital developmental reasons, has breasts she considers too small. Like the girl with the port-wine stain, she can invoke no state of personal normality to which she might be restored. Indeed, she hasn't departed from her personal norm. All she can ask, as did the girl with the port-wine stain, is that she be brought to a social norm. But breast implants, as distinct from the removal of a port-wine stain, would not bring the woman seeking them to a social norm. Some might say that's because there's no such thing as normal breast size, but another reason is that a sac of silicon gel or saline solution or even transplanted abdominal fat isn't normal breast tissue. Implants might constitute this particular woman's personal view as to how she would like her breasts to be, but an implant is not a normal breast. She has a congenital developmental issue, but she is asking, as the girl with the port-wine stain is not, to be refashioned according to her personal view of what is desirable. The correct verdict: the private insurer's denial of coverage should stand.

What about breast reduction for women who believe their breasts are too large? In the absence of functional issues such as back strain, appeals panels usually deny coverage. Yet as Dr. Elvin Zook, chair of plastic surgery at Southern Illinois University, acknowledges, there is no question that "people are more sympathetic to claims for breast reduction, even when there's no impairment of function, no rash or spinal issue, than to breast enlargement."[25] The procedures for both reduction and enlargement respond to congenital developmental discontents, and with neither of them can the woman point to a personal norm from which she has been deflected, only a social norm from which she deviates. But in the case of breast reduction, there is an achievable social norm. What remains after a breast reduction, and not after a breast enlargement, is a body part that corresponds to the social norm of a breast: Breast tissue has been removed, but nonbreast tissue hasn't been added.

We are also more sympathetic to insurance coverage for breast reconstruction after a mastectomy than to coverage for breast enlargement. We regard the reconstruction as both a necessity—because other substitute options do not exist—and legitimately medical. But why so? After all, in both enlargement and reconstruction procedures, nonbreast tissue is generally added. But in the case of reconstruction, the woman has been subjected to a trauma, breast surgery, that diverted her from a personal norm that had existed previously. If, in her own view of what it means for her to be normal—to be restored to herself— breast implants are required, then that should be her call. When, by contrast, a Massachusetts woman seeking insurance coverage for breast enlargement in 2001 declared that she was simply asking for "surgical correction of the same nature as that required by mastectomy patients," the physician-reviewer turned her down—and rightly so, for the analogy does not hold.

To make contact with the book's larger theme: Those who seek to expand the domain of public control over the decisions of private health insurers— beyond the strict natural-functioning criterion that physician panels currently employ—must rely on a duo of very distinctive public sphere and private realm values to do so. The comparatively public value is of course the societywide norm to which the port-wine stain patient—who never attained that norm—asks to be taken. The relatively private value is the personal norm to which the facially scarred patient—who has been diverted from that norm— asks to be returned. On this construction of public and private norms, the state, through the physician review panels it establishes, could justify extending its reach further into the marketplace than it goes currently to require insurers to pay for these conditions. Such a construction would straightforwardly require conditions that represent departures from public norms to be remedied according to those public norms. And, likewise, it would require conditions that represent departures from private norms to be remedied according to those private norms.

Many who think that this would be reasonable, however, might well want to draw the line there, so as not to be seen to be arguing for indiscriminately unlimited coverage. But they then would have to confront those who would indeed like to go further to cover the next tranche—tummy tucks and breast enlargement—and yet who also rely on both public and private norms for justification, but in an inverse way. For them, individuals who have never embodied a public norm should be covered even if what they seek to attain is a personal norm (breast enlargement). And individuals who have been dislodged from a personal norm should be covered if what they now seek to attain is a public norm (tummy tuck). In other words, those who would expand the definition of *medical* to include breast enlargement and tummy tucks would apply private norms to conditions that represent departures from public norms and public norms to conditions that represent departures from private norms.

Each position—the one that would extend publicly mandated coverage only to port-wine stains and facial scars, and the one that would go further into the marketplace to cover breast enlargement and tummy tucks—thus relies on public and private norms, albeit in inverse ways. And yet, there is a sense in which any public-private tension involved is greater, or at least places a greater onus, on those who would go further to require coverage of breast enlargement and tummy tucks. They have to explain why—in the case of breast enlargement—it is appropriate to apply a personal norm to a condition that is a divergence, if at all, from a social norm. And—in the case of tummy tucks— they have to argue that it is reasonable to apply a social norm to a condition whose roots lie in a divergence from a personal norm. Those who seek to extend coverage only to port-wine stains and facial scars avoid this kind of tension.

Some years ago, the nation was transfixed by Oregon's attempts to reshape Medicaid, the public insurance program for lower-income families. After much passionate debate, what tended to be deemed less medically necessary were treatments that have little impact on a condition, such as certain kinds of back surgery, some transplants, or some end-of-life care, and conditions that resolve themselves on their own, such as measles, viral sore throats, and minor bumps on the head. America's debate over private insurance cuts much closer to the bone. Impotence, facial scars, and infertility are not conditions that will resolve themselves without treatment. And Viagra, revision surgery, and in vitro fertilization do not fall into the class of treatments that will have little or no impact on these conditions. Precisely for that reason, the debates surrounding them come closer to really grasping the nettle—to calling forth our deepest understandings of *necessity* and of *medical*.

What is notable about so many of these battles waged on the borders of medical necessity is that they have to do with matters of sexual attractiveness or ability. Why is that? Perhaps it's because, as Freud famously observed, we are creatures who work and love. What is medically necessary for work is now taken care of by workers' compensation and workplace disability laws (which have generated their own prodigious debates). Now that the workplace has been attended to, love has become the frontier where the fiercest contention occurs over the meanings of *medical* and *necessity*. We are evolving richer understandings of both words, and it is time that those new insights modified the natural-functioning criterion.

But if and as they do so—and if and as patient groups try to get the state to bring more and more conditions under the ambit of mandated coverage—those groups will have to rely on a mixture of quite distinct public and private values: values that take their bearings from majority choices or public norms, and values that take their bearings from private realm needs or personal norms. And in each case, whether the debate is over *medical* or *necessity*, they will meet opponents who will also rely on a mixture of public sphere and private realm norms, albeit in reverse ways.

9

FOR RICHER AND FOR POORER,
BUT NOT IN SICKNESS AND IN HEALTH

During the 2004 presidential campaign, a curious and revealing symmetry developed between Democratic and Republican approaches to the issue of private health insurance. John Kerry proposed that the federal government clamp a lid on premiums by relieving insurers of most of the expenses for catastrophic claims—those that exceed $30,000 to $50,000 annually for any given individual. Democrats, in other words, identified themselves with the idea that those who are richest—those who contribute proportionately more to the federal treasury through the progressive tax system—should heavily defray the medical expenses of those who are sickest. For their part, George W. Bush and the Republicans had for some time been pointing to the tendency for hospitals and health maintenance organizations to take money saved from premiums paid by their healthier clients—that is, patients who don't need much medical care—and use it to subsidize the expenses of the poor. This propensity, Republicans liked to say, functions more effectively as a safety net than anything government could do.

When it comes to private insurance, apparently, Democrats would have had the rich subsidize the sick; Republicans seemed largely content to have the healthy subsidize the poor. In their complementary if half-satisfactory ways, these two doctrines are nevertheless suggestive. The traditional purpose of private health insurance has always been to take premiums paid by the healthy and redistribute them to the sick. The time-honored principle underlying

America's public income-security programs has always been to take money from the rich and redistribute it to the poor. What the two parties' proposals together suggest is that private health insurance should be nudged toward some kind of middle ground between these two functions. But they also raise a question: Why not go all the way? Why not abandon altogether the notion of health insurance as privately managed redistribution from healthy to sick and make it become a form of publicly managed income security, a form of redistribution from rich to poor?[1]

Indeed, thanks to new developments in medical technology, we are on the brink of an era in which the traditional sine qua non of private health insurance, redistribution from healthy to sick, will make less and less sense. Not only might a public system have to take over anyway, but it would have to look less like a public version of private insurance, redistributing funds from healthy to sick as in Germany, France, and Belgium, and more like a public income-security scheme redistributing funds from rich to poor.

To consider what this possibility means, let us recall that the income-security components of the welfare state, those dealing with richer-poorer redistribution, typically fall into two categories. On the one hand, there are "social insurance" programs, such as Social Security or unemployment insurance, which, as the French writer Pierre Rosanvallon puts it, try to insure those risks to income that share two key characteristics: they are "equally distributed and largely unpredictable."[2] By unpredictable, Rosanvallon means not in a society-wide but in an individual sense; we may well be able to predict that one person out of ten thousand will be hit by a car and so lose earning capacity, but there is no way to tell who will be hit. As the Yale law professors Michael Graetz and Jerry Mashaw have written, when Social Security and unemployment insurance were devised in the wake of the Great Depression, "nearly everyone's family income was viewed [as] sharing the same risk characteristics." Any given family might have to rely heavily on the contributions of others: this is the essence of the equally shared and unpredictable risks that social insurance programs are meant to address.[3]

On the other hand, state provision also embraces "public assistance" programs, such as cash welfare payments or supplemental security income. Here, the idea is just the reverse: these programs cover needs that are unequally distributed and predictable for any given individual. One person (or family) may be poor, as determined by a means test; another may be wealthy, as determined by tax returns. Such verifiable inequality between them allows the state, through its tax and expenditure activities, to transfer funds from richer to poorer.

Each of these two halves of the income-security state—social insurance and public assistance—it is commonly said, counts on a particular human impulse to induce the wealthier to accept that some of their income should go to those who are poorer. For social insurance programs such as Social Security or unemployment insurance, which handle risks that are more or less "equally distributed" and "unpredictable," that impulse, as former labor secretary Robert Reich says, is self-interest.[4] Those whose incomes end up not being diminished by job loss or some other unforeseen risk accept that their contributions will go to assist people whose incomes were diminished. And they do so precisely because it might well have been the other way around. It is self concern, not generosity, that is said to motivate participation in social insurance schemes.

As for public assistance schemes, such as cash welfare payments or supplemental security income, which deal with predictable inequality, the political philosopher David Miller has captured the underlying motivation that must be at work for the better-off to contribute to the worse-off. To the extent that those who know they are better off "agree to enter schemes that they can see in advance will be adversely redistributive from their point of view," Miller writes, they must be motivated by "altruistic sentiments."[5]

In social insurance schemes, then, it is the self-interest of those who do better financially that allows the state to take their money and redistribute it to those who are worse off, and in public assistance schemes it is their altruism that allows such state action. In practice, most income-security programs blend elements of each. But conceptually, they all assume that equality goes with unpredictability and inequality with predictability.

There is a kind of embodied wisdom to this linking of equality with unpredictability, and of inequality with predictability. Suppose instead that the United States had constructed its income-security state around programs that reversed the equation. Suppose one set of programs assumed that, within particular bounds, all members of the community face predictably equal needs for income support—as with George McGovern's 1972 proposal to give every American $1,000 a year, or the suggestion of legal scholars Bruce Ackerman and Ann Alstott that the government provide every young person in America with a lump sum of $80,000 as a stake in life. And suppose the United States enacted a new income-security program that assumed that we face, or prefer to face, income unpredictability not in equal but in unequal degrees—in accordance, say, with George W. Bush's ill-fated proposal to set up "personal investment accounts" in Social Security.

Neither McGovern/Ackerman-Alstott nor a partially privatized Social Security system has gained much political traction in America. And that may be because, at the deepest level, programs like these are unable to tap into either the self-interest or altruism required to mobilize support from those who are better off. A McGovern/Ackerman-Alstott scheme would not appeal on altruistic grounds because the better-off would be getting back just as much as the worse-off would; nor would it be attractive on self-interested grounds, because the better-off would be getting back less than they gave in the progressive taxes needed to fund the program. As for privatizing part of Social Security, the ensuing inequality of portfolio sizes would vitiate any self-interested need, or reason, for better-off individuals to continue participating in the larger program. At the same time, the inevitable uncertainty besetting their own portfolios would dampen any altruistic motivation that they might otherwise have harnessed for contributing to the savings of others.

These tensions within U.S. public income-security programs are apparent in that other major area of the welfare state: private health insurance. It may seem odd to call private health insurance a component of the welfare state, but certainly its proponents believe it to be an adequate substitute for any public health insurance plan that might otherwise cover that part of the population that does not receive Medicaid or Medicare.[6] Of course, unlike income-security programs, whose linchpin is redistribution from rich to poor, with private health insurance, redistribution is from healthy to sick. But private insurance has always resembled public income security in that it, too, relies on linking equality with unpredictability and inequality with predictability.

More specifically, private health insurance has always relied on the idea that, to the extent that our health care needs are unpredictable, we face them equally: a spinal injury from a car accident, for example, or the onset of Parkinson's in an individual with no previous warning signs. Such risks are unpredictable because they have not yet manifested themselves in a symptom or a family history at the time the insurance contract takes effect. And they are equally faced precisely because—since their faintest glimmerings lie entirely in the future—no one member of the community can be said to bear such risks more than any other. We all (as far as one can calculate ex ante) face them equally. Conversely, to the extent that we know what our health care needs are or are likely to be, then, private insurance traditionally assumes, we face them unequally. If A has Type 1 diabetes and B does not, A will need insulin and B will not. Such expenses are predictable and are faced unequally because only those diagnosed with certain symptoms will predictably need insulin.

Of course, there are innumerable gradations between the equally faced unpredictability with which accidents may strike and the completely predictable inequality that arises because A has diabetes and B does not. Insurers, for example, will charge the cohort of seventy-year-old men a higher premium than that of fifty-year-old men. As a group, the former's predictable risk of prostate cancer is greater than in the male community as a whole, even if, within the group, it is not possible to tell which individuals will or will not develop it. Within the group, in other words, there is equal unpredictability, but between the group and the community, there is a predictable inequality. The group collectively has a comparatively predictable and unequally greater likelihood of developing cancer cases.

The existence, for the purposes of setting premiums, of such groups as seventy-year-old-men testifies to the larger point: the less predictable the onset of any given condition is for any given person—the less we can tell who will experience it—the more equally the risk of it confronts members of the community. And the more predictable a need is for any given person—the more we can tell who will experience it and who not—the more we face it with interpersonal inequality. Because of this, private health insurance has, at least up until now, always been able to call upon both self-interest and altruism to motivate redistribution from healthy to sick—not perfectly, of course, but enough to make for a functioning (if often perilously unstable) system.

To the extent that private health insurance covers risks that we face with equal unpredictability, the motivation for those who turn out to be healthy to help those who turn out to be sick is self-interest: it just as easily could have been the other way round. As for needs that are more predictable for any given individual and hence faced with greater inequality across individuals, private health insurance relies on altruism. A nondiabetic worker in a given workplace will pay the same health insurance premium as a diabetic worker, thereby helping to defray the latter's predictable, unequal, higher expense. Only an implicit altruism could explain this. Or, as the Princeton health-policy analysts Tsung-mei Cheng and Uwe E. Reinhardt put it, "A positive externality in the consumption of health care occurs when individual A derives happiness from knowing that individual B receives health care of a given type."[7]

Even critics of private health insurance buy into these conceptual premises. Ron Pollack of Families USA, for example, speaks of health insurance participation as being partly "an issue of altruism for a discrete and disadvantaged population," and partly "one of self-interest for a very substantial part of the population."[8] Indeed, one recent innovation in private health insurance, the combination of catastrophic coverage with individual Health Savings Accounts, simply highlights this distinction. The catastrophic plan is meant to cover relatively large, unpredictable needs we face with equality, while the Health Savings Account is available for smaller, mostly predictable needs we each face to our own unequal degrees—and, on some such proposals, they would be subsidized for those whose medical needs are greater.

One question, however, nags: What if this fundamental intellectual premise underlying private health insurance—that health care arranges itself on a spectrum from unpredictable needs that we face equally to predictable needs that we face unequally—is not the only or even the best principle on which to divide up the universe of medical need? What if, in fact, our predictable medical needs are coming to be more and more the same, more and more equally held? And what if the unpredictability with which we develop other medical needs, far from facing us equally, more and more confronts each one of us with our own, individually differentiated odds? Can the private health insurance system continue to function in such circumstances?

It is true that we face many predictable medical needs—insulin for diabetes, dialysis for kidney disease—unequally on an individual-by-individual basis. But we have arrived at a point where, over the next few decades, we will begin holding many other predictable medical needs equally. The key here is the growing portion of health care that will be offered presymptomatically, in advance of any distinguishing or contingent symptoms at all. Preventive care, from vaccines to wellness treatments, is increasing as a proportion of all health care, and it is required by whole populations equally, hence predictably. For example, "If we know," says Philip Boyle, a bioethicist at Chicago's Park Ridge Center, that "ibuprofen has some effect on Alzheimer's, large numbers of people will want to take it."[9] Whereas typically the absence of individual symptoms or risk factors for a particular condition means that we each face it with equal unpredictability, here—where the idea is to prevent such symptoms or risk factors—we share the same medical needs with equal certainty.

The same is the case with genetic screening, another service that is offered presymptomatically. Indeed, the point of screening is precisely to discover symptoms, which means that, in many if not all cases, everyone will need it equally. And, because need for it does not depend on the contingency of manifesting a symptom, everyone will need it with a priori predictability. Hence references to "population screening," "widespread screening," and "mass screening" pervade discussions of the topic. The "number of tests that can be applied to all healthy people," says Robert Pokorski, chair of the American Council of Life Insurance's genetic testing committee, is "limited only by the imagination."[10] In June 2004 the *New York Times* reported that Baylor College of Medicine had introduced a "pilot program with perhaps the largest panel of prenatal tests ever offered. For $2,000, a pregnant woman will be able to have her fetus tested for some

50 conditions that cause mental retardation."[11] As Ted Halstead and Michael Lind of the New American Foundation say, a "new citizen-based health care system would encourage the development and use of new medical technologies, including genetic testing, which could ultimately benefit all citizens, and shift the whole focus of health care to disease prevention."[12]

Similarly, enhancement—whether of the genetic, pharmacological, or surgical kind—will also open up a range of medical services that all of us could claim to need equally and with predictable certainty. "The techniques of genetic engineering," the bioethicist Alexander Capron writes, "might be used not merely to bring all people up to a 'normal' level but actually to 'enhance' human capabilities by providing genes not usually found in a particular form in humans."[13] To the extent that enhancement becomes something that we regard as a medical need—as properly falling within the province of health care—it would, by definition, be something we would need predictably, relying as it would not on the contingent presence of symptoms but on the certifiable absence of desired traits. Additionally, if and as such enhancement becomes something that we come to regard as a need, it would by definition be something that we would all need equally, because it would instill physical traits that none, or very few of us, now have.

We need not focus on the more far-out putative enhancements such as IQ boosters or memory restorers. If the bar for what constitutes a healthy human being even rises to include something far less extravagant than "adding a few points to IQ," as the late Dorothy Wertz of the University of Massachusetts Medical School told me—for example, "immunity to pneumonia or HIV or flu"—then almost all of us "will fall short."[14] Put another way, what is now asymptomatic—not having pneumonia—will become symptomatic, and the symptoms will be ones we almost all know we have. The pattern has been set, Philip Boyle notes, by "people who use [Prozac] absent depression, or men who use Viagra absent impotence."[15] Normal anxiety or normal sexual performance are coming to be considered pathological. But the very fact that they are normal means that we harbor them with community-wide equality and predictability.

In many ways, then, as preventive care, genetic screening, and pharmacological, surgical, and genetic enhancement become more powerful and prevalent, our more predictable health care needs, which private insurance assumes are distributed unequally and differentially over individuals, may become more and more equally shared over whole communities. But this is only one half of the story. The other half is that our unpredictable health care needs, which private insurance assumes are distributed largely equally across the whole community, might be growing more and more individuated.

Although it is true that the ballooning opportunity for genetic screening will increase the number of predictable medical needs we all face equally, the results of such screening will, in turn, increase the individuation with which we face unpredictable needs. Even with the most sophisticated testing, people will confront unequal genetic futures not with predictability, but with newly individual-specific measures of uncertainty. If you have the breast-cancer gene BRCA1, your chances of developing breast cancer are 1 percent as opposed to 0.5 percent for the rest of the population. Eighty percent of individuals who test positive for the gene for fragile-X will manifest some kind of mental retardation—what kind lies beyond genetic prediction—but 20 percent never will. "We tend to hold unrealistic expectations about the accuracy and certainty of genetic information," Philip Boyle says;[16] according to Klaus Lindpaintner, vice president of research at Hoffmann-La Roche, new "diagnostic approaches—including those based on DNA analysis—will ultimately provide a measure of probability, not of certainty."[17]

What new diagnostic approaches will do is individuate risk profiles to a degree hitherto unseen in health insurance, which thus far has based its premiums either on the different risk profiles assigned to various groups or on the historic certainties (via preexisting conditions) that each medical biography offers. But now, suppose that A's positive test assigns a high probability to the chance that he or she might be afflicted by a particular condition, while B's negative test assigns a particular low probability to the same chance. Then, summed over further tests and other conditions, what distinguishes A from B is the unprecedented nuanced individuation with which they each face unpredictability. We will each have our own unique risk profile.

Advanced genetics will not only individuate the probabilities with which we face diseases, it will individuate the probabilities with which we will respond to different therapies. The new field of pharmacogenomics, as the geneticists Aravinda Chakravarti and Peter Little wrote in the January 23, 2005, issue of Nature, "will focus . . . uniquely and completely upon the individual," but, as an editorial in the same journal also says, the "popular and much-hyped image of a straightforward glide into perfect, personalized medicine is way off the mark."[18] Instead, individuals will face their own probabilities of responding to each of the various drug treatments for their conditions, depending on how their genetic makeup allows their bodies to transport, target, metabolize, and eliminate the drugs. And these are, very much, probabilities, albeit individually specified ones. If we are indeed heading into a world "where the complexities of genetic testing . . . are married with those of best drug prescription," the health policy expert Jai Shah wrote in the July 2003 issue of Nature

Biotechnology, then each individual will display his or her own host of risk factors for all diseases and "the issues surrounding [insurance] coverage will be particularly vexing."[19]

The preceding has been a kind of thought experiment. In reality, the unequally distributed predictable needs contemplated by traditional insurance—insulin for the diabetic, none for the nondiabetic—will not go away, but they will be joined by a flotilla of equally distributed predictable needs: for preventive care, genetic screening, or surgical or pharmaceutical enhancement. Nor will the equally distributed unpredictable needs anticipated by traditional insurance entirely disappear; accidents and acts of nature will still happen. But as genetic and other diagnostic tools and pharmacological and other tailored therapies grow increasingly sophisticated, more and more of what formerly were risks equally unpredictable for the entire community will resolve themselves into unequal degrees of probability for each individual.

Whatever its actual dimensions, to the extent that this new world comes into being, it will pose serious problems for the possibility of redistribution from healthy to sick. Consider first that growing range of predictable medical needs we would all share equally: the needs for prevention, screening, and enhancement. To the extent that we require these services, we do not do so with the predictable inequality that induces those with fewer medical needs altruistically to allow their payments to help those with more. Nor do we do so with the equal unpredictability required to motivate a self-interested participation in health insurance. Rather, to the extent that "you and I have equal, predictable needs," says Julie Taylor of Blue Cross/Blue Shield of Idaho, "where's the sense in my paying for yours or you for mine?"[20] With respect to prevention, screening, and enhancement, we are all equally and predictably needy; hence, the possibility of redistribution from healthy to sick no longer even exists.

Now consider those medical expenses we would face, as a consequence of genetic diagnosis and pharmacogenomic therapy, with unequal, individuated measures of unpredictability. Here, it is not the very idea of health that would ebb, but the very possibility of insurance. To the extent that we each make up our own risk category, then we each will be charged a premium that covers our own risk and ours alone, negating any idea of our participating in a broader insurance scheme that embraces others. The self-interested reason for participating in insurance that emerges when we each face unpredictability equally—as with acts of nature and ailments for which there are no current risk factors—ebbs, certainly, for person A, when A's odds of developing multiple sclerosis are far less than B's. Nor can the altruistic reason for participating in health insurance emerge easily as long as we're talking about inequality that is merely probable instead of certain. As South Carolina insurance director Ernest Csiszar says, individuals with low probabilities of being sick are nevertheless inclined to fix on that possibility, however minuscule: routinely, those with low probabilities of prostate cancer as determined by increasingly sophisticated diagnostic tools seek to treat it aggressively. Their doing so saps any motivation they may have to participate in insurance as an altruistic giver. Resources that I otherwise might have been willing to devote to "those worse-off if I was sure I'd be better off," Csiszar says, "I will want to keep for myself just in case" and so will be more hesitant to pay a premium of an amount sufficient to help others.[21]

Private health insurance has historically relied on either the principle of self-interest or the principle of altruism. Yet it is far from clear that either will work, or work as well, in a world in which our predictable medical needs are ever more equally faced, while our unpredictable needs are faced to ever more unequal degrees. The basic impulses of self-interest and altruism that all private insurers have to balance may well be changing so that they contradict the basic assumptions of the private health insurance industry.

If so, then we might have to abandon the idea of health insurance as a means of redistribution from healthy to sick and accept that it too should become a mechanism of redistribution from rich to poor, part of America's income-security programs. There is no shortage of proposed schemes by which we might effect such a transformation; the *New York Times*, the American Medical Association, many prominent academics, and (especially during the summer and fall of 2009) numerous legislators have offered such proposals.[22] Yale's Graetz and Mashaw, for example, argue that "the role of health insurance should be to protect families against two types of risks to income." First, by calling, public assistance style, upon whatever altruism the rich feel for the poor, the government should ensure that "out-of-pocket [medical] costs for the poor [are] fully subsidized with public funds."[23] Put another way, if you and I both need preventive care of some sort, altruism will not motivate me to pay for yours because you are medically needier than I—you're not—but altruism could prompt me to pay for yours if you are financially needier and can ill afford it.

Second, by calling, social insurance style, upon the self-interest that all people, rich or poor, harbor to protect themselves against income loss, government could ensure that "no family, however high its income, [is] required to spend more than 15 percent of its income on health care in any one year." Doing so, Graetz and Mashaw say, will eliminate "the risk of encountering an unacceptably steep decline in living standards because of large medical expenses."[24] Put another way, even if individual health risk profiles are becoming more and more individuated, we still face risks to income with a much more equal, more widespread unpredictability: almost any of us may be unable to meet the cost of any given health need. An income-security scheme that protects 85 percent of a wealthy person's income from health care expenses, just as it does for a poorer person's, will appeal to the self-interest of the financially better off.

Indeed, the logics of both Medicaid and Medicare point in this direction of transforming health insurance into a two-part public assistance and social insurance income-security program. Viewed as an income-security program, Medicaid is a form of public assistance through which the rich (altruistically) assist the poor, but it is famously unsuccessful as a social insurance program. It fails to insure the rich or the middle class against the income loss that comes from catastrophic medical expenses, requiring them actually to suffer that loss, actually become poor, before they can become eligible for Medicaid. Hence the widespread dilemma imposed on those who have to spend down their assets before they become eligible. As for Medicare, it indemnifies the elderly rich and poor alike against catastrophic medical expenses and so succeeds fairly well as an income-security social insurance program, serving the self-interest of the rich, the poor, and everyone in between. But it fails as a public assistance program because people of very different income levels, notwithstanding some recent modifications, pay the same premiums for Medicare Part B (physician services).[25] And anything Medicare does not cover—including Medicare Part A's deductible for stays in hospital of more than sixty days—remains out of reach for the poor.

Viewed within the context of the broader debates that frame this book's inquiry, the conflict here, on a traditional understanding, pits private against public. It pits private health insurers and their supporters, who believe that private insurance should continue to carry the freight it does, against those—from state insurance commissioners to scientists to doctors—who are dubious of that prospect over the medium term, believing that some sort of broader public scheme will ultimately be necessary.

That is a battle that is being joined in the opening phase of the Obama administration. As the debate unfolds, though, it might be helpful to understand in what ways it might be less aptly described as a battle between partisans of public sphere values and private market norms than as a clash in which each side looks to both public sphere values of altruism and private market norms of self-interest but sees them applying in inverse ways.

Consider first private health insurers. They tap as much into the public sphere value of altruism as they do the private market value of self-interestedness, relying on both for the viability of private health insurance. A realm exists within the universe of health conditions, certainly, wherein the self-interested motive for participating in health insurance remains alive and well: conditions that we all face with equal unpredictability, such as trauma care for accident victims. But private insurance also covers a comparably robust realm of medical needs that—at any given time—are predictably unequal, such as diabetes care, where the public sphere values of altruism and concern for others must be in play at some level. Both self-interest and altruism work together—they need to work together—to sustain participation even in a private health insurance system.

For private insurance skeptics such as Julie Taylor or Ernest Csiszar, too, the equality and unpredictability that underlie the self-interested motivation to participate in health insurance, and the predictability and inequality that underlie the altruistic motive, still exist. It is just that to some extent they threaten to reshuffle their relationships. Self-interest's prerequisite of unpredictability is beginning to commingle with altruism's prerequisite of inequality in areas like pharmacogenetics, where we will each face particular medical conditions with our own individuated and unequal degrees of unpredictability. Here, neither self-interest (there is too much inequality) nor altruism (there is too much unpredictability) may be sufficiently robust to motivate workable participation in any kind of health insurance, public or private.

Conversely, self-interest's prerequisite of equality and altruism's prerequisite of predictability are, increasingly, commingling in areas like prevention, screening, and enhancement. Here, we will each face the same medical needs with equality and predictability. And here, again, neither self-interest (there is too much predictability) nor altruism (there is too much equality) are as likely to be able to motivate participation in health insurance, public or private. The ultimate consequence, for those who side with this view, must be the advent of a public income-security program: either generally or one that deals specifically with the impact of health care costs on income.

So each side in this debate—private insurers defending a private system and those from many quarters advancing a public scheme—in fact sees the constituent parts of both the public sphere value of altruism and the private sphere value of self-interest at play. It's just that where private insurers see altruism and self-interest each continuing to work robustly to motivate participation in and support for private health insurance, others see them as increasingly prone to break up into their elements and recombine, so that aspects of self-interest and altruism act to counter and dilute each other. This portends an eventual untenability of private health insurance and a takeover by a public income-security program.

We are living at a moment in which medical technology—prevention, screening, enhancement, pharmacogenetics—is beginning to undermine both the self-interested and the altruistic motivations for the healthy to aid the sick. The time is thus ripe for America to set out for where it is headed logically, even if not quite yet ideologically: to a public health care system whose premise is income security and whose redistribution flows not from the healthier to the sicker, but from richer to poorer.

WELFARE

10

MORAL ECONOMY IN AMERICA

"Leave those vain moralists, my friend," Rousseau advised, "and return to the depth of your soul." His great contemporary Edmund Burke lamented that "the age of chivalry is gone; that of . . . economists . . . has succeeded." One can only imagine, then, what the two thinkers might have said about our age—the age when moral and economic thought combined to produce moral economy. From the former Republican House majority leader Dick Armey, who claimed that "poverty [is not] a material but a moral phenomenon," to the liberal public intellectual E. J. Dionne Jr., who argues that "many aspects of the economy that conservatives celebrate . . . undermine the very virtues that conservatives . . . revere," the political air is thick with postulated links and counterlinks between moral and economic growth or decay.[1]

Moral economy has always commanded intellectual interest in America. But when moral-economic arguments get pressed into the service of the dominant ideologies of liberalism and conservatism, as is the case today, they display a pronounced tendency to turn in on themselves and self-destruct. At the very moment when moral-economic arguments seem to define contemporary liberalism and conservatism, they have also developed the capacity to expose liberalism and conservatism alike to considerable tension and pressure.

In times past, liberal and conservative moral economies were both relatively straightforward. Liberals argued that wealthy societies are not necessarily moral ones—that the creative destruction of capitalism lays waste to communities and to their moral fabric through plant closings, onerous labor conditions, or forced migrations—and that government is therefore needed to compel the malefactors of wealth to meet their moral obligations.[2] Moving from the social to the personal level, liberals also argued that morally virtuous individuals, even though they work hard and play by the rules, will not necessarily become economically well off, without redistributive assistance from the state. The notion that personal economic failure is not automatically attributable to personal moral failings, that unemployment and bankruptcy are not necessarily one's fault, is often cited as the psychological breakthrough of New Deal liberalism.

Conservatives, at the social and individual levels, have always claimed the opposite. Seeking to minimize the need for redistributive government, they argue that wealthy societies, left to their own devices, will adequately take on the moral burden of caring for those less well off—those displaced or cast aside by the waves of economic change—through private charity, philanthropy, and voluntarism. And conservatives have for generations insisted that morally virtuous individuals—honest, reliable, cooperative—will, left to their own devices, eventually make their own way up the economic ladder without help from the government.

Liberals and conservatives, of course, still make these arguments. At the social level, liberal political economists such as Lester Thurow worry that wealthy societies, in the absence of government intervention, will inevitably show insufficient concern for the disadvantaged whom they leave in their wake.[3] At the individual level, liberal intellectuals such as Robert Reich heap skepticism on the "story of the little guy who works hard, takes risks, believes in himself and eventually earns wealth and fame."[4] On the other side, conservative scholars such as Marvin Olasky counter that society, once freed of government's heavy hand, will indeed unleash both the wealth and the previously repressed altruistic spirit necessary to ameliorate a host of social ills.[5] And at the individual level, Irving Kristol and other conservative intellectuals speak of an enduring connection between such "bourgeois virtues as honesty, sobriety [and] a concern for family and community," on the one hand, and personal "worldly success" on the other.[6]

In the last decades of the twentieth century, however, two political issues—one at the individual level, the other at the social level—emerged to torque both liberal and conservative moral economy in inconsistent ways. The first was the debate over welfare, which operates at the individual level. Here conservatives, who have long believed that an individual's moral character has a positive influence on his capacity to accumulate wealth, began arguing that an individual's wealth has a negative influence on his moral character. Whether we are talking about the small increments of wealth that the welfare state provides the poor, or the large amounts of wealth that rich parents provide their children, economic largesse affords individuals the wherewithal to indulge in moral depravity: to buy drugs, leave their spouses, give birth out of wedlock, lead a life of indolence. "In very different ways," the neoconservative intellectual Norman Podhoretz has written, "groups at both ends of the . . . economic scale . . . have been liberated from . . . traditional [moral] norms."[7] Or as the conservative writer David Frum puts it, "Big government does for the 98 percent of society that is not rich what her millions did for the late Barbara Hutton—it enables them to engage in destructive behavior without immediately suffering the consequences." Frum concludes that "without welfare, people would cling harder to working-class respectability than they do now."[8]

Liberals, put on the defensive, took to arguing that it is precisely when an individual becomes economically deprived that he or she becomes morally depraved. Unsatisfactory work prospects lead the poor to take it out on their families—to abuse them, abandon them, or else turn to crime for a living—in much the same way that unsatisfying family relationships lead the rich to plunge into their work. Only when individuals are enabled to earn a decent living wage—through a combination of income support, social assistance, and progressive labor policies—is moral behavior possible; no longer will they have to resort to larceny, drug use, or desertion.[9] Whether the moral ill is family breakdown or teen pregnancy, as the economist David M. Gordon wrote in the *Nation*, "we can find falling real wages or job insecurity lurking in the background."[10] For decades liberals have argued that possessing an admirable moral character does not necessarily ensure that one will reap economic rewards. More recently they have come to argue as well that economic well-being is the single most important ingredient in the development of individual moral character.

Globalization is the other new issue stretching liberal and conservative moral economy into new shapes, this time at the social level. Liberals, who argue that economically prosperous societies do not typically win high marks for moral conduct, now claim in addition that it is the morally advanced society that stands the best chance of prospering economically in a competitive international system. Dionne writes that a moral society—one in which the social virtues of "loyalty, commitment, generosity, and community-mindedness" abound—is a prerequisite for economic success.[11] Conservatives "may choke on the fact," as Century Foundation president Richard C. Leone has put it, "but capitalism works best when . . . the system is fair and democratic

. . . when it is mixed with community and public values."[12] Consumers will purchase from, employees will give their all to, and the physical environment will be there only for those companies that treat them well; the notion that a society can "do well by doing good" is very much a contemporary liberal refrain. It underlies the movement for much social welfare legislation, from family leave to occupational health and safety to consumer protection, and the impetus to embody such standards in global trade agreements.

Yet conservatives such as David Brooks have disputed such claims, arguing that moral decency—social habits of "trustworthiness, respect, responsibility, caring, and citizenship"—can in fact hamstring the audacity, ambition, and high-spirited competitiveness necessary for a society's economic expansion.[13] As the neoconservative historian Gertrude Himmelfarb has written in describing this argument, "traditional manners and morals"—a "more civil, more pacific, more humane society"—are inconsistent with the "qualities that encourage economic . . . progress—individuality, boldness, the spirit of enterprise and innovation."[14] Conservative critics of corporate social responsibility, such as Milton Friedman, have echoed this refrain, arguing that societies whose businesses are overly concerned with doing good are less likely to do well, especially in a fiercely competitive global environment. For fifty years, conservatives have claimed that when societies are economically prosperous they will be more than sufficiently morally virtuous. Now they argue, in light of globalization, that when societies are shot through with moral virtue, they are likely to risk becoming less-than-optimal economic performers.

Are liberal and conservative moral economy ideologies internally contradictory, each one carrying the seeds of its own destruction? If they are, it is not because it is inconsistent to believe (as many conservatives do, for example) that personal moral virtue brings an individual economic success, but that personal economic well-being undermines an individual's moral virtue. Nor is it illogical to hold, as many liberals do, that a morally virtuous society is likely to become an economically successful one, but that, assuming it does reach economic supremacy, it will not necessarily acquit itself well morally. These propositions may simply describe with considerable accuracy the natural cycles—the organic rises and falls—in the lives of individuals and societies. They may bespeak catch-22s in the human condition, not contradictions within liberalism and conservatism.

But now let me slightly reshuffle these arguments to suggest that liberals and conservatives do contradict themselves, because each ideology argues that what is good for societies is not necessarily good for individuals—and vice versa. Much of what we call American liberalism, for example, would seem to be traceable to one or another of the following views. First, growth in national income risks unraveling a society's moral fabric, but growth in personal income strengthens an individual's moral fiber. Second, if a society is morally decent it will prosper economically, but if an individual is morally decent there is no similar guarantee. American conservatism is the designation we give to the contrary set of doctrines, that economically well-off societies have a greater tendency to behave morally than do economically well-off individuals, but that morally punctilious individuals have a greater tendency to do well economically than do morally fastidious societies.

Is it possible that societies and individuals are so different that what works for one fails for the other? At the core, this is what liberals and conservatives are now telling us.

Societies are fractured while individuals are unitary: if there is a difference between the two, this would seem to be it. Certainly this is why liberals think that a growing national income poses greater moral hazards for societies than a growing personal income does for individuals. Within society as a whole, liberals say, some groups that become wealthy will inevitably behave badly toward others that do not. When liberals speak of the morally corrosive effects of wealth accumulation at the social level, they have in mind corporations tearing apart or abandoning communities, or the rich seceding from and turning their backs on the poor. But why, liberals implicitly ask, should an individual whose income goes up—whether because of welfare or other state programs—abuse himself in any analogous way as a result? Even if all of society does not benefit from a given increase in national income, all of an individual does benefit from a rise in his or her personal income.

But what if individuals and societies are in fact not so different? Indeed, in the welfare debates of the last twenty-five years, conservatives in effect argued that individuals are best understood as minisocieties. In his 1992 book *The New Politics of Poverty*, Lawrence Mead wrote that for decades it was assumed that "if government and the economy took care of workers, . . . employees would be able to take care of their families. . . . Debates in progressive politics largely took the family for granted."[15] Today, however, the debate over welfare does not stop at the threshold of the home—treating each as an individual (that is, indivisible) black box represented by a sole breadwinner—but rather opens it up, there to confront a small fractured society with multiple players. "What was once offstage," as Mead says, has "come onstage."[16]

What had come onstage during the period leading up to the 1996 welfare reforms, specifically, was the conservative claim that when the income of some family members goes up as a result of a welfare check, they may very well treat other family members badly—abandoning them, seceding from them, turning their backs on them. "Family affection," as David Frum puts it, is "one of the weakest of human ties"; instead, the "glue of mutual [economic] self-interest" is what keeps families together.[17] A welfare entitlement, however, dissolves this glue by making it financially possible—indeed desirable—for women to leave the fathers of their children, or for teenage single mothers to set up housekeeping apart from their parents, in order to qualify for or keep their grant. According to conservatives, poor mothers will not get or stay married, nor will they turn to their broader family for support if their marriages fail, unless they are constrained to do these things by economic self-interest. Welfare, especially if it is too generous or unconditional, removes any such constraints.

Conservatives may or may not be right about this—the empirical evidence is mixed[18]—but the point here is that, to the extent that a family is better understood as a fractious minisociety, then whatever wealth's consequences happen to be for society at large, they should be much the same for the individual family unit. So if liberals are going to argue that wealth tends to have a disintegrating, "I'm all right, Jack" effect on the moral fabric of societies, it would be hard to reason why wealth should not have the same effect, at least to some degree, at the family level.

But conservatives are not out of the woods either. In effect, their moral economy has forced them to characterize "society at large" as a more fraternal, less fractured entity than the family. Consider Newt Gingrich's confidence, often expressed during his early years as Speaker of the House, that if only the welfare state's choke hold on the economy were to be relaxed, corporations and other groups would provide laptop computers for poor children, adopt all the homeless in America, and free up their employees to do three hours of volunteer work a week. "When the American people have more they give more," the 1996 Republican presidential aspirant Steve Forbes told his campaign audiences; "the American people are known as a generous people, a giving people."[19] Conservatives, in other words, argue that at a social level we are moved by altruism, prepared to use our private largesse to help out strangers as the welfare state retrenches.

Yet this jars, because at the same time conservatives have been arguing that at the family level we are actuated (in the conservative policy intellectual Charles Murray's terms) by a keen "self-interest," prepared to abandon family members at the drop of a hat when largesse from the welfare state or elsewhere makes that possible.[20] If, as a society, we are indeed prepared to use our wealth in a way that respects our moral obligations to strangers, then why as individuals would we use our wealth in a way that flouts our obligations to family members? Could the relationship between members of society be as altruistic and community-minded as conservatives say, when the relationship between family members is so self-interested and atomistic?

In effect, it is precisely this question that liberals pose whenever they argue that the intrafamily relationships between women and men and between mothers and children are governed far more by affective impulses than by calculations of self-interest. That is why, for liberals, it was never plausible that single women would become abstinent just because they are cut off welfare. "Almost all humans enjoy sex" and "[m]ost women also find infants extraordinarily endearing," as the liberal scholars Christopher Jencks and Kathryn Edin put it, and hence states that cut welfare are not likely to markedly reduce nonmarital birthrates.[21] Nor do married women leave their husbands just because welfare affords them the opportunity; the bonds of affection are stronger than that: and if they do leave their husbands, it is often out of mother-love, the desire to protect or preserve the well-being of their children. For conservatives, denying single mothers welfare allows economic self-interest to enforce abstinence and reinforce marriage. But for liberals, affection runs roughshod over calculations of economic self-interest in the familial realm: Welfare's disappearance will not stop women from having children. And its presence does not dissolve marriages.

Much recent American debate over welfare comes down to this: For conservatives, altruism and the bonds of affection are sufficiently strong within the social realm that the welfare state can afford to wither. But when it comes to the individual and her family, affective and altruistic impulses are not so strong that we can afford to ignore appeals to economic self-interest, or fail to exploit it, as a means of reinforcing the two-parent family. For liberals, altruism and the bonds of affection between citizens are not sufficiently strong that we can afford to ignore appeals to economic self-interest in establishing a welfare state; as Robert Reich says, America's major social programs came into existence only because they successfully appealed to the "enlightened self-interest" of middle-class America. They prevailed not because the average middle-class American cared about the poor, the unemployed, the sick or the elderly, but only because the average middle-class American understood that he himself could become poor, unemployed, sick or elderly. "Altruism," Reich says, "never figured prominently in . . . liberal public philosophy."[22] But when it comes to the individual and her family, affective and altruistic impulses dominate self-interest. Married mothers do not break up their marriages just because welfare may give them an incentive to do so; single women will become mothers even if welfare's disappearance gives them an incentive not to do so.

In the welfare debate, then, both liberals and conservatives assume—in ways that subject their argumentation to tensions and contortions—that individual families and societies display very different moral economies when the arrow runs from economics to morality. Conservatives rest their arguments on the claim that wealth makes societies behave morally but not individuals; liberals the reverse. In the debate over appropriate social policy in the wake of globalization, it turns out, the same pattern emerges, this time with the arrow running from morality to economics.

Consider Francis Fukuyama's 1995 book, *Trust: The Social Virtues and the Creation of Prosperity*. Societies, Fukuyama argues, prosper economically to the extent that they are able to replicate, on a nationwide scale, the moral virtues of trustworthiness, affection, cooperation, and mutual responsibility that traditionally characterize the individual family. In some societies, like those of southern Italy and China, there is still sufficient trustworthiness at the family level, between close relatives, to create prosperous small domestic enterprises. But there is insufficient trust between strangers at the social level to go the next step and create the huge private corporate enterprises that, in Germany and the United States, have brought fantastic economic growth.

Whatever its weaknesses, Fukuyama's argument at least has the virtue of consistency. It sees the same moral-economic dynamics—moral virtue leads to economic prosperity—operating at the individual-familial and social levels, which is why it provides a useful reference for pointing up the inconsistency that globalization has wrought in both liberal and conservative moral economy. If liberals believe that a morally virtuous society—one in which employers are required by social policy to curb their self-interest and pay higher wages, tend to the environment, and be solicitous of consumers—will be rewarded in a wildly careering global economic system, then why should they be less sanguine that moral behavior by individuals—those who curb their self-indulgence, work hard, and play by the rules—will be rewarded by their domestic economic systems? Conversely, if conservatives believe that individuals who display the moral virtues of solicitousness, scrupulousness, trustworthiness, and cooperativeness are not chumps but will in fact be rewarded economically within their own societies, then why shouldn't societies that display these same virtues, requiring them if necessary through social policy, attract business and prosper within the international system?

It goes against the grain of American political argument—maybe it is even heresy—to suggest that individuals and societies resemble one another. For many purposes, those having to do with basic freedoms, for example, we

rightly insist on treating the individual (or his family) and society as profoundly different entities. But when it comes to the everyday politics of welfare
and globalization at the beginning of the twenty-first century, the distinction
carries less weight. The debate over welfare, in essence, requires that we not
stop at the threshold of the individual household, but instead cross it and
approach the family as if it were a small society. Globalization, by contrast,
requires that we not stop at the frontiers of our own society but cross them,
recognizing that each society is but one individual actor in a roiling international economy. Because liberalism and conservatism now define themselves
so substantially as competing moral economies, each must ensure that the
links between morals and economics it posits for societies do not chafe against
the links it posits for individuals. This they have not done.

Why? Because support for a strong regulatory and redistributive state
requires liberals to distinguish between societies and individuals. If economic
prosperity at the societal level fails to bring moral responsibility in its wake,
then we need progressive labor, consumer, and environmental legislation. But
only if economic prosperity at the individual level does bring moral
responsibility—only if a decent wage is the surest antidote to "larceny, drug use
or desertion"—can we justify generous welfare and redistributive policies.
Likewise when we reverse the arrow: If moral decency at the societal level
brings economic prosperity, then we need progressive labor, consumer, and
environmental legislation. But only if moral decency at the individual level is
no guarantee of economic security can we justify generous welfare and redistributive schemes. Conservatives, who oppose the regulatory and redistributive
state, are required to make just the opposite set of moral-economic arguments.

Already there are signs that these liberal and conservative moral economies
are both coming unraveled—that liberals and conservatives themselves recognize that tensions emerge when they say different things about individuals
and societies. For example, historian Gertrude Himmelfarb has long argued (as
have most conservatives) that at the individual level, wealth, whether from
private sources or the government, does not necessarily bring personal moral
elevation. But she also quite consistently goes the next step, chiding her fellow
conservatives for failing to recognize that, at the social level as well, a booming free-market "economy does not automatically produce the moral goods
that they value."[23] Conversely, conservative followers of the late Jack Kemp, the
prominent Republican—who do believe that a booming economy will inspire
virtuous behavior (altruism, generosity) at the social level—also argue that tar-
geted injections of economic assistance at the individual level will cultivate
personal moral virtues such as familial responsibility, industriousness, and

respect for property. This certainly makes for a moral economy consistent at the social and individual levels. But it also led Kemp and his followers to propose an array of government programs, such as tenant ownership of public housing and enterprise zones, for which they have then been duly chastised by other conservatives.

Similarly, some important fault lines within contemporary liberalism are traceable to a struggle on the part of both paleoliberal "old Democrats" and neoliberal New Democrats to reach some level of consistency in liberalism's moral economy: a struggle that began under Bill Clinton and continues to this day. For example, one of the original paleoliberals, the economist Jeff Faux, argues—as most liberals do—that personal economic well-being is the surest curative for a host of moral ills (indolence, illegitimacy, desertion) at the individual level; hence Faux and other paleoliberals support robust welfare programs. But Faux then goes further than many liberals in arguing that, at the broadest social level, roaring economic growth stands the best chance of expunging a host of moral ills (corporate abandonment of employees, white flight from urban centers, and public disaffection from politics). Adopting such a moral economy allows Faux and other paleoliberals to urge a stimulative macroeconomic policy of high government spending and low interest rates.[24]

This certainly makes for a moral economy consistent at the social and individual levels, but it also creates tensions within political liberalism. Will Marshall of the Progressive Policy Institute and other neoliberals twit what they see as the simplemindedness of the paleoliberal nostrum ("get the economy booming again and the rising tide will cover our blighted social landscape"[25]), dismissing it on the ground that "such economic reductionism drains politics of moral sense." At the social level, in other words, neoliberals are hesitant to assume that economic well-being—whether fostered by government or the market—will cure all moral blights. But Marshall goes further, arguing that at the individual level as well, economic well-being in itself does little to bring about personal moral improvement. In fact, Marshall and other neoliberals, perhaps propelled by an instinctive urge toward moral-economic consistency, depart from traditional liberalism in entertaining the possibility that a welfare check might indeed be morally corrupting—an antigovernment stance for which they are duly chastised by paleoliberals.

Perhaps the one contemporary political current that comes closest to arguing a consistent moral economy is communitarianism.[26] Communitarians, by and large, believe that economic well-being does not automatically translate into moral decency at either the social or the individual level. Like liberals, they worry that unbridled capitalism has a tendency to weaken the moral fabric of society; like conservatives, they fret that overgenerous or unconditional welfare support weakens the moral fiber of individuals. So, for example, the communitarian thinker David Blankenhorn maintains that "more prosperity" will not in itself "generate a revival of American civil society"—a position with affinities to liberalism—while insisting that at the individual level, "welfare . . . cannot turn children into good citizens," a position that resonates with conservative argumentation.[27]

Now reverse the economic-moral causal arrow and consider that many thinkers who advance or support strands of communitarianism believe that moral virtue does reliably translate into economic prosperity and that it does so at both the individual level (as conservatives claim) and at the social level (as liberals would have it). In the political theorist William Galston's view, for example, there continues to be "a nonrandom relation between the effort, contribution, and skill [individuals] display and the rewards they receive," while at the social level, "modern industry requires as much cooperation as competition."[28] Since moral behavior leads to economic well-being at both levels, communitarians recommend traditional familial and educational values for individuals, while often counseling progressive consumer, labor, and environmental legislation for societies.

Yet although communitarians may have evolved a fairly consistent moral economy, they for that very reason have no coherent position on whether government should grow or shrink. This is why there are—and always will be—what Philip Selznick, in *The Moral Commonwealth*, calls "communitarians of both left and right."[29] As Berkeley professor David Kirp aptly observes, "Those who proffer a different vision of the commonweal—the promoters of civil society or a communitarian ethos—frequently find themselves warding off antagonists of all political shades."[30]

As for liberals and conservatives, no matter how well defined their respective views on government might remain, the moral-economic arguments underlying those views, at least during much of the last twenty years, have displayed internal fault lines and tensions. One of those tensions in particular dovetails with the discussions of welfare that follow. For while liberals and conservatives—on a traditional understanding—clash over the public and private border, with liberals championing expansive welfare policy and conservatives resisting it, at another level each side relies coequally on the same two kinds of public sphere and private realm values: the public sphere norm of concern for others; and the private market norm of self-interest.

It's just that they apply them in inverse ways. Conservatives claim that social behavior between strangers is sufficiently imbued with the public sphere value of altruism to compensate for the state's retrenchment in welfare. At the same time, they claim that individual behavior at the familial level is so actuated by private-market-style self-interest that poor women will keep having children, and then leave the father, unless welfare stops rewarding them for so doing. Liberals, by contrast, believe that strangers in the social sphere operate preponderantly according to individual self-interest and so will fail to take up the slack from a retrenching welfare state, while altruism—feeling and caring for others, whether a lover or one's own children—characterizes the domestic sphere, the minisociety of the individual and her family. That is why individuals are unlikely to stop procreating or altering their marital relationships to any great degree, even if the conditions placed on welfare make it in their interests to do so.

II

WORK AND WELFARE

Few domestic issues in America during the last twenty years have con-
tributed more centrally than welfare policy to opening up political fault lines.
I look here at four American contests over the boundaries of the welfare state:
the controversies over workfare, the Earned Income Tax Credit (EITC), income
disregards for determining welfare eligibility, and the merits of in-kind aid
such as food stamps. Together, this quartet of issues displays a certain symmetry in the realms of work and consumption. Workfare has to do with the work
that welfare recipients might be required to do, while in-kind aid has to do with
the consumption that welfare recipients should be compelled to undertake.
The EITC has to do with increasing an individual's income above the level she
earns at work, while disregards have to do with decreasing an individual's
income—notionally, of course—to exclude certain items she consumes for
the purposes of determining her welfare eligibility.

Over the past twenty years each of these debates has engaged not only academics and think-tank analysts, but state legislators (especially those serving on
legislative human services committees), as well as officials in state welfare agencies and poverty activists. All of these debates feature a conservative side—a side
arguing for a more restrictive, less generous version of the workfare, EITC, disregards, or in-kind aid in question—and a more liberal side, one advancing a
more generous, less restrictive version. The conservative side advances a position
that would restrain the state, and the liberal side a position that would extend it,

but both rely equally on exactly the same public sphere *and* private market values to make their cases. They just apply those values in converse ways.[1]

WORKFARE

Workfare transforms welfare from a grant based on need, for which the welfare recipient might well do little in return, into a quid pro quo, in which the recipient is required to work—generally at a state-subsidized or community-service job—in return for a cash payment from government. By moving that cash a substantial distance from its previous status as a public entitlement into a private market exchange or contract, workfare, for conservatives, helped make welfare appropriately less open-handed. Workfare "weakened the concept of entitlement . . . by replacing its rights-based underpinnings with the market-based concept of exchange," as Hunter College social policy professor Mimi Abramovitz says in describing its attractiveness for conservatives.[2]

A significant strand in the argumentation of conservative lawmakers reflects this view: that, with workfare, welfare has taken a giant and very salutary step out of the public sphere and into the private market. Workfare "is just like work. . . . [Participants are] part of the workforce," says Republican state representative Chuck Damschen of North Dakota; workfare "creates genuine work habits."[3] His Republican colleague Representative Todd Porter agrees: "If you treat [workfare participants] as if they're volunteers who aren't earning their keep, [as if] they're just welfare recipients, then you'll never get them out of the rut."[4] With workfare, says Republican senator Larry Mumper of Ohio, "folks get an idea of paying their own way. This country stands for that."[5] As the father of workfare, former Wisconsin governor and Health and Human Services secretary Tommy Thompson, puts it, workfare expects "the people it helped to get up in the morning and go to work! . . . earn a paycheck and support your family. . . . Giving something for nothing does not work."[6]

Yet having taken workfare a significant way from the public toward the private market realm, conservatives hesitated, in the final analysis, to fully endow workfare with the private market connotations of a real employment contract and retracted it into the public sphere. A *New Yorker* cartoon from April 2006 captures the unwillingness of conservatives to take workfare that last step into the marketplace. It depicts two men in business suits on either side of a desk, the one behind saying to the one in front, "I'm so glad you decided to participate in our Money for Employment program." If one works for what she is paid, the cartoon asks, is that not simply work—a regular private market transaction—not workfare or "work for welfare"?

Conservatives resist this interpretation, however, preferring to portray the workfare relationship not as a market employment contract, but as a civic covenant, a "social contract" as the state of Iowa calls it, a "contract of mutual responsibility" as the state of Delaware conceives it, or a "social contract [of] mutual obligations" as Harvard economist David Ellwood describes this view: all very much terms with public sphere connotations.[7] Workfare is here depicted as an arrangement between an individual and government, not as employee and employer (wage recipient and wage payer) but in their public roles: as citizen and state. Such an arrangement sets forth the "reciprocal obligation" of "citizenship on welfare recipients"—their obligation to use the assistance being provided, the hand up, to develop the capacities necessary to become self-supporting citizens—and on government to provide that assistance.[8] The recipient is said to work "off," not for, her payment, as if she were discharging an obligation, not performing a "quid" in a private market quid pro quo. They're "[w]orking off a debt," says Republican state representative Ron Stoker of Montana, who describes himself as conservative in his philosophy.[9] Workfare recipients, as social policy professors Sarah K. Gideonse and R. William Meyers say, "work off their grants in public service jobs [or other] unpaid work assignment[s]."[10]

If one is getting cash from the government for an "unpaid work assignment," though, why is it not a paid work assignment—or, simply, work? Why do conservatives, having taken welfare such a long way in the direction of a private market relationship, making payments contingent on work, then hesitate to describe such arrangements as ordinary labor market work? Because to do so would validate the relationship as "real work," and endow the recipient of government funds with the same dignity-of-labor status as is bestowed on those who work for private employers. The recipient, however, cannot be treated as if she has fully ascended to the private market. Workfare, as the welfare policy scholar Mildred Rein describes this view, "is not to be construed as work performed," because such a pretense will only drag out dependency.[11] And so conservatives alight on the idea that workfare is not, in the final analysis, a quid pro quo, a form of private market exchange, so much as a simultaneous execution by recipient and government of obligations that they bear within the public sphere.

Thus North Dakota state representative Damschen, who at one point had lauded workfare for being "just like work," endowing the participant with the pride that comes from earning what one gets, says in the next breath that workfare "is not really earned as wages for the work they're doing, it's a benefit paid by government." Likewise, his colleague Representative Porter, who had said that those on workfare must be treated as if they're "earning their own keep," also says that "when you're directly attached to a federal program, you're still on welfare."[12] Tommy Thompson, in addressing a Heritage Foundation audience five years after he had described workfare as work and its payment as a paycheck, depicted it as a period of "transition" during which individuals are characterized by "dependence on a welfare check," the "independence of a paycheck" coming only when they get a real job.[13]

Ohio state senator Bill Seitz, a Republican, believes that those on workfare are "not working, they're on welfare . . . it's called welfare *to* work." Yet he also praises workfare for sending the message that "we're not going to give you something for nothing; the recipient has to work." On reflecting, he sees a "dichotomy between those two positions."[14] But this dichotomy is necessary to advance what is a recognizably conservative position: that workfare should carry not only the no-free-handout philosophy of the private market sphere, but the stigma of a public program.

The problem for conservatives, however, is that they cannot go too fully in this public sphere direction either. After all, unlike in a market quid pro quo, reciprocal obligations in the public sphere—obligations one bears not because of what the other does but because of who one is or what role one occupies— need not be an exchange of equivalents; of work performed in return for a wage reflecting the worth of that work. When the *pro* is knocked out of the equation, and each party is executing a public sphere civic obligation, it may well be that one party's obligations dwarf those of the other in value. Government, then, is vulnerable to the claim that its obligations to the welfare recipient might be much larger once it no longer has recourse to the private market notion that it is obligated only for a wage in return for work, a quo that is worth the quid. On the most common "civic obligation" model, the state bears a much more open-ended obligation: one that goes beyond simply paying cash as a wage for work done. It would include anything necessary to assist the recipient in becoming a full-fledged participant in the private market, the workplace, because on this understanding she is not yet one—not yet a worker giving a quid for a quo but a citizen struggling toward that status, toward self-support.[15]

But of course conservatives do not want the public to be on the hook for training, child care, food stamps, and housing assistance.[16] "It's legitimate to pay people for what they do, but they haven't earned the extras . . . they're receiving more than the job's actually worth," says Republican state senator Randy McNally of Tennessee.[17] The best way to cut off this possibility is to move workfare back out of the public sphere toward the market realm—to reintroduce the idea that workfare is in fact just work for a wage, meaning that the government's only obligation would be the market one, to pay the minimum wage for the work it gets. Although government might choose to do more beyond that—few conservatives oppose all forms of additional assistance—what matters is that the state would have no obligation to do so, because the contract is essentially a market one, meant to teach the lessons of the market, and not a social one. But again, to go too far in that direction also poses problems for conservatives: If this is real private market work, it should not be stigmatizing, but rather command the appropriate respect. The Heritage Foundation's Jason Turner, who at one point praises workfare as "real work" that provides the "pride and satisfaction" that comes from relinquishing dependency and earning what one gets, at other times is careful to term it instead a "work-like activity."[18]

So a rhetorical cycle emerges. On the one hand, conservatives want to portray workfare as a market relationship, an arrangement in the private market sphere, in order to teach the recipient the satisfaction that comes from earning what one gets and to cap the amount of the civic obligations that the public otherwise might bear toward the recipient. On the other hand, they also want to depict it as a civic obligation in order to avoid normalizing it as a true private market employment relationship. By necessity, liberals—in countering these arguments—risk splaying themselves on the converse dilemma. On the one hand, they insist that workfare imposes a civic obligation on the public to provide generous support services whenever conservatives define the relationship as a private market one, where you earn what you get. On the other hand, they describe workfare as a market relationship—real work for wages—whenever conservatives want to stigmatize the recipient as dependent on the public sphere, not earning what she gets.

So on the one hand, Brigham Young University political scientist Gary Bryner, arguing a liberal position that government ought to provide a relatively generous range of services to workfare participants, denies that the participant has entered the labor market. It is precisely because "the welfare system prepare[s] recipients for the labor market" that it must provide training, job placement, child care, transportation assistance, and other kinds of aid.[19] Here, the government's obligations are as a government—as a public entity to do whatever it can to help the welfare recipient into the private market by providing a raft of training services—and not merely as a private market employer. In the same vein, liberal thinkers such as Harvard law dean Martha Minow speak of workfare as a "mutual obligation."[20] Urban Institute scholar Pamela A. Holcomb, advocating generous programs, says approvingly that workfare "embraced the concept of a social contract—recipients had an obligation to work toward self sufficiency . . . and the government had an obligation to assist them" by helping "recipients prepare themselves for work through basic education, vocational and on-the-job training."[21]

But of course this "social contract" language echoes the claims made by conservatives, when they want to deny that workfare involves a dignity-conferring private market contract. So some liberals, on the other hand, feel pressed to insist that the recipient must be treated as if she's already in the private labor market, giving a quid for her quo. She must be accorded the nonstigmatizing dignity that attaches to anyone who earns her keep.[22] Government, in this view, is not doing the welfare recipient a favor, supplying anything more than what the recipient is giving in return; government is getting what it is paying for. Both the welfare recipient and government are operating in a full private market employer-employee relationship; hence it is not work for welfare; it is work.[23]

"If welfare recipients [are] doing useful work," liberal policy scholar Leonard Goodwin writes, "they should be paid prevailing wages for that kind of job in the form of a paycheck, not a welfare check."[24] "To me," says West Virginia Democratic delegate Sharon Spencer, "it is a job. It is not welfare, it's a state job, though [the money] comes from welfare. Single women get up and go to work in the middle of the night. It gives them dignity."[25] Democratic state senator Gilda Jacobs of Michigan agrees: "We should call it work, and call it a paycheck, with the dignity that comes with it."[26]

So, in this perspective liberals insist that workfare be viewed as a full-fledged private market relationship, in order to claim for the participant the dignity that comes from her being said to earn what she gets. To the ear of the first set of liberals, however, this market framing undercuts the notion, which they want to advance, that the state has an obligation to provide the recipient with much more than just a wage. If what lends the welfare recipient dignity is the fact that whatever she gets from the state is not a gift but earned—if the standard is a market quid pro quo—then, these liberals fear, government will labor under no civic obligation to provide anything more than a payment commensurate with the work done.[27] Such a view pretends that what she has is a real job, when in fact the state has much more to do before she gets there: she needs the child care, training, food aid, housing allowances, and transportation assistance that only public agencies, not private employers, can be obligated to supply. Democratic delegate Don Perdue of Virginia says, "The last thing anyone wants to be told is that they're on welfare," yet it's "compelling to say no, it's not a job. . . . The more it looks like it's in the private market, the more you normalize [recipients], but then you ignore what's special about these folks"—and their needs.[28]

That is why, in advocating generous welfare programs, Gordon Lafer of the University of Oregon, in contrast to other liberal voices who seek to destigmatize workfare, asks us to remember that "workfare is not a real job."[29] Workfare, says Democratic state representative Linda Coleman of North Carolina, "is not a job . . . and should not be seen that way. Families need more than what any job can provide them."[30] Democratic state representative Shalonn "KiKi" Curls of Missouri believes that we should have "no problem looking at workfare as a public program. . . . The state has an obligation to support [participants] with child care, training, housing assistance, [and] transportation assistance," although she also says that workfare should be viewed as if it were "any other kind of work in the private sector." There's a "tension here," she acknowledges.[31]

In sum, conservatives characterize workfare as an arrangement in both the public and the private spheres to advance a more stigmatizing, less generous approach to the program. What is public about workfare justifies its not being dignified with the terms "work" or "wage," as if it were earned, while what is private about it justifies the state in using workfare to communicate the message that, in America, a person must earn whatever she gets. A private market framing also justifies the state in assuming no broader human development obligations toward the recipient—no obligation to serve her needs for training or transportation—beyond simply providing her with minimal support (that is, a minimum wage), as any private employer would do. Liberals, by contrast, apply private market norms to nudge the enterprise closer to being called what it is—nonstigmatizing work for a wage, with the dignity implied in earning what one gets—and public sphere norms to argue that government has a more generous set of obligations to welfare recipients, to see to their needs, beyond simply paying them cash for work done. Each side, liberal and conservative, finds itself straddling the same two competing pools of values, public sphere and private market, drawing on each, albeit in contrary ways, to make its case.

THE EARNED INCOME TAX CREDIT

The federal EITC is available to low-wage workers; it first increases in amount as wages rise, then plateaus, then falls, phasing out entirely at income levels above $25,000. If an eligible worker is at an income level at which she pays taxes, the EITC will simply reduce the amount owed. For workers who owe no or a small amount of taxes, the EITC is refundable: a worker receives the full amount of the credit through an infusion of extra funds, from the government, added to her paycheck. There are also numerous state and even some municipal versions, many of them refundable.[32]

Although the EITC is available to all low-wage workers, the focus here is on its normative status for someone leaving welfare and beginning work, thereby becoming initially eligible for the credit. For her, the EITC will generally be refundable, because the wage she earns generally will fall below taxable levels. Without the refundable EITC, the welfare-to-work transition could result in her losing a dollar of government welfare funds for every dollar gained from work. The EITC, by continuing to provide public funds of around 40 percent of the lowest wage that a transitioner might earn, is intended to mitigate the work disincentive caused by the withdrawal of welfare.

Liberal-conservative disagreement on the EITC focuses on two questions. First, especially in its refundable aspects, is the EITC simply a continuation of welfare by another name, or is it in some real sense—as the term itself suggests—income earned by the newly working recipient? Here, the conservative position is that the EITC is (stigmatizing) public welfare; the liberal position is that it is income constructively (and nonstigmatizingly) earned in the private market by the recipient. Second, is the EITC sufficiently generous or not? Conservatives believe it is; liberals that it is not. But to so argue, conservatives have to reverse their previous position and frame the EITC as a wage supplement earned in the private market. Viewed in that private market frame, the credit can be construed as taking the recipient's earnings generously above the market level. Liberals, also reversing themselves, frame the EITC as a partial extension of the welfare grant, meant to offset what would otherwise be the grant's incentive-dampening total withdrawal. Viewed in that public welfare frame, the EITC will seem insufficient by comparison with the larger but now forgone welfare grant. Each side, then, is internally divided over whether the EITC recipient should be seen as falling into the public or the private sphere.

To begin with, conservatives argue, the very term *earned income tax credit* is a misnomer when the EITC is refundable. It is not a return to the worker of income she earns in the private market that was taxed away but rather a straightforward infusion of public money. On this view, as social policy expert Christopher Howard aptly describes it, the EITC is seen as a vestigial element of the welfare grant that accompanies the transitioner into the workplace.[33] In 1995 Senator Phil Gramm of Texas said of the EITC, "It's just welfare, it's a subsidy";[34] Florida official Michael Poole described it as "probably the most direct welfare program that we have in our country."[35] Even though the transitioner is working in the private marketplace, for conservatives the EITC cannot really be seen as earned, because it consists of public funds and eligibility is confined to needy, lower-income families. It must be regarded as a remnant of the public sphere welfare grant. Democratic state representative Patricia Serpa of Rhode Island, who describes herself as a conservative, says that because "the EITC helps the working poor with a gift of public money . . . it's welfare."[36] Republican state senator Dave Syverson of Illinois says that his state's EITC "is not earned . . . it's a welfare handout," and he did not support it.[37]

For liberals, by contrast, the fact that the recipient is working in the private market trumps the fact that the money is public. As soon as one crosses the border into the working world, any money that one gets from government—especially if explicitly awarded, as the EITC is, only to those who are working—is earned. A welfare grant has been withdrawn, the needle goes back to zero, and then something new—a wage supplement called the EITC, contingent on work but designed to make up for work's inadequate wages—takes its place. The principles here are private market ones: the transitioner earns both her wage and the EITC. That is because, in the liberal view, low wages alone are an inadequate quo for the quid of her work. Only with the EITC does the transitioner actually get what she earns, the furthest thing imaginable from a vestigial welfare grant. Just because the transitioner was getting public money before she entered the workforce and continues to get it after does not mean the money has the same character in both cases. It was welfare. It is now earned.

The EITC thus "makes work pay," policy scholar Lawrence E. Lynn writes[38]; it is "like a pay raise for the working poor," as Harvard's Mary Jo Bane and David Ellwood put it.[39] "Given how low the minimum wage is," says Democratic state senator Gilda Jacobs of Michigan, which had just passed a refundable EITC, "you earn it."[40] State Senator William E. Peterson of Illinois, a moderate Republican, sponsored his state's original EITC bill and also supported its having been made refundable. "It's earned," he says, because market wages are "less than they should be to be livable."[41] "I bristle when I hear the EITC described as public welfare; it's not welfare," insists Democratic state representative Al Riley of Illinois; "it's earned."[42]

The EITC, however, provokes another kind of debate. Here, the question is whether, in amount, the credit is under- or instead overgenerous. For liberals—that is, those who take the position that it is inadequate—although the transitioner gains a wage when she begins working, nevertheless by giving up a roughly equivalent welfare grant, she actually earns virtually nothing by going to work. As liberal policy scholars Joel F. Handler and Yeheskel Hasenfeld say, "If every dollar of earned income reduces assistance by that amount, the recipient is [paying] a 100 percent tax."[43] The EITC needs to "be made more generous," says Democratic delegate Ana Sol Gutierrez of Maryland, speaking of her own state's version, "since there comes a point where losing the grant has a negative impact on [a person's] ability to take a job. The EITC right now makes up for only some of the withdrawn grant."[44]

What presumptions underlie this strand of liberal argument? When a person leaves one job, at which she is earning a private market wage, to take another, we do not subtract the income lost by quitting the first from the income earned in the second to say that her new wage is actually, on a net basis, a fraction of what it appears to be. If, though, a wealthy legatee goes to work for a salary and then has to forgo an equivalent amount of her legacy as a result, we would indeed say that she earned nothing by taking the job. We would say that the job cost her as much as she made. In the same way, it makes sense to deduct the lost welfare grant from the welfare-to-work transitioner's work income—in the way liberal argumentation here does—only if, by being compelled to surrender the grant, she is relinquishing something to which she would and should have been entitled anyway, without having to work for it. Then we would say that, by going to work, she gave up precisely what she gained, since she already had it without having to earn it.

The EITC, on this view, is meant to mitigate that loss. It is a "restoration of part of the grant," says Democratic state senator Edward Flanagan of Vermont.[45] If it is to be effective, that is how it must be seen by the transitioner: as a vestige of her public welfare entitlement that accompanies her into the workforce, not something for which she should have to work in the private market. Only if the proper frame for assessing the generosity of the EITC is the unearned grant she relinquishes will the EITC—which generally makes up only part of that amount—look inadequate. If instead it is framed as a supplement earned in the market on top of the wage (as conservatives view it) it will seem generous. Hence those arguing for an increase describe the EITC as a "public benefit" that, at current levels, falls well short of entirely restoring the public benefit the transitioner loses by going to work.[46] "We need to make the EITC more liberal to restore some of that grant; otherwise you fall off a cliff," says Democratic state representative Riley of Illinois.[47] Or as Gary Bryner puts it, "incentive programs"—incentives to work such as the EITC—"are successful only if some welfare payments continue to be received"; such "incentives are benefit payments in and of themselves."[48]

To see this further, consider the conservative response to the claim that the revocation of the welfare grant constitutes a loss that almost entirely offsets the wage earned. "When I first heard this argument," conservative policy analyst Blanche Bernstein says,

> I made some calculations of the comparable earnings of a cop in New York City. It turned out that the cop, under the illusion that he was being paid $15,000 per year, was really working for $1.75 an hour—the difference between what he would have obtained on welfare and what his wages, plus fringe benefits and minus taxes and the welfare grant, left him and his family. The welfare officials were not, however, either impressed or moved by this analysis.[49]

To reject the idea that the welfare-to-work transitioner essentially receives an income equal to a mere $1.75 or less an hour—her wage minus the confiscated welfare grant—conservatives have to believe that once the welfare recipient is able to enter the world of work, her eligibility to receive a welfare grant legitimately and entirely ceases. "[G]overnment benefits and work," in this conservative view, are "mutually exclusive categories to be kept fully separate."[50]

To withdraw income to which a person is no longer entitled under the circumstances is not to impose a cost on her. Once the recipient crosses the border into the workplace, the needle goes back to zero, and any public funds she gets must be seen as earned income: a wage supplement having nothing to do with the previously received welfare grant but rather earned, on top of the wage, as a result of work in the private marketplace. This is Illinois Republican state senator Syverson's view: "The EITC is definitely a wage top-up. You'd never look at the net of what a person would be getting if they were still on welfare, since they're no longer entitled to it."[51] "The EITC is a wage supplement; to put it in the same class as the welfare grant is not the right way to look at it, since that's something you're not entitled to keep when you're working," says Republican state representative Anne Donahue of Vermont.[52]

This way, far from being an inadequate attempt to make up for a confiscated public sphere grant that no longer is legitimately the recipient's to claim, the EITC is a more-than-generous "supplementary wage."[53] The "EITC has become too generous," says American Enterprise Institute economist Marvin Kosters. "Instead of making $15,000 a year, you may make $17,000."[54] Far from earning a wage a mere fraction of what it appears to be, the welfare-to-work transitioner is actually earning—"making"—a total wage considerably higher, because we must count the EITC as money she earns on top of the wage by working in the private market.

To sum up, each side in the EITC debate draws on both public sphere and private market values, viewing them as equally applicable. On the one hand, liberals want to frame the EITC as part of "pay"—a wage supplement legitimately earned according to private market principles—and not a public sphere grant hanging over into the working world, to reinforce the idea that recipients, who must work in order to get it, should not be stigmatized as vestigial dependents. Yet on the other hand, liberals do want to view the EITC as a way of restoring, to the greatest extent possible, a much larger revoked public sphere grant, hence a vestigial "public benefit" that legitimately persists into the world of low-wage work. Only in such a frame will the EITC appear inadequate, insufficient to make up for the "100 percent tax"—the withdrawal of the entitlement—that the transitioner pays by going to work. Liberals, then, draw equally on private market and public sphere norms to paint the EITC as both unstigmatizingly earned and insufficiently generous.

As for conservatives, on the one hand, they want to stigmatize the refundable EITC as a welfare grant—a hangover of public sphere welfare into the world of work—and not income earned by working according to private market principles. Yet on the other hand, conservatives very much want to treat the EITC as income that accrues to work in the private market, not as a partial continuation of the public welfare entitlement. Only in this way can it be deemed a supplement to the recipient's market wage—making her wage generous by private market standards and hence an incentive to work—and not a fraction of the public welfare grant that fails to provide a sufficient incentive to transition. In order to take a view on which the EITC is both stigmatizingly unearned and more than adequate, conservatives shuttle back and forth between framing it as allocated according to public sphere principles (which make it seem unearned but inadequate) and private market principles (which make it seem more than adequate but also earned).

DISREGARDS

For any given welfare program, almost every state "disregards" a certain amount of earned income—generally that spent on food, clothing, transportation, shelter, or medical care—in determining a potential recipient's income eligibility level. What is of interest here are the arguments that underlie a liberal position—one supportive of disregards, which have the effect of increasing the number of families eligible for a program—and a conservative position, which questions them. Why should we disregard expenditures on food, housing, and transportation—items of consumption every bit as much as are toys and televisions—in determining a household's income for welfare purposes?

We do not do that in calculating the income, and derivatively assessing the well-being, of people who are not on welfare.

We do not, that is, except in two broad cases: when, for tax purposes, an expenditure can be deducted from income either as a work expense or as a charitable contribution (the standard deduction is meant to cover both categories for those who don't itemize). Neither type of expenditure is considered personal consumption: work expenses might be personal, but they are ostensibly incurred not for consumption but for income generation. Charitable expenses may well furnish items of consumption, but not personal consumption; instead, they constitute primarily the consumption of others. Pursuing and upgrading one's own capacities to earn income is recognizable as a private market value, while charity—helping needy others less well off—is recognizable as a public sphere value. The norms of the tax system see a sufficient tension between the two that any attempt to deduct an expense on one criterion bars the attempt to do so on the other. The question here is whether disregards for welfare purposes can be analogized to deductions for tax purposes.

Before looking at the liberal and conservative positions here, it is necessary to briefly set out the basic logic of work and charitable expenses as they are understood for tax purposes. Work expenses are typically distinguished from personal consumption items in the following kinds of ways: education required to advance in one's current job is a work expense; education to begin a new career as a matter of personal choice is a personal consumption item. The flight to an out-of-town business meeting is a work expense; the subway required to get to work from the residence one has selected as a matter of personal choice is a personal consumption item. The foie gras one consumes at a business meal is a work expense; the ordinary lunch one consumes as a matter of personal necessity is a personal consumption items. The fancy home one buys to provide business entertainment can in part be a work expense, but the ordinary residence that is a personal necessity is a personal consumption item. There is no need, for current purposes, to inquire into the principles that distinguish these two classes of consumption items; all that matters is that work expenses rely on the idea that for a given consumer, it can be possible to divide her consumption items into two different classes—personal and work related. For a good to be work related, it must lie beyond a class of goods that are already being or have been used for personal reasons. Even if a personal consumption good can be said to double as a work expense—one needs to eat to work—that is not enough.

As for charitable expenses, they involve not one consumer's purchasing two different classes of consumption goods, but two classes of consumers' enjoying one consumption good. Imagine a wealthy benefactor who contributes to a food bank or a walk-in clinic in a poor neighborhood and who gets a "warm glow" as a result. In effect there is only one consumption item here, be it food or health care. But both parties, benefactor and beneficiary, "consume" that item, in the sense that each derives utility from its being used by the beneficiary. The beneficiary does so directly and self-interestedly, and the benefactor derivatively and altruistically (according to the major body of economic research analyzing charitable expenditures, this imputed "warm glow" is their defining feature). Just as the archetypal structure of the work-expense deduction is "one consumer, two classes of consumption goods," the archetypal structure of the charitable-expense deduction is "two classes of consumers, one consumption good."

Can the rationales for excluding consumption items from taxable income, whether as work or as charitable expenses, be made to apply to income disregards? As a first cut—and before turning to liberal and conservative views on the question—it is important to outline one kind of distinction that exists between work and charitable expenses as just described, and disregards. Because welfare recipients are not fully in the work force, they have less opportunity to segregate consumption items into two classes—-one set that is clearly personal and the other work-related. The differences between the subway and the plane ride, between education for a new career and upgrading within one's current vocation, or between the ordinary lunch and the foie gras do not apply to the welfare recipient. There is, generally, only the subway, the training to get a job in the first place, and the ordinary lunch, all of which are personal consumption items that fail to rise to the level of traditional work expenses.

Welfare recipients would seem no more able to justify disregards by claiming that some of their consumption is an analogue of charitable contributions; instead, welfare recipients are more often beneficiaries of charity than benefactors. To the extent that welfare recipients' consumption purchases are said to benefit others, it is when a welfare recipient and her family are enabled to purchase food or housing and are thereby deemed less likely to descend into underclass status, thus contributing to the safety and security of others. Likewise, a welfare recipient's personal consumption can benefit others when she is enabled to purchase basic job-skills training—including, as is often the case, training in punctuality, diligence, and the like—thereby contributing to the civility and order of the workplace as a whole. But in these cases, the "benefactor"—the welfare recipient doing the purchasing—is not deriving a warm glow from the beneficiary's consumption of a good. There is not one good whose consumption is enjoyed by two classes of consumers, as with recognized kinds of charitable expenses. Rather, the welfare recipient is consuming one good in the ordinary personal consumption way (food, housing, education), while the beneficiary—that is, the rest of society—is consuming a second good (safety, civility, security, order). The altruism inherent in charity is absent here.

So the traditional rationales for work-expense and charitable-expense deductions do not seem to apply to the welfare recipient's world—do not, at first glance, seem to provide any analogous rationale for disregarding expenses from income for purposes of welfare eligibility. Yet there is a lively debate over the principle of disregards between liberals and conservatives. And with this particular difference between deductions and disregards now in mind, we are better able to examine its structure.

Liberals make two principled arguments in defense of disregards: arguments that can be understood as seeking some kind of broader analogy with work and charitable expenses. First, it may well be true that when the welfare recipient spends on her own food, housing, and education, others benefit because of the consequent increase in safety, civility, security, and orderliness. But instead of attempting to view this as a (concededly implausible) kind of charitable contribution from the less well-off to the better-off, because of the two classes of consumers involved, we could regard it as a kind of work expense particular to welfare recipients, because of the two classes of goods involved. The first class—food, housing and education—constitute personal consumption, but the second—safety, civility, security, and orderliness ("social capital")—can be interpreted as a contribution to the work-related costs, or more specifically, the costs involved in earning the private income, of those who already are fully working in the marketplace. After all, the essence of goods that are work related is that they differ from personal consumption goods, and here they do. It is just that since welfare recipients are not fully in the workforce, the income-earning benefits—the social capital created—flow mainly to those who are.

This seems more in line with what liberals actually argue when they are defending the principle of disregards. As political scientist Carl P. Chelf puts it, we should look at the food, clothing, housing, and training expenditures of those on welfare as an "investment" in creating a greater social "capital resource"—allowing for the generation of greater income in society as a whole—rather than as consumption "expenditure for the support of non-productive elements of our society."[55] Barb Caruso, program manager of Iowa's Family Investment Program, says that "disregards play their part in contributing to the social capital of the economy," because the consumption items being disregarded—including shelter and medical expenses—"contribute to broader social stability."[56] The items that families eligible for a particular welfare program are able to disregard, says George Cahlandt, administrator of economic assistance in Nebraska, advance the "income-generating capacity of society as a whole."[57] Cherie Jamason, executive director of the Food Bank of Northern Nevada, says that disregarded purchases are an "economic development opportunity for the community itself" because they contribute to "greater social stability and less crime."[58]

Liberals have available a further argument, one that need not rely on the idea that a second set of income-generating social goods—safety, civility, security, and orderliness—derives from the welfare recipient's personal consumption of food, education, housing, and the like. We could view that food, education, and housing as, themselves, a kind of charitable contribution. After all, much charity consists of such items. It is just that usually their consumption is enjoyed by two classes of people: better-off benefactors indirectly and worse-off beneficiaries directly. Here, in the case of disregards, we have just one class of person, but it is the class of person who would ordinarily be eligible for charity—those worse off—buying those items for themselves.

In effect, it is on this basis that another strand of liberal discourse argues that such expenditures should be disregarded. Celia Hagert, senior policy analyst at Houston's Center on Public Priorities, puts it this way: "You could make an analogy to the charitable deduction," since disregarded expenditures "serve the same purposes as charity . . . a poor person is spending on the poor, it just happens to be herself. She can purchase a sweater without it counting against her welfare eligibility."[59] Barbara Van Burgel, director of Maine's Office of Integrated Access, says that "philosophically, you can argue that disregards fulfill the same function as the deduction for charitable contributions. . . . We have to do a better job of making that connection."[60] Sandra Hamill, a policy analyst with the Kentucky Cabinet for Health and Family Services, says that with the goods that are being disregarded, the purchaser is "helping the needy, just as you would with charity."[61]

"Policymakers," policy researcher Deanna Lyter and her colleagues say, "must increase income disregards for those transitioning away from welfare so that families can earn enough money to meet their basic needs, and, ultimately escape poverty."[62] Expenditures on personal consumption items by the poor are here portrayed as eminently disregardable in the name of a recognizable charitable purpose: they meet the basic consumption needs of poor families, helping them escape poverty.[63]

Disregards, then, get located by liberals in both the private market and the public sphere. They are meant to support both the private market purposes of helping those who generate their own earned income and the public sphere purposes of helping those who cannot or do not generate their own earned income. Of course, the welfare recipient is not yet fully a worker but is herself an eligible charity recipient. Hence, her income-generating expenditures are largely for others in the workforce, not herself, and her charitable expenditures are for herself, not others: unlike for the middle-class taxpayer deducting work-related and charitable expenses.

Conservatives, in responding, also draw on both public sphere and private market values but in ways that differ from the liberal interpretations. Applying private market values, conservatives find the welfare recipient's type of "work expenses" too other-oriented, too public-good-focused—devoted as they are to the creation of broad social capital (safety, civility, security, orderliness)—to be considered work expenses, which typically have to do with investing in one's own private income generation. A person who incurs work expenses in earning her own income can deduct them because, if she could not, her income would be overstated. If, however, the earned income being generated is not her own but that of others, then this rationale would not apply, and the expenses would simply be ordinary personal consumption. By the appropriately self-focused standard of private market work expenses, then, the welfare recipient, not yet fully in the work force or a true income earner, is in no position to legitimately claim disregards for income-generating, work-related expenses.[64]

Even for working people not on welfare, such expenses are not excludable from income for tax purposes, because they do not constitute a second class of items that go beyond personal consumption. Former Reagan adviser Martin Anderson, who frowns on allowing "work related expenses to be deducted from earned income before the amount of the welfare grant is determined"— expenses for transportation, clothing, and training—observes by analogy that "[w]orking people not on welfare are, of course, not allowed to deduct such expenses in determining the taxes they must pay."[65] Ken Furr, a Republican state representative in North Carolina and a self-described conservative, says that disregards cannot be analogized to work expenses: "These are really personal consumption items; most people wouldn't be able to deduct them from their income on the grounds that they were undertaken to generate that income."[66]

At the same time, conservatives apply public-spirited altruistic standards to disregards. On those standards—the traditional other-focused standards for recognizing charitable expenditures—the welfare recipient also falls short. By spending on her own consumption of food, clothing, transportation, and the like, she is not engaging in public-spirited giving. "That charitable analogy," says Sara Mims of the North Carolina Division of Social Services, "doesn't fly in North Carolina. You're helping yourself, not another person."[67] Hence, as a Heritage Foundation study says, expenditures that currently fall under the class of disregards should by rights be included in a welfare recipient's "official count of income," as part of her personal consumption, just as they would be for anyone. In fact, disregarding such expenditures when determining her welfare eligibility gives an exaggerated account of her neediness, her fitness as an object of charity. A "family's actual living conditions are likely to be far higher" than income minus disregards suggests.[68] For conservatives, then, disregarded expenses are at one and the same time too public (other focused, focused on the income earning of others) to be excluded from the welfare recipient's income on the basis that they are private income-generating work expenses, and too private (selfish, focused on their own consumption) to be seen as public-spirited charitable expenses.

To sum up, both liberals and conservatives bring private market and public sphere values to bear, in equal measure, to the disregard debate. Liberals, describing disregards as instruments to both private market earned-income generation and public sphere assistance for the needy, justify them on the norms of both realms. Conservatives likewise bring both sets of norms to bear, but they focus on the ideas that public sphere norms require that charitable expenditures be for others, not oneself, and that private market norms require that income-generating expenditures be for oneself, not others. They conclude that disregards fail on each.

IN-KIND ASSISTANCE

The debate over whether welfare should take the form of cash or should instead be provided in kind—as with food stamps, housing assistance, or transportation aid—flows back and forth through a number of public-private border stations.

To begin with, a conservative position—in which welfare should be more restrictive and stigmatizing and less generous—favors the idea of in-kind aid. Such aid requires the recipient to consume only a constrained set of items, items that the benefactor, in this case the public, deems of preeminent importance: food, housing, health care, and so forth (as opposed to nonessential market commodities, such as the cigarettes or alcohol it is feared recipients might purchase if that in-kind aid were converted to cash). Any comparison to private market earnings, which the earner is free to spend on anything she chooses, is inapt, testimony to the fact that anyone who receives welfare is still in the public sphere, not a full-fledged participant in the market, where control over the income one earns is a fundamental value.[69] And, of course, an implicit stigmatization is involved here: the stigmatization of not being trusted to properly control one's cash expenditures.

A public welfare frame also allows a less generous amount of aid than otherwise. For if private earnings are the right comparison, then any food stamp allotment—and, in what follows, food stamps will be taken as a proxy for in-kind aid in general—is arguably worth less than its cash equivalent. And so, at least by that measure, it is stingy. That is because the welfare recipient's choices are constrained by the in-kind aspect of food stamps. And so, liberals say, stamps are worth less to her than their cash equivalent value would be, thus not as generous as supposed.[70]

Conservatives tend to deny this as an irrelevant private market framing. If it is appropriate to allow the public to constrain the disposition of welfare to certain commodities such as food, housing, and medical care—if in other words it is the public's preferences, not the recipients', that form the appropriate measuring rod—then in-kind aid is worth its cash value. Conservatives, then, see food stamps in public sphere terms. They are a form of public welfare whose disposition should be guided by public purposes: assistance directed at the genuine needs of the poor on the path to self-sufficiency. The disposition of welfare cannot be guided by the recipient's wishes, as if she had earned the money in the private market; private market earnings are not the proper normative frame. As Republican representative Lynn M. Luker of Idaho says, the in-kind nature of food stamps is a "mechanism of accountability to the taxpayer. The public's preferences should govern."[71] State representative Linda Miller of Iowa says, "It's the public's money, and should be directed to where the public wants to spend it. . . . We are teaching [recipients] how to be consumers."[72] They aren't, in other words, consumers—full inhabitants of the private market—yet.

By contrast, liberals—those seeking to loosen the restrictions inherent in in-kind aid or to boost its generosity—resort to private market earnings as the appropriate comparator. Recipients, liberals say, should be allowed to use their welfare benefits anywhere in the private market—just as anyone can with the cash she earns—instead of having to conform their consumption to the preferences of public benefactors. Although academic economists are among those making this point on efficiency grounds, its greatest political support comes from liberals who believe that welfare recipients should be treated not paternalistically, but as sovereign over the use of their resources as if they had earned them.[73] "The program," writes Anne Kim of the Progressive Policy Institute, "is . . . highly paternalistic—an attitude much at odds with the spirit of welfare reform, which sought to instill recipients with the dignity and self-determination that comes from work and personal responsibility. . . . The program mistrusts the ability of families to allocate their income as they see fit."[74] This view would respect the fact that for any given individual, at the margin, buying toys for her children might be more important than food for herself. "There is something paternalistic" about food stamps, says Gina Cornia, executive director of Utahans Against Hunger, and in an "ideal world, you'd get the money to spend as you see fit . . . you could spend that money on a child."[75] The proper frame of reference for assessing food stamps, for liberals, is private earnings, and by that standard food stamps come up short: too stigmatizing and constraining, hence less generous than their cash equivalent.[76]

Many food bank operators take this view, even though they are in the business of privately raising food aid for the very same clientele that food stamps serve. Matt Habash of the Mid-Ohio Food Bank in Columbus says that although "there is some rationale to the in-kind argument, cash assistance would be better from a philosophical standpoint. We have talked a lot about this, and people find [food stamps] paternalistic. [Recipients] shouldn't be treated as if they're on welfare."[77] "A lot of antihunger groups," too, "oppose the in-kind aspect of food stamps" or "seek increases that recognize the constraints it imposes," according to Berry Friesen of the Pennsylvania Hunger Action Center.[78] Kevin Seggelke, president of Colorado's Food Bank of the Rockies, says the in-kind nature of food stamps is an "insult to the intelligence" of recipients; they should be "treated as if they're grown-up consumers able to make their own market decisions."[79]

If, however, we look at a different attribute of in-kind aid—if we switch from spending to receiving—then we see that it is conservatives who argue that the proper criterion for assessing in-kind aid is indeed private earnings, while liberals say no, we do better to remember the program's public aspect, and regard it as a form of public welfare.

The point that conservatives want to make is this: Because private market wages are earned, they require work. But in-kind aid by and large does not, and so, at least by private market standards, it is too generous. In fact, if the value of the leisure time the welfare recipient freely controls by not having to earn her in-kind aid is taken into account, she is enjoying a benefit much higher than the stamps' cash equivalent, testifying to the program's beneficence. Economics professor Morton Paglin advances this conservative line of argument, the one that relies on assimilating food stamps not to public welfare but to private earnings: A "comparison with earned income," Paglin writes, "is appropriate," and on that criterion, those "households receiving a large part of their incomes from transfers in kind . . . have more leisure and are spared the monotony of deadend jobs."[80] State representative Mark Anderson, an Arizona Republican, says that "someone in the marketplace has to work for the food basket for their family, and so food stamps," which require no work, "are more than generous."[81]

To deny this gambit, liberals have to be able to reply that the standards of public welfare, not earnings in the private market, offer the right comparator. Food stamps *should* be a program for which no work is required—in other words, they should conform to the governing principle of public welfare, distribution according to need—and by that standard they are not too generous. They do not have to be reduced to a smaller cash equivalent reflective of the fact that recipients need not earn them as in the private market; that is the wrong frame.

Liberals, as we have seen, oppose using the cash value of food stamps as a measure of their worth when the issue is spending. They are worth less than their cash value according to the right measure, namely, private market earnings that come with the added utility of free choice over disposal. Here, though, when the issue is receiving, liberals do use cash value as a legitimate measure of food stamps' value, denying that they are worth more than their cash value by the right measure, the measure of public welfare according to need. Therefore food stamps are not overgenerous even if they do not come with the disutility of work involved in private market earnings.[82] Says Patty Whitney Wise of the Oregon Food Coalition, "Work should not be a requirement for food stamps, and the fact [that] work isn't a requirement for food stamps is irrelevant in measuring their generosity or appropriate level."[83] Lucy Nolan of End Hunger Connecticut says, "Working and . . . market earnings are the wrong frame of reference; the traditions of public welfare and [the criteria] of need are what's appropriate in assessing the program's generosity or lack of generosity."[84] Kevin Seggelke of the Food Bank of the Rockies likewise says that "the market frame is the wrong one" for assessing food stamps' generosity; "these folks are receiving aid on the basis of their need and should not be required or expected to work for it."[85]

In sum, each side views in-kind aid as appropriately governed or assessed by both public sphere and private market principles. It is precisely on the basis of this double premise that conservatives view in-kind aid as both properly constrained in a way that cash is not and more generous than liberals like to see it. Liberals, likewise, premise their opposing view that in-kind aid is too constraining and hardly overgenerous on a combination of private market and public sphere norms. But of course liberals want to place in-kind aid in a private market frame where conservatives want to view it in a public one, and in a public frame where conservatives prefer a private market one.

In all four of these welfare debates, a traditional interpretation would go as follows. The liberal side would be said to champion the expansion of the public sphere, proposing that workfare, the EITC, disregards, and in-kind aid be made more generous or less restrictive. The conservative side would be said to advance private market norms, proposing that restrictions on these programs be tightened, thereby forcing individuals to participate more in the labor market than they would otherwise, or that the programs be made less generous, thus throwing more individuals back on their own private resources.

Such an interpretation might be perfectly valid, but such validity need not exclude the aptness of others. The suggestion here is that discourse reveals an alternative animating structure. In that alternative interpretation, each side draws on both sets of values, believing that the norms and imperatives of public *and* private are equally apt, equally to be called upon, in judging the policy issues at hand. Each side views workfare or the EITC or disregards or in-kind aid as policies that lend themselves to public sphere *and* private market norms of assessment. As the two sides come to apply them, however, each set of values, public and private, lends itself to disagreement over what it suggests. *Public* and *private* jointly imply a more open-handed and generous, less restrictive and stigmatizing approach to liberals. And they jointly imply a more restrictive and stigmatizing, less open-handed and generous approach to conservatives.

The fact that the two sides in these debates each share the same couplet of values, however, affords possibilities for principled compromise. As a suggestive example, consider the debates over the refundable EITC. We could appraise the credit on either wholly public sphere or wholly private market norms. If we located the refundable EITC in the public sphere, we would view it as a continuation of welfare, in the way conservatives do. But then we would also have to view it—taking the forgone welfare payment as our standard—as inadequate as an incentive to work, in the way liberals urge. If instead we located the credit in the realm of the private market, we would, along conservative lines, view the refundable EITC as more than adequate as an incentive, taking as we would the prevailing market wage as our standard. But then, in viewing the credit as a supplement to the wage earned in the marketplace, we would—as liberals want—be forestalled from stigmatizing it as welfare. Either possibility would involve a compromise, but one derived from a shared principle: a principled compromise.

12

CHARITABLE CHOICE:
THE HIDDEN CONSENSUS

American social policy finds itself engaged in two grand arenas of constitutional controversy over the separation of church and state. The first, in the realm of education (and discussed in chapter 5), surrounds school choice: programs through which the government funds busing, textbooks, field trips, remedial instruction, tuition vouchers, and more for parochial school children. The second, in the realm of welfare policy—and to be examined here—concerns charitable choice, programs through which government funds religious organizations to provide services such as child care, shelter for abused or neglected children, foster homes and adoption placement, teen counseling, homeless shelter, literacy training, career and life counseling, drug and alcohol abuse therapy, marital counseling, and more to those in need.[1]

Charitable choice came into existence with the 1996 welfare reforms. Its key innovation was to broaden the long-standing government practice of funding religiously affiliated social-service organizations that operate in a wholly secular fashion, such as Catholic Charities, Lutheran Services in America, and Jewish Family Services. With charitable choice, the state could now support "pervasively sectarian" organizations such as churches, synagogues, and mosques in their provision of welfare services. The charitable choice law, however, subjects any such aid to a double proviso meant to address constitutional concerns. First, a nonsectarian alternative must be available "for any beneficiary who objects to the religious character of the service provider." And second, public money may never be used by a faith-based organization for proselytization, religious instruction, or worship services. A majority of states have enacted their own "legislation that includes reference to FBOs [faith-based organizations] either as potential participants in social service program functions, or more directly in legislation intended to increase state/FBO partnerships."[2]

Each side in the school choice debates has its counterpart in charitable choice discourse. Those who oppose school choice tend preponderantly to resist charitable choice, worrying that both risk transgressing constitutional norms prohibiting public money from supporting sectarian purposes. Those who favor public funding for parochial schools tend as well to support public funding for faith-based social service providers, believing that neither necessarily entails constitutional violations. But the arguments each side deploys differ markedly across the two debates. Differences in the structure of the two kinds of organizations, schools and churches, contour the two controversies, channeling them in distinctive directions. Norms and arguments that make sense in school choice debates lose utility when the issue is charitable choice, and vice versa.

More specifically, as the debates over each reveal, there are two senses in which public funding for faith-based social-service providers provokes more profound constitutional worries than public funding for parochial schools, and two senses in which the reverse is the case. The focus here is on charitable choice, and what this quartet of differences with the school choice conflict— the first two surrounding the possibility of "direct" constitutional violations, and second two having to do with "indirect" transgressions—suggests about the unique ways in which concepts of public and private contour charitable choice debate.[3]

MONEY: DIRECT ISSUES

State aid to parochial schools, as discussed in chapter 5, usually goes to any given school through the intermediating channel of parental decisionmaking. Whether vouchers, or money for field trips, or support for the administration of exams, it typically flows per capita: "only as a result of the . . . private choices" that parents make to send their children to a given school.[4] For proponents of such aid, this intermediating parental control over the disposition of the funds acts as a circuit breaker. It converts the aid from public into private funds. State aid for parochial schools is no different, on this view, from Social Security or student loans, money that comes from the government, but which recipients can contribute to parochial purposes without raising concerns that public money is supporting religion. Precisely because private citizens—and not the government—make the decisions that send the money in a sectarian direction, school choice money is deemed no longer public but private: at least in a direct sense. For if the question is "who directed the money to the school?" or "from whom does the money directly come?" the answer is private individuals.

Proponents of charitable choice, as currently practiced, cannot as easily make the same claim. For a variety of reasons, charitable choice money is far more likely to flow directly from government to churches through contracts and grants than it is to make its way per capita, through the choices made by those seeking drug counseling or foster-home placement, say, to use any given church-based deliverer of those services. In the case of school choice, because parochial schools get state aid—whether for textbooks or field trips or remedial instruction—per capita on the basis of yearly enrollment, funding based on the choices of parents to send their children to parochial schools is guaranteed for a year. For churches, however, attendance at drug-counseling sessions or the take-up of adoption services is a week-by-week matter. If charitable choice funding were based on the choices of social service recipients, it would often not be sufficiently reliable for most churches to feel secure enough to launch a program.

Paula Parker Sawyers of Indiana's Office of Faith-Based and Community Initiatives puts it this way: "Parochial schools . . . enroll for a year, so there's more reliability with students. That's a little different from a small church that operates social services from Sunday to Sunday where your cash flow would take a hit if you relied on vouchers or other funding mechanisms that follow individual clients and their use." That is why, Parker Sawyers says, charitable choice projects get funded far more frequently through "contracts or grants, where you receive money up front from the government and you wait for clients to come." With vouchers or per capita support, she observes, "you're paid only if they come," and this "prevents church-based social services from going the per capita route."[5]

It also, however, prevents them from taking routine advantage of any argument that public money flows to them through the private choices of consumers, thus mutating into private money free from constitutional restrictions. The sole exception here is the one church-based social service that most closely resembles schooling: day care, which does lend itself to vouchers.[6] Janet Scott, who manages faith-based initiatives in the Arizona government, says that "vouchers maybe [work] for child care . . . but beyond this, they're not really practical."[7] Church-based social services, says Tiffany Fisher of Kansas' Office of Government Grants, are "just not well set up" structurally to "deal with vouchers or aid that flows through the decisions of service users more generally."[8] And so public monies that flow through charitable choice are "most likely to be contractual," says Cheryl Swartley, director of Bridge of Hope, a faith-based mentoring service for the homeless in Buxmont, Pennsylvania.[9]

The constitutional upshot is that since government decides directly which churches get public support for their charitable outreach, state money retains its public form. The "flip switch" or circuit breaker that arises when private individuals decide whether and which service providers should get public money—thereby converting it into private money—is nowhere near as prominent in charitable as in school choice.[10]

But another structural distinction looms between parochial schools and faith-based social service providers. And it is one that renders per capita or voucher-based aid—even to the extent that it is practicable in charitable choice—less routinely able to deliver the same kind of constitutional protection that accrues to per capita or voucher-based aid for parochial schools.

Public schooling is a state responsibility, guaranteed by all state constitutions. This means that there will always be available a nonreligious choice for parents. But no similar obligation falls upon the state to provide public or secular social services. States certainly are not required to do so to any particular minimum threshold. Yet unless there exists a nonsectarian alternative for consumers of faith-based organizations' services, those consumers—even if the aid flows per capita—cannot be said to have sent the state's money to the church-based provider as a result of their free, independent choices: the stipulation that must be met for the money to be converted from public to private, thereby eluding constitutional concern.

"Indiana just received an Access to Recovery Grant" from the federal government, Paula Parker Sawyers told me; "it's voucher based, and we will need to identify service providers. The logistical issue is that just for this single grant . . . we will need to fund equal numbers of faith-based and non-faith-based providers, which is time consuming and costly and not guaranteed to succeed . . . and this is why you don't see social services being 'voucherized,' if that's a word."[11] With schools, she continues, "you have existing institutions—you already have a public school on one corner and a parochial school on another." Even in rural areas where there are no schools, local boards must pay for children to attend schools in other districts. But when it comes to social services, according to Holly Hollman of the Baptist Joint Committee for Religious Liberty—an organization opposed to charitable choice—there is "rarely a variety of social service providers in many areas of the country, and so the court's acceptance of vouchers [or per capita aid] in school cases is not automatically transferable to charitable choice."[12]

It is not that there is *never* any nonsectarian alternative to church-based social services. It is only that—as a structural matter and by comparison with the case of schools—this is less likely to be the case. And so even with proposals that would send state funds to a church-based social service provider only to the extent that clients choose to use it, if the client has no nonsectarian alternative available, then it cannot be said that it is his choice that determines their disposition. Using the constitutional doctrine that governs school choice as a template, it would seem that far less circuit-breaking—far less private choice—exists in charitable choice. And so the money, as a general statement, remains public, subject to constitutional strictures.

PURPOSES: DIRECT ISSUES

A circuit breaker, of course, is strictly necessary only if the money is going directly to parochial, sectarian purposes. That is because, in rendering the money no longer public but private, the circuit breaker avoids (recall the Social Security recipient donating to his church) constitutional problems. If, however, the money is going exclusively to public, secular purposes—whether in parochial schools or church-based social service providers—then a circuit breaker is not constitutionally necessary: public money can legitimately flow to such ends.[13] But here arises a second structural difference between parochial schools and churches offering social services. It is much easier to carve out a realm of purely public, secular activities—activities that even public money could legitimately directly support—in parochial schools than in church-based social services.

True, church food pantries can easily bracket out any sectarian element from the services they offer, just as parochial school cafeterias can. But when we move on to "verbal services"—teaching in the case of education, counseling pregnant teenagers, say, in the case of social services—what is sectarian in education can more readily be bracketed out, without spilling into the secular. Government money for math tutorials or English textbooks in parochial schools, for example, need not in any way support a sectarian message, instead funding entirely a public purpose: the purpose of training children in language and mathematics. But government money for church-based drug or teen-pregnancy counseling is more likely to be funding programs into which a sectarian element would more naturally creep; hence it is more likely to comprise constitutionally prohibited public money for private, parochial purposes.[14] As Isaac Kramnick and R. Laurence Moore write, a "teenager receiving pregnancy counseling in a church ... vehemently opposed to abortion... is far more likely to be susceptible to covert religious indoctrination than a non-Catholic studying algebra in a parochial classroom."[15]

Individuals on both sides of the charitable choice divide agree with this kind of observation. Wade Matthews, a retired foreign service officer who is president of the Sarasota and Manatee chapter of Americans United for the Separation of Church and State, says that in the case of social services, the sectarian element is "more difficult to separate . . . out. A math course probably is not going to have any tinge of religious content."[16] Suzanne Yack of the Volunteer Florida Foundation, the state's faith-based initiative, believes the same: it is "much less easy," Yack says, "to tease apart secular and sectarian—it's extraordinarily difficult—in charitable choice as opposed to school choice."[17] Robert Linthicum is president of Partners in Urban Transformation, a Los Angeles–based organization that trains staff for "on-the-ground agencies working among the poor," combining a faith-based approach with "Saul Alinsky-style" activism. Linthicum says that there is "very much a distinction between school instruction separating secular and sectarian and the blur in counseling between the theological and the community approach. . . . Churches and FBOs have not figured out how to detach the theology from their community ministering."[18]

So to sum up thus far: First, government dollars flowing to religious institutions in the realm of welfare are more liable, in comparison with those in the realm of education, to be considered public funds rather than the monies of private consumers. That is because they do not, as a rule, flow to churches through the free choices of circuit-breaking private individual welfare recipients. Second, the drug-counseling or life-coaching purposes to which that public money is put are—in comparison with the math or language curriculum supported in parochial schools—more plausibly considered private, or more pointedly, parochial. That is because, as a general statement, the secular welfare services that churches provide are more naturally permeable to sectarian influence. So, compared with state aid to parochial schools, which on the whole displays neither of these characteristics, state funding for faith-based social welfare services seems more vulnerable to the charge that it amounts to public money for private, that is, parochial, purposes.

IS THERE A DEBATE HERE?

But to the extent that state aid to churches dispensing welfare services fits this description, it provokes little controversy about its constitutional illegitimacy. Conservatives every bit as much as liberals agree that so understood—as public money flowing directly to religious institutions for programs into which sectarian elements seep—charitable choice would violate the Establishment Clause. That is why President George W. Bush's charitable choice rules prohibited public support for parochial purposes, so understood. They state explicitly that no public money may be spent on social services that involve any form of "sectarian worship, instruction, or proselytization." The degree of consensus that exists on this point is illustrated by John J. DiIulio's recollection that, when he set up the White House Office of Faith-Based Initiatives for Bush,

> I tried to hire Julie Segal, who was the legislative counsel for Americans United for Separation of Church and State, I tried to hire her to work in the White House Office. Now, why would the director of the new faith-based and community initiatives office . . . try to hire somebody from Americans United for Separation of Church and State? Answer: I knew that if it got by Julie, it would certainly get by anybody else.[19]

Charitable choice, DiIulio emphasizes, is utterly constrained by "black-letter language that says, 'No [public] funds shall be used for religious instruction, sectarian worship,' and so on. It's black-letter language."[20]

Any disagreement, then, is not about principle but about practice, or, more exactly, about whether this black-letter principle can be put into practice.[21] But when one turns to the level of practice—the grass-roots level of implementation—one finds a relatively quiet front. As I canvassed state officials whose job it is to assist faith-based organizations in developing their social service capacities, I found little dispute, no hedging or trimming on the constitutional points. "The rule is simple," says Sydney Hoffman, director of the Alabama Governor's Office on Faith-Based Initiatives; "if you can separate the religious element out, then you can accept government money; if you can't then you get no government money."[22] In fact, of the debates surveyed in this book, the one over charitable choice is the least heated on the ground. There are, as Hoffman says, "no real controversies" because the constitutional parameters are clear. Paula Parker Sawyers similarly reports that there are "no significant issues in Indiana regarding government partnering with faith-based organizations because we've taken great pains to ensure that we aren't funding any activity where there's an inkling that it's religious in nature."

But a question remains: The whole point of charitable choice—of funding faith-based social services—is that, because of the spiritual resources they tap, churches are presumed to provide a kind of assistance that secular social service providers cannot replicate. And yet if all are agreed that that "something" can have nothing to do with religious content, then what, precisely, is it? One answer, as Kathy Myers of Chicago's Interfaith Youth Core, says, is that "even in the absence of direct religious content," there still is an ill-defined penumbra quotient of "spirituality that faith-based service providers can and do impart."[23]

True, withering skepticism falls these days on notions of generic spirituality untethered to the specific rituals of any particular religion.[24] Certainly some faith-based social service providers insist that their counseling cannot reach full effect without an explicitly sectarian content. But these providers then also tend to eschew public funding, deeming it inappropriate.[25]

Within the parameters of charitable choice, however, *spirituality* has, without anyone intending it, acquired a particular term-of-art meaning. Consider the trilogy of faith, hope and charity. Charitable choice certainly involves charity. But beyond that, its initiatives might better be called *hope-based* than *faith-based*. As Brookings scholars E. J. Dionne and Ming Hsu Chen say, "Having faith as a core value" enables a person to "'persevere in the face of stress, uncertainty, and disappointment. . . .' Faith keeps hope alive."[26] Faith may be the instrument, then, but hope is the goal. Spirituality here gets understood not so much in metaphysical terms—as connoting a higher, nonphysical being (that would be explicitly sectarian)—as in aspirational terms, implying a higher, nonmaterialistic purpose to life. Hope is easier to come by if the object of one's worldly struggles is not worldly gain per se but a deeper, inner satisfaction. Faith, by contrast, entails the quest for other worldly help in working through this worldly life's daily travails. "We instill hope, not faith," says Shelley Appel, director of New Focus, a faith-based training organization in Allendale, Michigan; "we look at the different forms of hope that the world offers you. Statistics show that if people have hope, they have the power to make their lives better."[27] In effect, in areas where they receive public funds, faith-based organizations would be better termed hope-based organizations.

As we have seen, schools can segregate religious content from their math or English instruction more easily than churches can from their drug or teen-pregnancy counseling. Any such religious component in the school curriculum—since it is not being publicly funded—is thus free (think of parochial school religious classes or prayer services) to take on the full parochial flavor of the particular denomination in question. In church social service offerings, by contrast, the religious content, being more difficult to exclude entirely, must remain more generically spiritual: instilling generic hope, not sectarian doctrine.

In fact, the difference between the two terms, *parochial schools* and *faith-based social service providers*, speaks loudly here. The word *parochial* emphasizes the doctrinal differences between religions that sectarian schools are free to convey because they can segregate doctrine from any publicly funded secular curriculum. The term *faith-based* emphasizes what is common and spiritual in faith-based providers, which is all that they can infuse into their publicly funded counseling without risking constitutional transgression. It is no accident that parents who want to send their children to a Catholic parochial school are unlikely to see a Jewish school as a direct substitute; nor, as a rule, do different denominational schools get together to offer interdenominational education for their students. But those who seek drug abuse counseling or homeless aid at a local church are quite apt to see the same services offered at a synagogue as a substitute. And "many congregations," John Bartkowski writes, "engage in collaborative benevolence work under the auspices of parachurch organizations."[28]

There exists, then, a penumbra realm beyond the parochial: a realm of generic spirituality where the operative concept is hope, and where what is sought to be transcended is the materialistic world, not the mundane world. It is a realm that many charitable choice providers feel they can occupy. Of course, it is possible even here for critics of charitable choice to legitimately feel uneasy. The point, though, is that it is not a grand abyss that separates them from defenders of charitable choice but rather a narrow strait. There is wide agreement on barring anything that involves public funds—as charitable choice does, because of the direct, contractual support it tends to provide—going to parochial purposes, as charitable choice would risk doing because of the permeability of church counseling to sectarian influence. Hence the charitable choice rules prohibit direct state funding for any social service with parochial content. The penumbra realm, the possibility that public funds might still support a message of hope and generic spirituality—a message that life is more than material pursuits, not that an afterlife transcends the physical world—is all that remains in the way of ground for any real battle. But so far it has proved too wispy or chimerical to stage much controversy. As John DiIulio says, there actually exists "great consensus" in charitable choice discourse. So "why," he asks, "do we miss this consensus when we talk about [charitable choice]?"[29]

MONEY: INDIRECT ISSUES

But this is not the end of the story. For beyond this, when we turn to the indirect risks, charitable choice finds itself on much stronger ground than school choice. And, again, there are two reasons, one having to do with money and the other with purposes.

First, recall that with school choice, critics can acknowledge that a given program of aid flows on a per capita basis, going to any given parochial school only to the extent that parents choose to send their children there. But, critics will then note, sending a child to parochial school has just become cheaper, thanks to the program that—by reason of its very coming into existence— provides a brand-new incentive for parents to go parochial where none existed previously. And that incentive in and of itself, school choice critics will say, constitutes a sufficient nudge by the state in the parochial direction that the money must still be considered public, its disposition indirectly influenced, if not directly controlled, by the government.

Second, with school choice, even if public money goes directly to the non-parochial aspects of the parochial school's offerings—fulfilling the public purpose of sectarian education in science, math, and English—it might still, because money is fungible, indirectly free up funds that the school was obligated to spend on those secular subjects and that can now be devoted to its parochial curriculum. Hence, school choice critics will say, the state would be indirectly supporting sectarian purposes.

So, even if school choice—with its per capita funding and ability to segregate parochial curricula—can avoid directly sending public funds to parochial purposes, in indirect terms it is a different story. School choice, critics say, still risks crossing into the constitutionally forbidden realm of money that is indirectly public—because of the incentive the state creates—for purposes that are indirectly parochial, because it frees up other funds for such purposes. Defenders of school choice, as we have seen in chapter 5, have responses available. But while school choice at the very least provokes a debate as to whether it amounts to the indirect channeling of public funds to parochial purposes, charitable choice involves no comparable dispute. This means that once charitable choice evades the direct constitutional threats that it could involve public money for parochial purposes—as the law requires it do, and that all agree it should—it as a general rule poses no indirect threats. And on this, too, there is considerable consensus.

Consider money first. With school choice, as Andy Aldrich, director of Wyoming's Office of Faith Based Initiatives, notes, "Parents would otherwise have to pay to send their child to private school. If all of a sudden they get a windfall in the form of a voucher that materially alters their capacity to do so [and hence] their incentive structure, this can be said to involve some form of . . . public direction of the funds."[30] Broadly speaking, however, this concern does not apply in the case of charitable choice. The welfare "consumer," Aldrich says, "is not paying anything to begin with." Whether she is getting shelter from spousal abuse or counseling for alcohol addiction from, say, a secular nonprofit entity supported by the local United Way, or a public entity like the local community center, she is not paying for it. A voucher that she could now use as well at the local Episcopal Church might open up a new option to her. But it would not provide any new incentive for her to go there as opposed to elsewhere. It would not nudge her in any particular direction.

What this means is that if and when charitable choice money does take a form in which recipients directly control its disposition—if it ever does flow per capita, with consumers afforded a choice of nonparochial and parochial providers—it would then involve no remaining indirect public control through a nudging incentive. The money would remain completely private, free not only of direct government control but of indirect government influence. It would defeat any claim that the money is still vestigially public in nature.

Again, there is little controversy between sides on this score. James Sell, president of the Houston chapter of Americans United for the Separation of Church and State, acknowledges that because "charitable choice welfare recipients are not paying for the services they get . . . new public funding that they could at their discretion take to church providers would in no way tilt the playing field. It would give them no new incentive to go to the church as opposed to the nonchurch entities."[31] Likewise, Lori Wiersma of Grand Rapids' Volunteers in Service, a faith-based organization that has never taken government money but that has partnered with agencies that do, says that there wouldn't be any "incentive argument against assistance for church-based social services as there would be for parochial schools, since very few [of the former] charge."[32]

PURPOSES: INDIRECT ISSUES

The second "indirect" difference that exists between school choice and charitable choice, again to the benefit of the latter, has to do not with the public-private nature of the money but of the purposes it supports. As long as charitable choice aid avoids directly funding social services with sectarian content, as it is required to do, there is far less danger than there is with school choice of its doing so indirectly. As we saw in chapter 5, one of the concerns with parochial schools is that even if they were not providing the secular service that a new school choice program underwrites—whether field trips, textbooks, or remedial instruction—these are nevertheless educational services that a parochial school can be deemed *obligated* to provide, on plausible philosophical norms about the responsibilities of schools. So when the state then funds these secular services, critics will say, it is essentially relieving a school of a responsibility it should otherwise have assumed—whether or not it actually was—and thereby freeing up funds that the school can then devote to parochial purposes.

Unlike with parochial schools, which are in the business of providing secular education courses such as English and math, there is no comparable consensus that churches bear any normative responsibility for secular welfare provision, such as literacy training or homeless shelter. It is in fact opponents of charitable choice who would be less likely than supporters ever to say that churches bear such a normative responsibility, since by and large they tend to place such obligations on the shoulders of government. But then, by channeling money to wholly secular church-based social service provision, the government would not even arguably be freeing up money that churches should have had to spend on those services, hence indirectly supporting the church's parochial activities—the new choir books or the additional Sunday school teacher.

And even if churches were offering a service—whether foster care, homeless aid, or drug counseling—that charitable choice will now underwrite, they would generally not have been paying to execute it. Rather, they would have been relying on volunteers: another reason why charitable choice money tends, by comparison with school choice, to free up no church funds that could be diverted to parochial purposes. As Sydney Hoffman of the Alabama Governor's Office of Faith-Based Initiatives says, "A lot of time these services were provided voluntarily and so by providing reliable funding for them [through charitable choice] you're not putting any money back into the church for sectarian purposes."[33] Such "diversion," says John Baumann, S.J., executive director of the Pico National Network in Oakland, "is much more of a problem with schools."[34] Wade Matthews, of the Sarasota and Manatee Americans United for the Separation of Church and State, agrees that "diverting is not a concern" in charitable choice.[35]

Although most church-based social services are provided voluntarily if at all, in some cases the church might have been channeling donations specifically toward them. Any such monies could, once they are supplanted by public funds, theoretically be diverted to parochial purposes. But this would require the donors to agree that money intended for counseling assistance should go, for example, to pay the minister's salary. More often, government funds simply "crowd out" charitable giving, "causing donors to withdraw," says David Spickard, president of Jobs for Life, a faith-based antipoverty organization in Raleigh.[36] Such crowding out is less likely to occur with an entity like a parochial school, whose funds come preponderantly from tuition payments and less from donations. Such payments, because they are earned, become the school's to flow to whatever purpose it thinks most fit at any given time. Hence if government begins to fund an activity the school was previously underwriting, the school does not need the permission of payers to transfer its freed-up money to parochial purposes.

PEACE IN THE VALLEY

Charitable choice is controversial. But when we look more deeply into the issues and place them in the context of other American debates over public and private, particularly in the realm of school choice, the controversy appears to narrow. Both conservatives and liberals agree that in direct terms, and without the safeguards contained in its governing law, charitable choice would channel public money to parochial purposes, thus violating the Establishment Clause. Charitable choice, unlike school choice, does not lend itself easily to per capita form, in which it would flow to any given provider on the basis of the private choices made by consumers. Hence its funds typically remain public money, flowing directly from government to churches, synagogues, and mosques through grants and contracts. And church-based secular counseling programs do not insulate themselves so easily, again by comparison with parochial school secular curricula, from religious permeation; hence a greater risk exists that public money will go directly to parochial purposes. Both liberals and conservatives, though, agree that this would be unconstitutional. That is why the charitable choice law contains safeguards against it.

With those safeguards in place, however, both sides then agree that the structural tendencies work to minimize any *indirect* public funding for parochial purposes. That is because charitable choice is just that: charitable. Recipients—certainly by comparison with parochial school parents—don't pay. Any new public money that welfare consumers could take per capita to a church-based provider would not defray costs that those consumers would otherwise have incurred. By giving them no new incentive to use a religious provider, the state thus would not even be indirectly influencing their decisions to do so. The funds would thus remain the consumers' privately controlled money.

By the same token, church social service providers—certainly by comparison with parochial school teachers—don't get paid, because most are volunteers. Hence even indirectly, new public funds to support their work would not, as a rule, free up any monies that could then be used for parochial purposes: for prayer books or religious figurines. Charitable choice funds would remain confined to the public purposes of social service provision. In indirect terms, then, charitable choice carries a comparatively low risk of qualifying as "public money for private purposes." That is why so relatively little debate is provoked by the possibility that charitable choice might indirectly violate constitutional norms, as contrasted with the substantial school choice debate on the topic.

On a traditional understanding of charitable choice controversy, conservatives—in supporting charitable choice—are seeking the enlargement of the private realm, and the contraction of the public, in social services. Liberals, of course, would be seen as seeking to protect the public and push back the private. But at a deeper level, both sides locate charitable choice money—depending on whether it takes direct or indirect form—equally and by turns in the public sphere and in the private sphere, drawing as appropriate on the constitutional norms applicable in each of those cases. They each do the same, too, with charitable choice's purposes. Unlike the participants in the other debates discussed in this book, however, neither side inverts the position of the other, seeing matters in public terms where its opponent views them in private terms and vice versa. Instead, both "sides" are in substantial agreement, an agreement that remains obscured in the traditional picture.

No wonder that a recent "left-right" dialogue on charitable choice, sponsored by the American Jewish Committee and Temple University, concluded that "significant points of agreement" exist between the two sides.[37] One would not say this about the other debates discussed in previous chapters. John DiIulio's words bear repeating: There is "great consensus" in the charitable-choice debate, even though we tend to "miss this consensus when we talk about it."[38]

13

CONCLUSION

Over the course of decades, commentators have offered scores of master narratives to interpret American political conflict. None is more popular than the idea that, in one way or another, political controversy in America consists of an unfolding series of struggles between the values of the public and the private realms. Partisans of public sphere values such as redistribution according to need, civic equity, communal obligation or secular neutrality are locked in a continuing contest for policy dominance with champions of private realm values, which, depending on the debate, might embrace anything from self-reliance or property rights to a focus on one's family or religious purposes.[1]

In the previous chapters, I labeled this understanding of American political debate the traditional interpretation. On this traditional interpretation, for example, those who would like to rein in the food stamp program—conservative state legislators, say—would be portrayed as stressing the importance of private market values such as personal responsibility and self-reliance. Their more liberal opponents—welfare activists or food bank managers—would be depicted, in their quest to make the program more generous and less restrictive, as resting their case on the public sphere values of compassion and redistribution according to need.

My argument is that in the debates I discuss—traditionally cast as clashes between champions of public and partisans of private values—something else more subtle and complex is going on. Each of those debates can be interpreted, either directly or in some variation, as a conflict in which both sides draw equally on exactly the same public *and* private values. Each side, however, then parts with the other over what policy course those public and private values jointly suggest.

Consider again the food stamp debate. On the interpretation I am advancing, those who would like to maximize the program's open-handedness—liberal welfare activists or food bank managers—certainly do cite the public sphere value of redistribution according to need. If the point of the program is to meet basic needs, they argue, then there is no justification for reducing food stamps' value to take account of the fact that recipients are not required to sweat for them, in the way those with jobs must earn their daily bread. But in another way, liberals do want to treat recipients just as if they were earning their keep in the market. No one in the private market is restricted in how she spends what she gets, and that same private market norm should be applied, many liberals argue, to food stamp recipients. In which case, stamps should be converted to cash to correct for the fact that they paternalistically compel a recipient to spend on food, even if that's not her priority.

For their part, those who would resist making food stamps any more open-handed—conservative state legislators, for example—cite that very same public sphere value, that redistribution is meant to help the poor with their basic needs, to deny that the program should be cashed out to allow the recipient to purchase goods other than food, even if they happen to be her personal priority. But conservatives also want to measure food stamps by private market norms—an individual should normally have to incur the onerousness of work for any food she brings to her family—to argue that if anything, food stamps are too generous.

All of the debates I analyze are traditionally seen as clashes between champions of public and partisans of private values, with the public values implying a policy course contrary to that indicated by the private. But, I argue, these debates can also be interpreted as clashes in which each side relies coequally on public and private values. It is just that both sets of values are capable of jointly supporting—depending on which side is applying them—the same two contrary policy courses. The debates I discuss certainly do not all display this structure in exactly the same way. But each does exhibit it in the form of a "family resemblance" with the others. There are substantial variations, but they are variations on a theme.[2]

My point is not that these two interpretations, the traditional one and the one I am advancing, are mutually exclusive. There is no reason to believe that rich and complex strands of American political discourse cannot lend themselves to illumination by more than one interpretation.[3] Nevertheless, the interpretation I offer does have some advantages. It has the capacity to account for those strands in discourse that the traditional approach would emphasize: for example, the way in which liberals in welfare debates rely on public sphere values of helping the needy and conservatives on private market norms of earning what you get. But the interpretation being advanced here can additionally accommodate strands that the traditional approach would not: those in which conservatives rely upon the norms of the public sphere and liberals call upon private market values. The approach I am advancing weaves these strands of argument into its interpretation.

In fact, there is no reason to think that the framing being advanced here is restricted to the education, health care, welfare, or space-related cases discussed in the previous chapters. Think, for example, of the policy debates over the last decade leading up to the near-collapse of the financial system in 2007–08. Many have depicted those debates as traditional contests between champions of a largely unrestricted private market and defenders of public sphere norms, under which government should have constrained everyone from Wall Street bankers to credit agencies to low-income homebuyers to bridle their own self-interest in the name of a broader social good.

That is certainly a fitting interpretation. But here is another way of framing the economic debate that has been unfolding in America, one suggested by the interpretation I am advancing. On the one side, politicians in both parties, over the past decade, wanted to use market mechanisms—and in particular, the mortgage market—to accomplish a redistributive goal, enabling more and more lower-income Americans to buy a home. The tension at the heart of this endeavor ultimately proved key to the financial failures of 2008. This outcome then led politicians—again, in both parties—to deploy blunt redistributive mechanisms, namely, bailouts of over a trillion dollars, to accomplish a goal that the market should have handled with the appropriate pricing structures, namely, transferring indemnification from those whose ventures turned out to be less risky to those whose ventures turned out to be more risky.

Over the last decade, in other words, a bipartisan consensus supported the use of a private sphere mechanism, the mortgage market, to pursue public sphere goals of wealth transfer, and then a public sphere mechanism, redistribution by the state, to accomplish private market goals of risk transfer.

On the other side of the debate there have emerged various critics (such as the CNN commentator Lou Dobbs or author and columnist Kevin Phillips), also to be found spanning both parties. These critics would have used redistributive mechanisms (low-income housing subsidies earlier, bailouts directly for homeowners more recently) to pursue the redistributive aims of helping low-income homeowners. And they would have deployed market mechanisms (letting financial institutions fail if they price risk inappropriately, creating open markets for hitherto privately exchanged financial instruments) to enforce the market purposes of appropriately handling risk.

Certainly, then, there are elements of the recent economic debate that resemble a straightforward clash between proponents of private market norms and advocates of public sphere values. But that interpretation excludes some important strands, which come to light only if we view the debate as one in which both sides drew equally on public (redistributive) *and* private (market) values. It is just that one side would have relied on a redistributive mechanism in matters where the other preferred a market mechanism, and a market mechanism where the other side favored a traditional wealth transfer by the state.[4]

INTERNAL INCONSISTENCY AND EXTERNAL CONSENSUS

To the extent that these debates lend themselves to the interpretation I am advancing, the competing sides each display greater internal argumentative inconsistency (public and private values can be mutually jarring) but also more compatibility with each other (both sides appeal to the same public and private values) than is commonly realized. I want to make some suggestions about what follows from this. But to do so, I first need to distinguish what I am saying from other critiques that have found either internal inconsistency within sides, or external consensus between them, in American political debate.

Charges of inconsistency are not new in American politics. But generally they are leveled at groups that take propublic and proprivate positions across different debates, not at groups that rely coequally on public and private values in the same debate, as discussed here. The conservative legal scholar and judge Richard Epstein, for example, has criticized pharmaceutical companies for inconsistently advocating an interventionist state in the debate over whether the government should restrict drug imports from Canada, while touting the laissez-faire virtues of the private market in the debate over Food and Drug Administration safety requirements.[5] In a similar vein, "Joe Lunchbucket" voters might avidly support state-imposed strictures in moral debates over abortion or gay rights, while remaining free-market partisans in economic debates, such as those over the minimum wage or health insurance, even though such a position thwarts their own interests. This is the mentality that liberal political commentator Thomas Frank attributes to the typical Midwestern Republican voter in his influential book *What's the Matter with Kansas?*

But this is a far cry from observing that within a particular debate, both sides rely equally on public and private values. Epstein and Frank are making points about personal or corporate ideologies, about the often inconsistent public and private values that an individual actor might advance across a number of different debates. I am making a point about the structure of individual debates and the way in which the different actors within them may marshal what are often inconsistent public and private values.

It is true, as well, that commentators since Tocqueville have noted that both sides in a given controversy might share an underlying consensus on public and private values. But where such consensus reigns, the public and private values concerned are seen as coherent with one another, not, as with the debates discussed here, as potentially jarring against each other in various ways. According to the great mid-twentieth-century scholar of American politics Louis Hartz, most prominently, the fundamental values of democracy (the public sphere) and capitalism (the private market) do not, in America, rankle with each other. Instead, they meld into a coherent democratic capitalism.[6]

True, for Hartz and others this coherence between America's public and private values exists only at an abstract level, across all debates.[7] When applied to any given concrete policy debate, two sides emerge because one lends a greater emphasis to the public values and the policy course they suggest, while the other side does the same with the private values. As the late Harvard political scientist Samuel P. Huntington wrote, in any given policy controversy, consensus disappears because "different groups assign different weights to each" set of values, those of the public and those of the private spheres.[8] But this, of course, is nothing more than what I have called the traditional approach.[9]

Commentators such as Epstein and Frank, then, have identified public-private inconsistencies in the positions taken by individual political actors, but these inconsistencies emerge across many debates, not within any given debate. And commentators such as Hartz and Huntington have identified a consensus on public and private values between different political actors, but—again—at a level that encompasses all debates: within each debate, such consensus disappears. My interest here lies in exploring the inconsistency within sides, and the consensus between sides, that can emerge within a given debate.[10]

MOVING FORWARD

But what follows from this? In my discussions of the various debates, I have in some cases come down on one side, while in others, I have suggested some kind of compromise. And there is a reason for this. On the one hand, the fact that each side rests its argument on both public and private values can mean that on occasion, one side or the other might find itself particularly vulnerable to the tension between those values. On the other hand, the fact that what divides the two sides is precisely the matter of how to apply values they share, whether public or private, means that room for a principled compromise may exist. Consider a couple of representative examples.

Think of the arguments advanced by parental fundraisers at public schools. They have to depict the act of parents giving to their own children's public school as legitimately self-concerned, an act within the private sphere undertaken to look after one's own family, to deflect demands that such money flow instead to a districtwide fund to benefit all schools. But fundraisers also have to portray the act of giving to the school as commendably altruistic, an act within the public sphere to benefit one's broader community, to reject demands by some parents that they be allowed to confine their contributions to their own child's classroom. Their opponents—whether those demanding districtwide giving, or those demanding own-classroom giving—face no such tension. And so, I argued in chapter 4, such a tension is unsustainable for fundraisers. Consequently, a percentage of parental monies raised at individual schools should go into a fund that benefits all schools in the district.

In other cases, *public* and *private* continue to mean contradictory things, but *both* sides are equally vulnerable to the resulting tension. Workfare is a good example here. Public sphere values entail the idea of redistribution based on need and the civic responsibility to care for others; private sphere values entail self-reliance and caring for one's own. For conservatives, the public sphere values they attribute to workfare mean that recipients are not entitled to be accorded the dignity that comes from earning what one gets: recipients cannot be allowed to forget that they are still dependents being supported on the basis of need. The private sphere values that conservatives attribute to workfare, however, mean that recipients must be made to understand that they will receive support only because they work for it, to inculcate into them the virtues of self-reliance and pride in earning. For liberals, by contrast, workfare's embodiment of public sphere values means that recipients cannot possibly be expected to earn all that they need by way of state assistance. Workfare's embodiment of private sphere values, however, means that recipients should be accorded the dignity that comes from earning what one gets.

Here, their coequal embrace of inconsistent public sphere and private market values places both sides in equal tension. One way of ameliorating the conflict between them would be to adopt only one of the two contradictory values they share—whether public sphere or private market—and then combine each side's interpretation of it. Suppose, for example, that we viewed workfare entirely in private market terms, as income earned by the recipient through an employment contract. That would mean that we could endow the participant with dignity as a worker, as liberals urge. We would recognize that she has a real job, and so time limits and other forms of harassment and stigmatization would not apply, just as they don't apply to regular jobs in the private labor market. But then, along conservative lines, government's obligations in the way of education, child care, transportation and the like, would be limited to whatever benefits the state as a state is prepared to supply to all workers, those whose wages it is paying and those whose wages it is not—state tax credits for vocational training, for example—and whatever benefits the state as an employer gives to its own employees, such as health insurance.

Alternatively, we could choose to view workfare entirely in public terms, as an endeavor meant to assist those who cannot support themselves. In this case we would see it as a compact based on mutual civic obligation. On the one hand, such a compact would—as liberals urge—bind the state to care for workfare participants in a host of ways that go far beyond whatever government provides to all workers or its own employees. After all, workfare participants, if they are denizens of the public sphere, are not yet full-fledged workers or employees in the private market. But then on the other hand, as conservatives would argue, government would also be entitled to view workfare as something prior to real work, as a transitional state. Workfare would then be properly subject to time limits, sanctions concerning family size, and other conditions that do not apply to a real private market job. Either approach, viewing workfare as wholly public or as wholly private, would involve each side in compromise. But in a principled, not an ad hoc, way.

Finally, in some debates the public and private values that each side advances do not frontally contradict one another, as do "altruism" and "self-interest" in the debate over parental funding for public schools, or "redistribution according to need" and "earning what you get" in the workfare debate. In the Medicaid debates, for example, the public sphere value to which each side recurs is "civic validation;" the private market value is "quid pro quo, in the form of an appropriate return for effort or expenditure." We can still, however, look to see if the schism between the two sides over how to apply one or the other of these values can be productively melded together. I argued, for reasons set out in chapter 7, that the private market value of appropriate return for an individual's work effort or Medicaid's expenditure is the superior one to go with. Sometimes it would point to expanding Medicaid up the ladder from poor to less poor; sometimes to expanding coverage out the spectrum of medical conditions from more serious to less serious, but in a principled, not an ad hoc, way. [11]

A commentator who offers a traditional interpretation of these debates—on which partisans of the public confront champions of the private—will find herself, if she wishes to take a stand, upholding public values while downplaying private ones, or vice versa. In the interpretation I am advancing, in which both sides advance the same public and private values but apply them in converse fashion, a principle of resolution would not take the form of championing the public over the private, or vice versa. Instead, it would set out the ways in which one or both sides fall victim to a contradiction, or in which one or both of the consensually shared values can sustain a principled compromise.

WHAT'S GOING ON?

What, finally, do these debates say about understandings of public and private in America? Many social commentators and theorists think of the basic units or spheres of activity in society—individuals, families, businesses, nonprofits (aka civil society), and the state—as arrayed on a spectrum from private to public. Thus, for example, feminist theorists argue that the family is a public—political—realm of power and violence by comparison with its individual (and especially weaker) members.[12] But they also characterize the family as a private realm of intimacy compared with the business world or the state, which is why, for these theorists, to confine women to roles within the family is to consign them to the private realm, denying them the public standing that comes from careers in business or government. Thus, the family gets situated at a particular point on a spectrum from private to public: a point relatively more private than the business world, while by comparison with its individual members, the family emerges as a public institution.[13]

Or, to move further up the spectrum, when social critics claim that the business world displays ambiguity—that it can in some ways be described as a public and in other ways a private sphere—what they generally mean is that, relative to the state, it is a private entity, while relative to the family, it is a public arena.[14] Consider, for example, the political theorist Michael Sandel's deft criticism of the contemporary tendency to auction off the memorabilia of political heroes such as John F. Kennedy or Martin Luther King. On the one hand, Sandel says, an auction "privatize[s] what should be public." By making the disposition of the hero's personal effects a business matter, an auction takes them out of the sphere of the state—perhaps a public museum where they would belong to everyone—and puts them in the hands of a private collector. On the other hand, Sandel says, an auction at the same time risks "publicizing what should be private." By making the disposition of the hero's belongings a business matter, an auction takes them out of the hands of his family—where, on a view that emphasizes privacy and discretion, they might be regarded as properly belonging—and brings them into a more public realm, where they will wind up with strangers. Thus, with respect to the state, the business world privatizes; with respect to the familial domain, it "publicizes."[15]

Under the standard conception, then, the private-public arrow flows in one direction. It flows from the most private entity (the individual), through family, business, and civil society, to the most public (the state).[16] What is crucial about the debates I have examined, however, is that in them, the arrow shows itself capable of flowing in both directions. Any given unit—individual, family, market, civil society, or state—can lay claim, often at one and the same time, to both a more public and a more private character than any other.

So for example, even with respect to the state, businesses can assume both a private *and* a public role. Think of business improvement districts, which claim to embody both private market principles—so that they are charging a legitimate fee to, not imposing an unconstitutional tax on, the state properties they protect and keep clean—but also public sphere values, so that, in laying claim to the aura of a state actor, they can escape having to compete with other suppliers in doing so.

Likewise, civil society institutions may well assert both a public and a private role with respect to the family; think of the relationship between civil society entities such as school booster clubs and the families from which they seek to raise money. On the one hand, booster club fundraisers will try to depict the school as a repository of public values, so that giving to it and not to one's own child's classroom would be commendably community minded, not like simply spending money on one's own family. On the other hand, they will depict the school as a site of private values, one within the ambit of the private sphere, so that giving to it and not the district would be legitimately self-concerned, just like spending to fulfill one's own family responsibilities. Toward the family, then, the civil society institution of the school, as portrayed by fundraisers, shows both a public sphere and a private realm face.

Or think of the debate over state aid to another kind of civil society institution: parochial schools. Here, any money that flows from the state to those schools through, say, parental vouchers is deemed by some to be public—just like any state grant, hence subject to constitutional strictures—but by others to have become private, more like a government employee's paycheck, whose disposition lies beyond constitutional concern. Toward parochial schools, then, what comes from the direction of the state can assume both public and private form.

Or consider debate over state mandates requiring insurers to cover particular medical conditions. In its dealings with insurers, the state is depicted by some as a custodian of public, majoritarian values—which would justify mandated coverage of treatments such as wigs for alopecia patients, which a majority of those eligible seek—and by others as a champion of private realm, domestic sphere, personal, intimate considerations, which would justify mandated coverage of Viagra.

Or think of debates over food stamps, in which the state is seen at one and the same time to be asserting public sphere values and private market values with respect to the families who are program beneficiaries. Or think of the more doctrinal debates over welfare discussed in chapter 10. Here, strangers in civil society are characterized by conservatives as more governed by the public sphere values of altruism, compassion, and responsibility for others—and by liberals as more imbued by the private realm values of self-interest and self-concern—than members of the (welfare) family manage to display to one another.

What is going on in much American political controversy, then, is more complicated than can properly be captured by the standard spectrum, in which individuals, families, businesses, civil society, and the state are arrayed in that order from private to public. At the largely grass-roots level at which the debates analyzed here play out, any major institution—individual, family, business, civil society, state—can find itself identified as a repository of both public and private values *with respect to any other*. Citizens and officeholders alike, depending on the debate and the position being taken, can and will—messily, pragmatically, complicatedly—see any one of these basic social entities, in its relationship with any other, as a redoubt for the imperatives of both the public and the private spheres. How, whether, and when to do so are precisely the questions that elicit some of the nation's most passionate political debates.

COMBAT AND CONTACT IN AMERICAN POLITICS

Now more than in a very long time, politicians—especially at the national level—are searching for new ways of forging consensus and framing disagreement. Often, they embark on such quests under the dispensation of the traditional understanding, in which one side in a given debate is understood to rely more heavily on public sphere norms, and the other on private realm values. Take as an example the politics, as it unfolded in 2009's opening months, surrounding President Barack Obama's stimulus package and budget. When the parties searched for consensus, they sought out points of contact between the public sphere values of a stimulative fiscal policy to restore middle- and working-class jobs, and the private market values embodied in a minimal governmental debt burden on private wealth creation. And, where consensus failed, each side tried to frame the underlying disagreement so that its preferred set of values—whether public sphere or private market—would seem the more appealing in combat with the other. Such would be a traditional, and indeed apt, understanding of the politics of consensus and disagreement surrounding the president's fiscal initiatives.

In the grass-roots debates discussed in this book—in which the opposing sides rely on the exact same values drawn equally from the public sphere and the private realm but apply them in inverse ways—the possibilities for both consensus and disagreement take on a profoundly different coloration. Searching for consensus might well involve picking only one of those two jointly held sets of values, public or private, and then finding points of contact between each side's interpretation of it. Framing disagreement, for its part, might rely on showing how your opponent's particular combination of public and private values falls into mutually undermining internal combat. To the extent that policy debates lend themselves to the interpretation being advanced here, they provide another raft of possibilities for both fashioning consensus and formulating disagreement in American politics.

The quest to productively combine consensus and conflict—to marry points of contact with points of combat—is what the historian Daniel Boorstin referred to as "the genius of American politics." Many American political debates lend themselves most suitably to a traditional understanding of this quest. But many others, including grass-roots debates over everything from tax rebates for private communities to mandated insurance coverage for in vitro fertilization, and from parental funding for public schools to the earned income tax credit, disclose, on a deeper look, a very different set of possibilities for pursuing the genius of American politics.

NOTES

INTRODUCTION

1. Interview, Cynthia Davis, October 15, 2007.

2. Interview, Dale Miller, October 15, 2007.

3. For examples of such an interpretation, see, for example, Theda Skocpol, *The Missing Middle* (New York: Norton, 2000), pp. 103, 145; William Julius Wilson, *When Work Disappears* (New York: Knopf, 1996), p. 21; and Lawrence M. Mead and Christopher Beem, "The Deeper Issues," in *Welfare Reform and Political Theory*, edited by Lawrence M. Mead and Christopher Beem (New York: Sage, 2005), pp. 249–69.

4. See, for example, Alan Wolfe, *Marginalized in the Middle* (University of Chicago Press, 1996).

5. Jeff Weintraub, "The Theory and Politics of the Public/Private Distinction," in *Public and Private in Thought and Practice*, edited by Jeff Weintraub and Krishnan Kumar (University of Chicago Press, 1997), p. 15.

6. Part of that public record includes the work of scholars and activists who have shed much empirical light on these debates. But the controversies being analyzed certainly have not been, and probably cannot be, settled on empirical grounds. Nor are they conducted exclusively or even fundamentally at that level. For example, as Mary Jo Bane and David Ellwood say of welfare policy, "Judging whether the poor are really willing to take the jobs that others think they ought to seems to hinge far more on political and moral philosophy than on well defined concepts of what constitutes an acceptable and appropriate attachment to the labor force." See Mary Jo Bane and David T. Ellwood, *Welfare Realities: From Rhetoric to Reform* (Harvard University Press, 1994), p. 88. See also Jacob Hacker, *The Divided Welfare State: The Battle over Public and Pri-*

vate Social Benefits in the United States (Cambridge University Press, 2002), p. 334; Henry M. Levin, "The Public-Private Nexus in Education," *American Behavioral Scientist* 43 (1996), pp. 135–36; and Gary Burtless, "The Economist's Lament: Public Assistance in America," *Journal of Economic Perspectives* 4 (1990), pp. 57–78.

7. For a helpful discussion of the kind of approach being taken here, see Rogers Smith, "Political Jurisprudence, the 'New Institutionalism,' and the Future of Public Law," *American Political Science Review* 82 (1988), pp. 91, 102, 104–06: "If one is attempting an interpretive narrative that shows [certain] structures of thought and argument to be visible in [the] text" of public discourse, one can do so only by focusing "on a few major cases that seem representative instead of documenting how those structures are visible in all or most of the relevant cases."

Smith also points out something else. The project of interpreting the structure of policy discourse is directed at uncovering not the interests or the strategic motivations that might drive participants to mount various arguments—a different endeavor—but rather the patterns in those arguments themselves. A "wealth of . . . internal psychological factors and personal interests . . . influences all political conduct," Smith writes. But even so, "the behavior of political actors . . . is influenced in part by the nature . . . of the ideas they possess, and the basic ideas of a given period . . . often have a discernible structure, which may be articulated in revealing fashion by political writers of the day." See *Liberalism and American Constitutional Law* (Harvard University Press, 1985), pp. 6–7; see also Martin Shapiro, "Of Interests and Values: The New Politics and the New Political Science," in *The New Politics of Public Policy,* edited by Marc K. Landy and Martin A. Levin (Johns Hopkins University Press, 1995), p. 5; and Jeffrey Hening, *Rethinking School Choice: Limits of the Market Metaphor* (Princeton University Press, 1974), pp. 74, 77.

8. David Kirp, *Almost Home: America's Love-Hate Relationship with Community* (Princeton University Press, 2000), p. 21.

CHAPTER ONE

1. Interview, Fred Gaines, October 17, 1997.

2. Interview, Irv Foreman, February 27, 1997.

3. Interview, Amanda Susskind, October 10, 1997.

4. See, for example, Evan McKenzie, *Privatopia: Homeowner Associations and the Rise of Residential Private Government* (Yale University Press, 1994); and Edward J. Blakely and Mary Gail Snyder, *Fortress America: Gated Communities in the United States* (Brookings, 1997).

5. Community Associations Institute, "Industry Data" (www.caionline.org/info/research/Pages/default.aspx); Haya El Nasser, "Gated Communities More Popular, and Not Just for Rich," *USA Today,* December 16, 2002, p. 1A; see also John Bruhn, "Communities of Exclusion and Excluded Communities: Barriers to Neighboring," in *The Sociology of Community Connections* (New York: Kluwer Academic/Plenum Publishers 2004), pp. 133–57.

6. Robert C. Ellickson, "Cities and Homeowners Associations," *University of Pennsylvania Law Review* 130 (1982), p. 1578.

7. California Assembly Select Committee on Common Interest Subdivisions, *Interim Hearing on Common Interest Developments and the Future,* October 11, 1990, Sacramento, pp. 50–51; 56.

8. California Assembly Select Committee on Common Interest Subdivisions, *Final Report,* December 23, 1990, Sacramento, p. 44.

9. Interview, Robyn Stewart, August 5, 1996.

10. *Flat Top Lake Association v. United States,* 868 F. 2d 108 (4th Cir. 1989).

11. Interview, Benjamin Lambert, March 17, 1997.

12. Interview, Benjamin Lambert, August 8, 1996.

13. Interview, Doug Kleine, February 10, 1997, and November 7, 1997.

14. See, as well, Nancy L. Rosenblum, *Membership and Morals: The Personal Uses of Pluralism in America* (Princeton University Press, 1998), p. 152.

15. Interview, David Ramsey, February 20, 1997, and October 16, 1997.

16. Interview, Steve Silverman, February 10, 1997.

17. See, for example, Theda Skocpol, *Diminished Democracy: From Membership to Management in American Civic Life* (University of Oklahoma Press, 2003), pp. 257–58.

18. Interview, Jeff Olson, February 11, 1997.

19. For a discussion of these motives by one of the intellectual pioneers of such initiatives, see Oscar Newman, *Community of Interest* (Garden City, N.Y.: Anchor Press/Doubleday, 1980), pp. 17, 128, 133.

20. Interview, Tom Benton, October 4, 1997.

21. Interview, Silvia Unzueta, April 15,1997; see also Fred Siegel, *The Future Once Happened Here: New York, D.C., L.A., and the Fate of America's Big Cities* (New York: Free Press, 1997), p. 171.

22. Interview, Monique Taylor, February 24, 1997, and October 3–4, 1997.

23. Interview, Mike van Dyk, October 10, 11, 1997.

24. See, for example, Josh Zimmer, "No Gates on Public Streets," *St. Petersburg Times,* August 28, 2002, p. 1B.

25. Interview, Randall Atlas, August 23, 1997.

26. Interview, Carol Pelly, August 27, 1997.

27. Interview, Mickey Munir, September 4, 1997.

28. Interviews with Addison city councillor Sue Halpern, September 9, 1997; Plano assistant city manager Frank Turner, July 29, 1997; Richardson deputy city manager Jerry Hiebert, August 27, 1997; Southlake city planner Chris Carpenter, May 12, 1997.

29. Interview, Carmen Moran, September 13, 1997.

30. Richard Stengel, "Bowling Together," *Time Magazine,* July 22, 1996, p. 3.

31. Andrew Heiskell, "Letters," *Time Magazine,* August 12, 1996, p. 6.

32. For a balanced and insightful analysis of BIDs from a legal perspective, see Richard Briffault, "A Government for Our Time? Business Improvement Districts and Urban Governance," *Columbia Law Review* 99 (1999), pp. 365–477. Briffault describes BIDs as entities less public than the state, because they cannot "enforce a vision of

public order," yet less private than the businesses within their perimeters, because they do not own any property (pp. 475–76).

33. Interview, Terry Miller, October 10, 1997.

34. Interview, Paul Levy, February 24, 1997.

35. Interview, Gretchen Dykstra, August 12, 1996.

36. Interview, Andrew Eristoff, November 13, 1996.

37. Interview, Dave Fogarty, September 10, 1996.

38. Jack R. Greene, Thomas M. Seamon, and Paul R. Levy, "Merging Public and Private Security for Collective Benefit: Philadelphia's Center City District," *American Journal of Police* 14 (1995), pp 9, 15. There is a subtlety involved in determining what is objectionable about this kind of practice. Viewed one way, it would be unfair to allege that, by offering to pay for a new station if the city staffs it, the BID is bribing the city, skewing municipal officeholders' judgment, or otherwise distorting their priorities. True, the city might not deem the provision of extra police in the BID to be its very next priority, as long as the price to it includes the cost of both station and personnel. But extra policing in the BID might very well jump to the city's number-one spot when the price to it is just that of personnel. This is nothing more than the economist's famous substitution effect, in which the lowering of the price of a good causes consumers to shift their consumption.

But the lowering of a price is also supposed to create an income effect, which can sometimes counter the substitution effect. If the price of a potato falls by half from $1.00 to fifty cents, to cite a typical example, then instead of using the $10 you budget weekly for potatoes to buy your usual ten, you might now buy twenty (substitution effect), but you might instead buy only five because now, with the $7.50 left over, you can afford that jar of expensive jam you always wanted (income effect). With the BID deal, however, any income effect cannot kick in, because for the lowered price of policing within the BID to have any effect on the city's budget, the city has to buy more of the commodity—policing in the BID—not less. What the BID is offering is not a market price, but a deal. Such a deal permits the city, as consumer, to act on any substitution effect, but not on any income effect, that it might experience as a result of the lowered price of police in the BID. In this sense, the municipality's judgment and priorities—to purchase police in the BID instead of something else—can be skewed by such deals.

A mirror image of the Philadelphia BID situation, one in which government can act on an income effect but not a substitution effect, arises in cases such as the Smithsonian recently faced, when entrepreneur Catherine Reynolds offered the museum a $38 million donation if it would establish an "Achievers' Hall of Fame," which Reynolds would also have funded; see, for example, Roxanne Roberts, "Where Cash and Culture Go Hand in Hand," *Washington Post*, February 7, 2002, p. C1.

The priorities of the museum, which turned down the deal, evidently would not have included an Achievers' Hall of Fame no matter how low the price, not even at the far-below-zero price being offered, if we imagine the $38 million donation as a kind of rebate. For this reason, the deal would not have passed muster on the substitution effect. Had the museum accepted the deal, however, it would have been wholly unencumbered insofar as it would have been able to act on the income effect. After all, it wouldn't have been parting with any of its own money for the hall, and so all the benefit of the price drop—the $38 million "rebate"—could have gone to purchasing whatever was genuinely next in the museum's order of priorities but which had until then been unaffordable.

39. Interview, Jim Flood, October 29, 1996.

40. Interview, Randall Gregson, November 1, 1996.

41. Interview, Larry Houstoun, September 11, 1996.

42. Interviews, Bob Jones, September 19, 1996; February 18, 1997; October 10, 1997.

43. Interview, Peter Pimentel, February 25, 1997.

CHAPTER TWO

1. Interview, Rick Lewis, February 6, 1998.

2. Interview, Norm Brewer, February 5, 1998.

3. Robert B. Reich, "Secession of the Successful," *New York Times Magazine*, January 20, 1991, p. 16.

4. Sandra Marquez Garcia and Jody Mailander Farrell, "Deliveryman Killed over Parking Space," *Miami Herald*, January 3, 1998, p. 1.

5. *People* v. *Zelinski*, 594 P. 2d 1000 (1979) at 1003.

6. Interview, Steve Teal, February 5, 1998.

7. Interview, Mike Levin, president and former manager, Black Butte homeowners association, January 26, 1998; interview, Bill Handy, Black Butte Ranch Special District Police, February 5, 1998.

8. Interview, Mike Torres, January 29, 1998.

9. Interview, John Winterstein, January 28, 1998.

10. Interview, Bob Diamond, January 21, 1998; February 23, 1998.

11. Interview, Cliff van Meter, February 9, 1998.

12. Interview, Daniel Nicholson, February 9, 1998.

13. *U.S.* v. *McGreevy*, 652 F. 2d 849 (1981); see also *Commonwealth* v. *Leone*, 435 NE 2d 1036 (1982) at 1041 and some of the discussion in Gary T. Marx, "The Interweaving of Public and Private Police in Undercover Work," in *Private Policing*, edited by Clifford D. Shearing and Philip C. Stenning (Newbury Park, Calif.: Sage, 1987), pp. 172–90.

14. *Griffin* v. *Maryland*, 378 U.S. 130 (1964). In two other cases, *Watkins* v. *Oakland Jockey Club*, 183 F. 2d 440 (8th Cir. 1950), and *Robinson* v. *Davis*, 447 F. 2d 753 (4th Cir. 1971), courts concluded that the public uniform was not sufficient to lend the color of public authority to a moonlighting cop who otherwise operates wholly within the confines of a private security role. But both cases were complicated by the fact that the publicly uniformed private security guard was a personal acquaintance of those against whom he was enforcing a private rule, known to them outside of both his public police and private security roles.

15. Interview, Jeremy Travis, February 5, 1998.

16. Interview, Marvin Nodiff , January 22, 1998. See *Maryland Estates Homeowners' Association* v. *Puckett*, 936 S.W. 2d 218, 219 (Mo. App. E.D. 1996).

17. Interview, Marjorie Meyer, January 26, 1998.

18. Interview, Kenneth Seguin, January 31, 1998.

19. Interview, Chuck Edgar, April 17, 1997.

20. Interview, Mike Shanahan, January 21, 1998.

21. Interview, Kevin Jones, February 13, 1998.

22. Interview, David Brennan, March 5, 1998.

23. Interview, Ron Perl, January 23, 1998.

24. Interview, Steve Hovany, February 5, 1998.

25. Interview, Barbara Wick, January 21, 1998.

26. Interview, Brian Johnson, March 5, 1998.

27. Interview, Wayne Hyatt, April 14, 1997.

28. Interview, Richard Zappelli, March 2, 1998. See also Elizabeth E. Joh, "The Paradox of Private Policing," *Journal of Criminal Law and Criminology* 95 (2004), p. 86.

29. Interview, Jon Epsten, January 21, 1998.

30. Interview, Bruce Benson, January 22, 1998.

31. Interview, Phyllis Matthey, January 23, 1998.

32. Interview, Mike Walker, February 5, 1998.

33. Interview, William Cunningham, January 28, 1998.

34. Interview, Mike Woo, October 3, 1997.

35. Interview, Mike Gambrill, January 29, 1998.

36. Interview, Charles Morgenstein, January 23, 1998.

37. In other criminal justice public-private border battles, however, both sides can be seen to rely on the same values drawn equally from the public and the private realms, while applying them in converse ways. Consider the practice known as "pay to stay," in which inmates convicted of nonviolent crimes can pay to upgrade their jail cells, purchasing private TVs, private washrooms, and other amenities. For their defenders, these kinds of payments should be seen not as private market fees but as public sphere fines. Just as, for certain misdemeanors, one is allowed to pay a fine in lieu of being deprived of one's freedom by a jail sentence, so here one in effect pays a fine in lieu of being deprived of a TV and a washroom during one's jail sentence. For critics, by contrast, to dignify such payments as fines—as if being required to pay for a TV or a washroom somehow represented a statement of disapproval by the state—is absurd; the payment is a private market act and cannot be so elevated, and hence justified.

So in the debate over inmate payments for TVs and washrooms, when it comes to their views of the payment, defenders see it as a penalty in the public sphere while critics identify it as a transaction in the private market. Yet when it comes to their views of the items that those payments are meant to purchase—the TV and the washroom—the two sides switch positions. Critics view the TV or washroom in public sphere terms, in that their being withheld from inmates is part and parcel of the deprivation of freedom that lies at the core of the public's communication of its disapprobation. To allow inmates to buy their way out of that penalty is offensive: tantamount to permitting people to buy their way out of any other civic obligation, such as the military draft. For defenders, by contrast, to suggest that the deprivation of a television or a washroom is part of the public sphere penalty that inmates face is to trivialize the accompanying (and far more fundamental) deprivation of freedom, which is the true penalty, the one that sends the message to the miscreant—in a way in which being barred from watching his preferred TV show never can—that he has violated his civic obligations. The correct framing for defenders of inmate payments is that the deprivation of the TV or washroom is merely a private market matter, much as a television salesman deprives anyone of a TV until it is purchased. Inmates should be allowed to make such ordinary private market purchases, just as (though incarcerated) they can buy a book or magazine subscription or other basic items in the private market.

In sum, for critics the payment is a transfer of private market value by which inmates scandalously buy their way out of part of the experience of public opprobrium, namely, the deprivation of the TV and washroom, which is very much a public sphere statement, part and parcel of the punishment being meted out. For defenders, by contrast, the payment is a serviceable public sphere fine, while the deprivation of the TV and the washroom are not part of the public's communication of disapprobation but are merely private market realities that can be legitimately overcome by an act of purchase. See, for example, Jennifer Steinhauer, "For $82 a Day, Booking a Cell in a 5-Star Jail," *New York Times*, April 29, 2007, p. 1.1; Police Chief Paul M. Walters and Russell Davis, "Government Entrepreneurship: How COP, Direct Supervision, and a Business Helped Solve Santa Ana's Crime Problems," *Michigan Law Review First Impressions* 106 (2007), pp. 71–75.

CHAPTER THREE

1. Otis Port, "The Mind Is Immortal," *Business Week*, August 30, 1999, p. 100.

2. Radley Balko, e-mail message to Andrew Stark, June 22, 2004. Interviews with bloggers were conducted by e-mail, not phone.

3. Joshua Claybourn, e-mail message to Andrew Stark, June 22, 2004.

4. Interview, Tasha Thomas, June 4, 2004.

5. Kathleen Teltsch, "Wanted: Contributors in Search of Immortality," *New York Times*, June 11, 1993, p. B1.

6. James Gleick, "Get Out of My Namespace," *New York Times* Magazine, March 21, 2004, pp. 44–49.

7. Megan McArdle, e-mail message to Andrew Stark, June 22, 2004.

8. Michael Wood, comment posted March 3, 2004, www.michaelwood.com.

9. Hetti Judah, "Will the Real Dave Gorman Please Stand Up?" *London Times*, February 3, 2001, p. 28; Will Marlow, "His Name Is Dave Gorman, Is Yours?" *Birmingham Post*, September 6, 2001, p. 16.

10. Quoted in Julian Morris, "Name Games: The Next Threat to Dot-Coms," *Asian Wall Street Journal*, August 17, 2000, p. 6. See also Stephanie Rosenbloom, "Names That Match Forge a Bond on the Internet," *New York Times*, April 10, 2008, p. A1.

11. Barbara Wamboldt, "Gimme a Break," *Kingston Whig-Standard*, January 20, 1998, p. 6.

12. Interview, Dave Koehler, June 1, 2004.

13. Interview, Andrea Dowd, June 4, 2004.

14. Larry Carter, "Letter," *Rock Hill Herald*, September 28, 2003, p. 3E.

15. Meredith E. Bynum, "Letter," *Rock Hill Herald*, September 28, 2003, p. 3E.

16. Interview, Vernon Smith, June 14, 2004.

17. Interview, Chelsea Stalling, June 14, 2004.

18. Interview, Jim Camanger, June 14, 2004.

19. Richard Simon, "Few Remember Cornelius Cole but the Name Lives On," *Los Angeles Times*, February 10, 1999, p. 13.

20. "Plates Still Available for Wall of Honor in Hopewell Building," *Richmond Times Dispatch*, October 4, 1990, p. 9.

21. New York Times News Service, "Man Claims Dullest Blog, and He Just May Be Right," *Chicago Tribune*, May 24, 2003, p. 4.

22. Craig Taylor, "Hello World," *Guardian*, February 22, 2003, p. 38.

23. Jeffrey Rosen, "Your Blog or Mine?" *New York Times*, December 19, 2004, pp. 24, 32.

24. Andrew Ferguson, "Happy Campers in Boston," *Weekly Standard*, August 9, 2004, p. 20.

25. Quoted in James Boswell, *The Life of Samuel Johnson LL.D.*, vol. 1 (London: George Bell, 1884), p. 7.

26. John C. Dvorak, "Co-Opting the Future: The Onerous Big Media Incursion Marks the Beginning of the End for Blogging," *PC Magazine*, December 9, 2003, p. 69.

27. Michael Holroyd, "Biographers, Get a Life Preferably Your Own," *Glasgow Sunday Herald*, November 26, 2000, p. 10.

28. Eric S. Raymond, e-mail message to Andrew Stark, June 22, 2004.

29. Joseph M. Dougherty, "To Blog or Not to Blog?" *Deseret News*, July 7, 2003, p. C1.

30. Hannah Arendt, *The Human Condition* (Garden City, N.Y.: Doubleday, 1959), p. 175; see also Richard Sennett, *The Fall of Public Man* (New York: Knopf, 1977), ch. 14.

31. Arendt, *Human Condition*, p. 211.

CHAPTER FOUR

1. Interview, Diane Mancus, August 9, 1999.

2. Jill Smolowe, "Beyond Bake Sales: Parents and Principles Collide as Fund Raising Becomes a Way of Life in the Public Schools," *Time*, April 24, 1995, p. 62.

3. Interview, Lydia Moss, June 3, 1999.

4. Interview, Kathy Christie, June 10, 1999; see also Robert L. Lineberry, *Equality and Urban Policy* (Beverly Hills: Sage, 1977), p. 15.

5. Interview, Wayne Sampson, June 28, 1999.

6. Henry M. Levin, "The Public-Private Nexus in Education," *American Behavioral Scientist* 43 (1996), p. 129.

7. Anemona Hartocollis, "Crew Pledges to Rule on Teacher Today," *New York Times*, September 25, 1997, p. B3.

8. Jacques Steinberg, "Alumni to Give Brooklyn Tech Huge Donation," *New York Times,* March 20, 1998, p. A1.

9. Ibid.

10. Interview, Steve Conn, June 11, 1999.

11. Interview, Jim Terrell, June 29, 1999.

12. Interview, Pat Lawrence, July 22, 1999.

13. Interview, Rebecca Daniels, March 3, 2000.

14. Interview, Anne Bryant, August 15, 1999.

15. Interview, Richard Goldstein, July 26, 1999.

16. Interview, Paul Vance, July 12, 1999.

17. Interview, Sam Skootsky, August 26, 1999.

18. Interview, Nancy Wainman, August 20, 1999.

19. See, for example, *Granger v. Cascade County School District,* 499 P. 2d 780 (Mont. 1972).

20. Interview, Peter Hamilton, June 22, 1999.

21. Interview, Neal Rosenberg, February 21, 2000.

22. Sarah Carr, "Private Funds Padding Public School Coffers; Gifts Cover Shortfalls but Raise Concerns of Education Inequalities," *Milwaukee Journal Sentinel,* November 15, 2004, p. 1.

23. Michael Specter, "The Dangerous Philosopher," *New Yorker,* September 6, 1999, p. 55.

24. Interview, Beth Dilley, August 13, 1999.

25. Bob Thompson, "Sharing the Wealth," *Washington Post,* April 13, 2003, p. W8.

26. Jon M. Bakija and William G. Gale, "Effects of Estate Tax Reform on Charitable Giving," *Tax Policy Issues and Options* 6 (2003), p. 1.

27. I note in passing that when economists speak of altruism, they are often talking about a person forgoing personal consumption in order to provide a gift or a bequest for his or her children. By contrast, when they speak of self-interestedness, they can easily be characterizing a person giving to a charity for children halfway round the world, because such activities return a satisfying "warm glow" to the donor. These oddities—in which altruism characterizes our helping our own and self-interest characterizes our helping distant others—stems from the economist's twin allegiances to methodological individualism and rational self-interest. Methodological individualism suggests that even one's own child is an "other," so giving to him or her is an act of altruism, whereas the universal motivator of rational self-interest suggests that if one is giving to another halfway round the world, it must in some way be self-benefiting.

28. Interview, Brenda Diehl, August 13, 1999.

29. Joshua Zumbrun, "Howard Schools Hope to Bolster Budget via Private Donations," *Washington Post,* January 19, 2006, p. T3.

30. Interview, Cynthia Guyer, June 14, 1999.

31. See also Paul Demko and Susan Gray, "When Public Agencies Seek Private Funds," *Chronicle of Higher Education,* December 12, 1996, pp. 1, 12–17; Kevin Lynch and Amy Carlsen Kohnstamm, "Portland Public Schools—School Equity? There's More to That Story," *The Oregonian,* October 5, 2006, p. B7.

CHAPTER FIVE

1. *State* v. *Nussbaum*, 115 N.W.2d 761, 771 (Wis. 1962); see also Cass R. Sunstein, *The Partial Constitution* (Harvard University Press, 1993), p. 307.

2. For good discussions of the nonconstitutional issues, see Jeffrey R. Henig, *Rethinking School Choice: Limits of the Market Metaphor* (Princeton University Press, 1994); Jennifer L. Hochschild and Nathan Scorovnick, *The American Dream and the Public Schools* (Oxford University Press, 2003), pp. 107–32; William Howell and Paul Peterson, *The Education Gap: Vouchers and Urban Public Schools* (Brookings, 2002); and Joseph P. Viteritti, *Choosing Equality: School Choice, the Constitution, and Civil Society* (Brookings, 1999), pp. 80–117.

3. I have conducted no interviews for this chapter, since it focuses on discourse in and surrounding court cases, legal briefs and commentary—discourse that, because of its use of precedents, extends back further than the last two decades.

4. *Lemon v. Kurtzman*, 403 U.S. 602 (1971). It is true that *Lemon* actually requires courts to execute three tests to determine whether a challenged program of aid to parochial schools runs afoul of the Establishment Clause. But the Supreme Court has "essentially collapsed the *Lemon* test so that the focus is on whether the challenged activity has the effect of advancing religion"; see *Porta* v. *Klagholz*, 19 F. Supp. 2d 290, 297 (D.N.J. 1998). Note, too, that the test is whether the challenged activity has "the effect," not whether it has the "primary effect," as *Lemon* would have it, of advancing religion. As one district court said as early as 1974, "In applying the 'primary effects test,' we must be guided by the realization . . . that this is no longer a primary effects test, but an 'any effects test'"; see *Minnesota Civil Liberties Union* v. *State*, 224 N.W.2d 344, 353 (Minn., 1974). See also Justice Powell's opinion in *Committee for Public Education and Religious Liberty* v. *Nyquist*, 413 U.S. 756, 783 (1973).

5. As the Supreme Court put it in *Everson*, a case concerning the constitutionality of a New Jersey plan to extend free busing to private school students, "To say that New Jersey's appropriation and her use of the power of taxation for raising the funds appropriated are not for public purposes but are for private ends, is to say that they are for the support of religion and religious teaching. Conversely, to say that they are for public purposes is to say that they are not for religious ones [or for] the private character of the function of religious education." *See Everson* v. *Bd. of Education* 67 S. Ct. 504, 528, 529 (1947).

6. *Mueller* v. *Allen*, 436 U.S. 388, 399 (1983).

7. Eugene Volokh, "Vouched For," *New Republic*, July 6, 1998, p. 12; see also *Witters* v. *Washington Dep't of Servs. for the Blind*, 474 U.S. 487 (1986); and *Rosenberger* v. *Rector & Visitors of University of Va.*, 515 U.S. 819, 848 (1995).

8. *Rosenberger*, 515 U.S. at 886.

9. *Mitchell v. Helms*, 120 S. Ct. at 2544–45. See also *Wolman v. Essex*, 342 F. Supp. 399, 415 (S.D.Ohio 1972), aff'd mem., 409 U.S 808 (1972); *Wolman* v. *Walter*, 433 U.S. 229, 250 (1977).

10. Brief Amici Curiae of the Institute for Justice, p. 24; *Mitchell* v. *Helms*, 120 S. Ct. 2530 (2000) (No. 98-1648); Lexis, 1998 U.S. Briefs 1648.

11. *Everson* 67 S.Ct. at 507.

12. Margaret A. Nero, "The Cleveland Scholarship and Tutoring Program: Why Voucher Programs Do Not Violate the Establishment Clause," *Ohio State Law Journal* 58 (1997), pp. 1103, 1113.

13. *Board of Education* v. *Allen*, 392 U.S. 236, 272 (1968).

14. See Christopher L. Eisgruber and Lawrence G. Sager, *Religious Freedom and the Constitution* (Harvard University Press, 2007), p. 199.

15. *Board of Education* v. *Allen*, 392 U.S. at 239; see also *Zobrest* v. *Catalina Foothills Sch. Dist.*, 509 U.S. 1, 8 (1993).

16. *Nyquist*, 413 U.S. at 781. See also *Walz* v. *Tax Commission of the City of New York*, 397 U.S. 664, 671 (1969) ("'Aid' to schools teaching a particular religious faith [is no] more a violation of the Establishment Clause than providing state-paid policemen, detailed to protect children [at the schools] from the very real hazards of traffic"); *Nyquist*, 413 U.S. at 821 (Burger, C.J., dissenting): "States do, and they may, furnish churches and parochial schools with police and fire protection as well as water and sewage facilities"; *Widmar*, 454 U.S. at 274, quoting *Roemer* v. *Board of Public Works*, 426 U.S. 736, 747 (1976): "If the Establishment Clause barred the extension of general benefits to religious groups, a church would not be protected by the police and fire departments."

17. *Zobrest*, 509 U.S. at 10.

18. Matthew J. Perry, "What Does the Establishment Clause Forbid? Reflections on the Constitutionality of School Vouchers," in *School Choice: The Moral Debate*, edited by Alan Wolfe (Princeton University Press, 2003), p. 238.

19. Note, "Government Neutrality and Separation of Church and State: Tuition Tax Credits," *Harvard Law Review* 92 (1979), pp. 696, 687. See also *Minnesota Civil Liberties Union* v. *State*, 224 N.W.2d 344, 351 (Minn. 1974); and *Committee for Public Education and Religious Liberty* v. *Nyquist*, 350 F.Supp. 655, 668 (S.D.N.Y. 1972).

20. *Zobrest* v. *Catalina Foothills Sch. Dist.*, 963 F.2d 1190, 1201 (9th Cir. 1992).

21. *Lemon*, 403 U.S. at 624 (Douglas, J., concurring).

22. David J. Futterman, "School Choice and the Religion Clauses," *Georgetown Law Journal* 81 (1993), pp. 711, 728.

23. *Minnesota Civil Liberties Union* v. *Roemer*, 452 F.Supp. 1316, 1321 (D. Minn. 1978) (one of the reasons the Supreme Court struck down programs such as the tuition tax credits featured in *Nyquist* is because of their "recent vintage," whereas in *Walz*, the contested property tax exemptions for religious institutions were upheld because they had been in existence "for many years").

24. *Nyquist*, 413 U.S. at 782.

25. Steven K. Green, "The Legal Argument against Private School Choice," *University of Cincinnati Law Review* 62 (1993), p. 67; see also Note, "Establishment Clause—School Vouchers—Wisconsin Supreme Court Upholds Milwaukee Parental Choice Program," *Harvard Law Review* 112 (1999), pp. 736, 740 (quoting *Nyquist*, 413 U.S. at 788).

26. See, for example, *Judd* v. *Board of Education*, 15 N.E.2d 576, 582 (N.Y. 1938).

27. *Zobrest.*, 509 U.S. at 10.

28. Elliot M. Mincberg and Judith E. Schaffer, "Grades K-12: The Legal Problems with Public Funding of Religious Schools," in *Vouchers and the Provision of Public Services,* edited by C. Eugene Steuerle and others (Brookings, 2000), p. 395.

29. Joseph P. Viteritti, *The Last Freedom: Religion from the Public School to the Public Square* (Princeton University Press, 2007), p. 126.

30. Note, "Government Neutrality and Separation of Church and State: Tuition Tax Credits," pp. 696, 707.

31. Jesse H. Choper, "The Establishment Clause and Aid to Parochial Schools," *California Law Review* 56 (1968), p. 340.

32. Ibid.

33. Hugh F. Smart, "Tax Deductions as Permissible State Aid to Parochial Schools," *Chicago-Kent Law Review* 60 (1984), pp. 657, 677. See also *School Dist. of Grand Rapids v. Ball,* 473 U.S. 373, 375–76 (1985); *Nyquist* 413 U.S. at 803.

34. Antonin Scalia, "On Making It Look Easy by Doing It Wrong: A Critical View of the Justice Department," in *Private Schools and the Public Good: Policy Alternatives for the Eighties,* edited by Edward McGlynn Gaffney (University of Notre Dame Press, 1981), pp. 173, 179.

35. *Rosenberger,* 515 U.S. at 862 (Thomas, J., concurring); see also *Meek* v. *Pittenger,* 421 U.S. 349, 389–90 (1975); and Michael W. McConnell, "Legal and Constitutional Issues of Vouchers," in *Vouchers and the Provision of Public Services,* edited by Steuerle and others, p. 378.

36. *Zobrest,* 509 U.S. at 10. See also *Kotterman* v. *Killian,* 972 P. 2d 606, 612, 613, 614 (Ariz. 1999); *Mitchell* v. *Helms,* 120 S. Ct. 2530, 2547 (2000); and Brief Amici Curiae of the Institute for Justice, et al, *Mitchell v. Helms,* p. 24.

37. *Kotterman* v. *Killian,* 972 P. 2d at 614, 616. I thus far have looked only at programs—textbook provision, aid for remedial instruction, tuition-tax credits, vouchers—that provide some new form of aid only to private schools (even if comparable aid was already being furnished to public schools). But some new programs—such as Title I aid for needy students, Title II aid for instructional material, or IDEA support for interpretive services—were conceived de novo as assistance for both public and private school students. Even here, though, aid opponents adopt an existential approach. They treat the "public" part of the program as a natural extension of previously existing and long-standing state support for public schools—as falling within the baseline, hence entirely valid—but the "private" part as a new departure from that baseline. It thus remains the case, as those taking this view have argued, that "new economic benefits are being extended directly to religion"; see *Rosenberger,* 515 U.S. at 889 (Souter, J., dissenting). In the 1997 Cleveland voucher case, the vouchers would have been made available to parents at failing district public schools to use at both private and nondistrict public schools. But because the latter would simply have involved shuffling the particular public schools that might get funding from Cleveland's public school budget, the only new beneficiaries of the program—by comparison with the preexisting situation—were, voucher opponents held, private schools, whose prices would become cheaper. In the eyes of its opponents, the antivoucher side was urging the court to "examine the [private] school program in isolation, as if it were enacted

out of whole cloth for the benefit of religious institutions" (Opening Brief of Appellants/Cross-Appellees Hope for Cleveland's Children, et al., In the Supreme Court of Ohio, *Simmons-Harris* v. *Goff*, Case No. 97-1117, p. 30).

38. Douglas Laycock, "Formal, Substantive, and Disaggregated Neutrality toward Religion," *DePaul Law Review* 39 (1990), p. 1006.

39. Ibid.

40. *Rosenberger*, 515 U.S. at 862 (Thomas, J., concurring).

41. *Lemon*, 403 U.S. at 641.

42. *Agostini* v. *Felton*, 117 S. Ct. 1997, 2019 (Souter, J., dissenting). See also Choper, "The Establishment Clause and Aid to Parochial Schools," pp. 260, 326. ("Even public aid that is itself immune from sectarian manipulation frees church funds either for uses subject to manipulation, or for strictly religious uses.")

43. *Ball*, 473 U.S. at 397.

44. See also *Nyquist*, 350 F.Supp. at 665; *Gatton* v. *Goff*, Nos. 96CVH-01-193; 96CVH01-721, 1996 WL 466499 (Ohio Ct. C.P., Franklin County, July 31, 1996), p. 10; Michael J. Stick, "Educational Vouchers: A Constitutional Analysis," *Columbia Journal of Law and Social Problems* 28 (1995), pp. 423, 470; *Zobrest*, 509 U.S. at 12; *Bagley* v. *Raymond School District*, 728 A.2d 127, 142 (Me. 1999) (describing *Agostini v. Felton*).

45. *Mitchell* v. *Helms*, 120 S. Ct. at 2547.

46. *Zobrest*, 963 F.2d at 1200 (emphasis mine).

47. *DiCenso* v. *Robinson*, 316 F.Supp. 112, 118 (D. Rhode Island 1970).

48. See as well *Cochran* v. *Louisiana*, 50 S.Ct. 335 (1930).

49. *Ball*, 473 U.S. at 396 (emphasis mine); see also *Wolman* v. *Essex*, 417 F.Supp. 1113, 1118 n. 2 (S.D. Ohio 1976), referring to *Meek*, 421 U.S. at 361; see also *Meek* v. *Pittenger*, 374 F.Supp. 639, 654, 655 (E.D. Pa. 1974).

50. See also *Meek*, 374 F.Supp. at 675 (Higginbotham, J., concurring in part and dissenting in part); *Aguilar* v. *Felton*, 473 U.S. 402 (1984) (O'Connor, J., dissenting); *Agostini* 117 S. Ct. at 2012; *Bagley* v. *Raymond School Department*, 728 A.2d 127, 145 (Me.1999); and *Felton* v. *United States Dept. of Education*, 739 F. 2d, 48, 50 (2nd Cir. 1984).

51. *Everson*, 330 U.S. at 67.

52. See also *Judd* v. *Board of Education*, 15 N.E.2d 576, 583 (N.Y. 1938).

53. *Lemon v. Kurtzman*, 310 F. Supp. 35, 50 (E.D. Pa. 1969). See also *Wolman* v. *Walters*, 433 US at 258 (Marshall, J., concurring in part and dissenting in part); and *Allen*, 228 N.E.2d, 796.

54. *Agostini*, 117 S. Ct. at 2021 (Souter, J., dissenting).

55. *Ball*, 473 U.S. at 396.

56. Ibid.

57. *Lemon*, 403 U.S. at 657 (Brennan, J., concurring).

58. *Ball*, 473 U.S. at 396–7; see also *Felton*, 739 F. 2d at 67; and *Americans United for Separation of Church and State* v. *School District*, 718 F. 2d 1389, 1405, 1406 (6th Cir. 1983).

59. Stick, "Educational Vouchers: A Constitutional Analysis," p. 471.

60. Suppose that we accept the existential criterion, noting that the busing or book

services in question are not ones the school was underwriting anyway, so that in paying for them, the state frees up no new funds that the school can devote to private purposes. Suppose instead that parents were in fact paying for them. We still, some aid critics argue, face a potential problem. Knowing that parents are now getting free busing services or textbooks, the school can simply raise its tuition commensurately so as to capture their gains. As Choper puts it, "Since tuition charges are flexible," they "could readily be adjusted upward to take advantage of the parents' subsidies . . . thus providing [the school] with funds available for strictly religious use." See Choper, "The Establishment Clause and Aid to Parochial Schools," pp. 315, 319. Or, as Senator Bob Packwood told private school officials at a 1981 subcommittee hearing on tuition tax credits, "What I want each of you to lay to rest, if you can, is [the concern] that . . . if we pass this [tuition tax-credit bill], you are all going to immediately raise your tuitions, and this is just going to become a federal subsidy for the school, and the parents will be no better off than if we never pass a bill." See *Tuition Tax Credits: Hearings on S.550 before the Subcommittee on Taxation and Debt Management of the Senate Committee on Finance* (Part 2 of 2), 97 Cong. 2 sess. (1981), p. 250.

In raising its tuition in this way, the school *would* be getting new money, money that would be new even on existential grounds: new, that is, compared with the immediately preexisting status quo. But note that to the extent that tuition goes up, any incentive that the aid provides to parents to send their children to parochial school would diminish. After all, if the now-free busing and books are countervailed by a price hike from the institution, then even on existential grounds—that is, compared with the preexisting situation—let alone on normative criteria, parents would face no new incentive to send their child to parochial school. In other words, with a tuition price hike, the purposes to which aid is devoted may become private (even on existential grounds), but then so does the money (even on existential grounds): For with a tuition hike, the aid creates no new incentives—on existential, let alone normative, grounds—to go private over public, leaving its disposition instead entirely up to parental choice.

61. Sunstein, *The Partial Constitution,* pp. 3, 76.

62. Despite the symmetry, there is one difference between the burdens the two sides have to bear. Notice that while those opposed to aid must depict it as public money flowing to private purposes, defenders of aid need only insist that the money is private *or* that its purposes are public. In other words, aid defenders' approach can be disjunctive, and occasionally they take advantage of this fact. So on the one hand, some aid supporters concede that on a normative understanding of school responsibilities, the aid might well free up funds for private, that is, parochial purposes. But they then insist that this doesn't matter because the money is also private, there being, on an appropriate normative understanding of state responsibilities, no state-furnished "incentive to use the aid at a religious institution"; see *Campbell* v. *Manchester Board of School Directors,* 641A.2d 352, 358 (Vt. 1994). And, of course, there is no constitutional violation when private money goes to private purposes. As Justice Thomas expresses this view, "any use of that aid to indoctrinate cannot be attributed to the government and is thus not of constitutional concern" (*Mitchell* v. *Helms,* 120 S. Ct. at 2547).

On the other hand, aid supporters sometimes concede that—on an existential understanding of state responsibilities—the money might well remain public, because it affords parents a new, publicly dispensed incentive, compared with existing government aid, to send their children to parochial school. But aid supporters then insist that this doesn't matter, because the purposes that this public money supports are also public. On the appropriate existential understanding, no school funds are ultimately being freed up for private purposes, because the school's existing responsibilities exclude any outlay for the now publicly underwritten purpose. Hence there is ultimately no constitutional violation: after all, public funds can flow to public purposes (Stick, "Educational Vouchers: A Constitutional Analysis," p. 470, n. 323). See also *Everson*, 330 U.S. at 67; and *McGowan* v. *State of Maryland*, 366 U.S. 420, 467 (1961) (Frankfurter, J., concurring).

These two lines of argument that aid supporters might make—that both money and purposes are public (where both are understood on an existential baseline) and that both are private (where both are understood on a normative baseline)—themselves contradict each other. By and large, though, aid supporters argue that the money is private (here using a normative understanding of baseline government responsibilities) and the purposes public (here using an existential understanding of school responsibilities), because that amounts to the strongest possible argument for their case.

CHAPTER SIX

1. Interview, Frank Kohler, August 16, 1999.

2. Interview, Ernest Fleishman, August 12, 1999.

3. Interview, Paul Folkemer, August 17, 1999.

4. Interview, Alex Molnar, February 15, 1999.

5. James Dao, "School News Show with Ads Clears a Key Albany Panel," *New York Times*, May 25, 1995, p. B1.

6. Mark Crispin Miller, "How to Be Stupid: The Lessons of Channel One," *Extra!* May 1997, pp. 18–19.

7. Interview, William Hoynes, January 31, 1999. See also William Hoynes, "News for a Captive Audience: An Analysis of Channel One," *Extra!* May 1997, pp. 11–17.

8. Michael Morgan, *Channel One in the Public Schools: Widening the Gaps* (Department of Communications, University of Massachusetts, October 13, 1993), p. 7; see also Alex Molnar, *Giving Kids the Business* (Boulder, Colo.: Westview, 1996), pp. 19, 49.

9. The Center for Commercial-Free Public Education, "What Is Commercialism in Schools?" (www.ibiblio.org/commercialfree/commercialismtext.html).

10. David Shenk, "The Pedagogy of Pasta Sauce; Pretending to Help Teachers, Campbell's Teaches Consumerism," *Harper's Magazine*, September, 1995, p. 53.

11. Suzanne Alexander Ryan, "Companies Teach All Sorts of Lessons with Educational Tools They Give Away," *Wall Street Journal*, April 19, 1994, p. B1.

12. Interview, Charlotte Baecher, February 7, 1999; see also Alex Molnar, 1999 Phil Smith Lecture, Ohio Valley Philosophy of Education Conference, Bergamo, Ohio, October 15, 1999, p. 1.

13. See also comments of Alex Molnar, "Commercialism in the Schools: Supporting Students or Selling Access?" Center for the Analysis of Commercialism in Education, Association for Supervision and Curriculum Development (ASCD), National Issues Forum, December 9, 1998, Washington, D.C., pp. 6, 13.

14. Statement of U.S. Senator Richard C. Shelby on Channel One, Commercial Alert, May 20, 1999 (www.commercialalert.org/news/featured-in/1999/05/statement-of-us-senator-richard-c-shelby-on-channel-one).

15. Gerald Jude Kowal, "Commercialism in Public Schools: A Study of the Perceptions of Teachers and Administrators on Accepting Corporate Advertising," Ph.D. dissertation, University of Nebraska, October 2003, p. 53.

16. Interview, Jim Metrock, August 13, 1999.

17. Interview, Kevin Gordon, August 19, 1999.

18. Interview, Andy Hill, February 9, 1999.

19. Interview, Brita Butler-Wall, August 18, 1999.

20. Consumers Union, "Captive Kids: A Report on Commercial Pressures on Kids at School" (www.consumersunion.org/other/captivekids/pressures.htm).

21. Consumers Union, "Captive Kids."

22. Butler-Wall interview.

23. Baecher interview.

24. Michael Tabor, "Ban School Vending Machines," Baltimore Sun, March 2, 2001, p. 17A.

25. Consumers Union, "Captive Kids."

26. Constance L. Hays, "Channel One's Mixed Grades in Schools," New York Times, December 5, 1999, Section 3, p. 1.

27. Center for the Analysis of Commercialism in Education, ASCD National Issues Forum, "Commercialism in the Schools: Supporting Students or Selling Access?" Washington, D.C. December 9, 1998, p. 28.

28. For a classic exposition of this value, see Milton Friedman, "The Social Responsibility of Business Is to Increase Its Profits," New York Times Magazine, September 13, 1970, pp. 122–26.

CHAPTER SEVEN

1. Interview, Leonard Teitelbaum, January 9, 2001.

2. Interview, Ginny Hamilton, January 17, 2001.

3. Interview, Karen Darner, February 5, 2001.

4. Interview, Paul Wallace-Brodeur, January 29, 2001.

5. Theda Skocpol, Social Policy in the United States: Future Possibilities in Historical Perspective (Princeton University Press, 1995), p. 6; see also the discussion in Neil Gilbert, Capitalism and the Welfare State: Dilemmas of Social Benevolence (Yale University Press, 1983), pp. 58–59.

6. Interview, Jane Chiles, January 24, 2001

7. Interview, Win Moses, January 12, 2001.

8. Interview, Janet Varon, February 16, 2001.

9. Interview, Alexis Senger, January 9, 2001.

10. For good academic arguments to this effect, see David Cutler, *Your Money or Your Life: Strong Medicine for America's Health Care System* (Oxford University Press, 2004); Jeanne M. Lambrew, "A Wellness Trust to Prioritize Disease Prevention," (Brookings/The Hamilton Project, April 2007); and Michael Sparer, *Medicaid and the Limits of State Health Reform* (Temple University Press, 1996), pp. 46–47.

11. Interview, Steve Cooper, January 28, 2002.

12. Unlike some other debates, the two sides here differ over *how* to expand (or contract) the public sphere—the sphere of public health insurance—and not over *whether* to expand (contract) it. Yet even in this variation the theme emerges in which both sides rely equally on the same public sphere and private market values, while applying them in inverse ways.

13. Interview, Tim Berthold, February 12, 2001.

14. Interview, Sam Thompson, January 16, 2001.

15. Catherine Hoffman and Marie Wang, *Health Insurance Coverage in America 2002 Data Update* (Washington: Kaiser Commission on Medicaid and the Uninsured, 2003).

16. Interview, Steve Rauschenberger, January 16, 2001.

CHAPTER EIGHT

1. New Hampshire Senate Insurance Committee Hearing, *SB 370—Relative to Health Insurance Coverage for Scalp Hair Prostheses,* January 1, 1992, pp. 4–6.

2. Jacob Hacker, *The Divided Welfare State: The Battle over Public and Private Social Benefits in the United States* (Cambridge University Press, 2002), pp. 11, 29. See also Christopher Howard, *The Welfare State Nobody Knows: Debunking Myths about U.S. Social Policy* (Princeton University Press, 2007), p. 2.

3. Interview, Wendy Royalty, January 15, 2002.

4. Bob Rosenblatt, "Viagra Spurs New Questions about HMO Drug Coverage," *Los Angeles Times,* June 8, 1998, p. 8.

5. Interview, Tracy Barnes, January 16, 2002.

6. New Hampshire Senate Insurance Committee Hearing, p. 14.

7. Norman Daniels, *Just Health Care* (Cambridge University Press, 1985), p. 33.

8. M. L. Lyke, "Viagra's Bitter Pill," *Seattle Post-Intelligencer,* May 14, 1998, p. A1.

9. Robert Scheer, "Dole Is Here to Remind Us: Sex Isn't Dirty; It's Been a Year—Viagra Notwithstanding—in Which Sexual Excitement Has Hardly Been Treated as a Good Thing," *Los Angeles Times,* January 5, 1999, p. 7.

10. Interview, Paige Shipman, November 29, 2001.

11. Interview, Jay Mahler, October 1, 2001.

12. Interview, Tom Bruckman, January 29, 2002.

13. Martha Fuller Clark, SB 175 Testimony, Senate Insurance Committee, New Hampshire, Document 2, March 29, 1999, p. 3; Candace White Bouchard, SB 175 Tes-

timony, Senate Insurance Committee, New Hampshire, Document 3, March 29, 1999, p. 1.

14. Blue Cross/Blue Shield of New Hampshire/Matthew Thornton Health Plan, SB 175 Testimony, Senate Insurance Committee, New Hampshire, Document 6, March 29, 1999, p. 1.

15. Rickie Solinger, *Beggars and Choosers: How the Politics of Choice Shapes Adoption, Abortion, and Welfare in the United States* (New York: Hill and Wang, 2001).

16. Interview, Ed Rivet, January 25, 2002; see also U.S. Newswire, "Right to Life of Michigan Commends President Bush as He Proclaims November as National Adoption Month," November 12, 2001.

17. Interview, Jennifer Gosselin, October 12, 2001.

18. See, for example, State of Illinois, 87th General Assembly, Regular Session, Senate Transcript, 46th Legislative Day, June 19, 1991, p. 48 (remarks of Sen. Raica).

19. Interview, Susan Scherr, December 7, 2001.

20. See, for example, Connie Ruggles, "Findings of Fact and Recommendation," Case No. 01-279, Subscriber vs. CIGNA HealthCare of Florida, State of Florida Statewide Provider and Subscriber Assistance Panel, July 31, 2001; Frank E. Iaquinta, M.D., "External Review Determination," IPRO, Lake Success, N.Y., July 26, 2001; John T. Price, M.D., "Rationale for Full Review Decision, Connecticut External Review Program, re. decision denying coverage of June 25, 1999."

21. Frank E. Iaquinta, M.D., "External Review Determination," IPRO, Lake Success, N.Y., May 8, 2001.

22. Frank E. Iaquinta, M.D., "External Review Determination," IPRO, Lake Success, N.Y., July 10, 2001.

23. Frank E. Iaquinta, M.D., IPRO, Lake Success, N.Y., "External Review Response—Full Review, Letter to Susan F. Cogswell, Insurance Commissioner, State of Connecticut," date redacted.

24. Interview, Jack Bruner, January 23, 2002.

25. Interview, Elvin Zook, January 23, 2002.

CHAPTER NINE

1. The first health care chapter, chapter 7, examined debate over the line between what public insurance should cover and what should be left instead to the responsibility of private individuals and their families. The second health care chapter, chapter 8, looked at debates over how government should draw the line between private insurance and the private individual's own responsibilities. This chapter completes the loop by examining discourse over the border between public insurance and private insurance, and whether that border can remain stable over time.

2. Pierre Rosanvallon, *The New Social Question: Rethinking the Welfare State* (Princeton University Press, 2000), p. 16.

3. Michael Graetz and Jerry Mashaw, *True Security: Rethinking American Social Insurance* (Yale University Press, 1999), p. 24.

4. Robert Reich, *The Resurgent Liberal: And Other Unfashionable Prophecies* (New York: Times Books, 1989), p. 279.

5. David Miller, "Altruism and the Welfare State," in *Responsibility, Rights, and Welfare: The Theory of the Welfare State,* edited by J. Donald Moon (Boulder, Colo.: Westview Press, 1988), p. 165. See also Karl Ove Meone and Michael Wallerstein, "Self-Interested Support for Welfare Spending," paper presented at the 1996 annual meeting of the American Political Science Association, San Francisco, Aug. 29–Sept. 1, 1996, p. 21.

6. See also the discussion in Jacob S. Hacker, *The Divided Welfare State: The Battle over Public and Private Social Benefits in the United States* (Cambridge University Press, 2002), p. 29; and Beth Stevens, "Blurring the Boundaries: How the Federal Government Has Influenced Welfare Benefits in the Private Sector," in *The Politics of Social Policy in the United States,* edited by Margaret Weir, Ann Shola Orloff, and Theda Skocpol (Princeton University Press, 1988), p. 147.

7. Tsung-mei Cheng and Uwe E. Reinhardt, "The Ethics of America's Health Care Debate," in *Uniting America: Restoring the Vital Center to American Democracy,* edited by Norton Garfinkle and Daniel Yankelovich (Yale University Press, 2005), p. 81.

8. Robin Toner, "Boiling Brew: Politics and Health Insurance Gap," *New York Times,* September 30, 2003, p. A27.

9. Interview, Philip Boyle, November 28, 2001.

10. Interview, Robert Pokorski, November 19, 2001.

11. Amy Harmon, "Burden of Knowledge: Tracking Prenatal Health in New Tests for Fetal Defects, Agonizing Choices for Parents," *New York Times,* June 20, 2004, p. A4. See also Andrew Pollack, "The Wide, Wild World of Genetic Testing," *New York Times,* September 12, 2006, p. G4.

12. Ted Halstead and Michael Lind, *The Radical Center: The Future of American Politics* (New York: Doubleday, 2001), p. 78.

13. Alexander Capron, "Which Ills to Bear, Revaluating the Power of Modern Genetics," in *Bioethics: Basic Writings on the Key Ethical Questions That Surround the Major Modern Biological Possibilities and Problems,* edited by Thomas Anthony Shannon (Mahwah, N.J.: Paulist Press, 1993), p. 497.

14. Interview, Dorothy Wertz, November 26, 2001.

15. Boyle interview.

16. Philip J. Boyle, "Shaping Priorities in Genetic Medicine," *Hastings Center Report* 25, no. 3 (1995), pp. S2–S8.

17. Klaus Lindpaintner, "The Impact of Pharmacogenetics and Pharmacogenomics," *Journal of Commercial Biotechnology* 10 (2003), p. 71.

18. Aravinda Chakravarti and Peter Little, "Nature, Nurture and Human Disease," *Nature* 421, January 23, 2003, p. 414; Editorial, "Pharmacogenetics to Come," *Nature* 425, October 23, 2003, p. 749.

19. Jai Shah, "Economic and Regulatory Considerations in Pharmacogenomics for Drug Licensing and Healthcare," *Nature Biotechnology* 21 (2003), p. 752.

20. Interview, Julie Taylor, October 30, 2001.

21. Interview, Ernest Csiszar, October 29, 2001.

22. See, for example, Charles Lockhart, *Gaining Ground: Tailoring Social Programs to American Values* (University of California Press, 1989), p. 22; Jacob S. Hacker, "Universal Risk Insurance" (Brookings/The Hamilton Project, September 2006); Linda Blumberg, principal research associate, Urban Institute, "Expanding Health Insurance Coverage to the Uninsured: Rationale, Recent Proposals, and Key Considerations," Statement to the Education and Labor Committee, Subcommittee on Health, Employment, Labor and Pensions, United States House of Representatives, March 15, 2007, p. 5.

23. Graetz and Mashaw, *True Security: Rethinking American Social Insurance*, p. 171.

24. Ibid. See also Jacob S. Hacker, "Health Care for America" (Washington: Economic Policy Institute, January 11, 2007).

25. Robert Pear, "Medicare Costs to Increase for Wealthier Beneficiaries," *New York Times*, September 11, 2006, p. A10.

CHAPTER TEN

1. Jacob Weisberg, *In Defense of Government: The Fall and Rise of Public Trust* (New York: Scribner, 1996), p. 51; E. J. Dionne Jr., *They Only Look Dead: Why Progressives Will Dominate the Next Political Era* (New York: Simon and Schuster, 1996), p. 49. I focus in this chapter on the published writings of American public intellectuals and commentators.

2. See, for example, Stephen H. Linder, "Coming to Terms with the Public-Private Partnership," *American Behavioral Scientist* 43 (1999), p. 40.

3. Lester Thurow, "Why Their World Might Crumble," *New York Times Magazine*, November 19, 1995, pp. 78–79; see also Rebecca M. Blank, "Viewing the Market Economy through the Lens of Faith," and "Reply to McGurn," in *Is the Market Moral?* by Rebecca M. Blank and William McGurn (Brookings, 2004), pp. 39–40, 96.

4. Robert Reich, *Tales of a New America* (New York: Vintage Books, 1988), p. 9.

5. Marvin N. Olasky, *The Tragedy of American Compassion* (Washington: Regnery Gateway, 1992); see also Howard Gleckman, "Rewriting the Social Contract," *Business Week*, November 20, 1995, p. 120.

6. Irving Kristol, *Neoconservatism: The Autobiography of an Idea* (New York: Free Press, 1995), p. 100.

7. Norman Podhoretz, "Contribution to a Symposium on 'The National Prospect,'" *Commentary*, November 1995, p. 100.

8. David Frum, *Dead Right* (New York: Basic Books, 1994), p. 4.

9. Dionne, *They Only Look Dead*, pp. 43–45; 97–98.

10. David M. Gordon, "Values That Work," *The Nation*, June 17, 1996, p. 16.

11. E. J. Dionne Jr., "The State of Our Civil Union," *Woodstock Report* 46 (June 1996) (woodstock.georgetown.edu/resources/articles/EJ-Dionne-The-State-of-Our-Civil-Union.html).

12. Richard C. Leone, "Taking Common out of Commonweal," *The Nation*, July 31, 1995, p. 130.

13. David Brooks, "'Civil Society' and Its Discontents," *Weekly Standard*, February 5, 1996, pp. 18–19.

14. Gertrude Himmelfarb, *The De-Moralization of Society: From Victorian Virtues to Modern Values* (New York: Vintage Books, 1996), pp. 253, 254, 255.

15. Lawrence Mead, *The New Politics of Poverty: The Nonworking Poor in America* (New York: Basic Books, 1992), p. 213.

16. Ibid.

17. Frum, *Dead Right*, p. 194.

18. See, for example, Mary Jo Bane and Paul A. Jargowsky, "The Links between Government Policy and Family Structure: What Matters and What Doesn't," in *The Changing American Family and Public Policy*, edited by Andrew J. Cherlin (Washington: Urban Institute Press, 1988), p. 231; and Marianne P. Bitler, Jonah B. Gelbach, and Hilary W. Hoynes, "The Impact of Welfare Reform on Living Arrangement," Working Paper 8784 (Cambridge, Mass.: National Bureau of Economic Research, 2002), p. 35.

19. Steve Forbes, Speech before the Conservative Political Action Committee, February 24, 1996, p. 11 (www.ontheissues.org/Celeb/Steve_Forbes_Tax_Reform.htm).

20. Charles Murray, *Losing Ground: American Social Policy 1950–1980* (New York: Basic Books, 1984), p. 156.

21. Christopher Jencks and Kathryn Edin, "Do Poor Women Have a Right to Bear Children?" *The American Prospect*, December 1, 1994 (www.prospect.org/cs/ articles?article=do_poor_women_have_a_right_to_bear_children); see also George Goertzel and John Hart, "New Jersey's $64 Question," in *The Politics of Welfare Reform*, edited by Donald F. Norris and Lyke Thompson (Thousand Oaks, Calif.: Sage Publications, 1995), p. 111.

22. Robert B. Reich, *The Resurgent Liberal* (New York: Times Books, 1989), p. 279; see also Charles Lockhart, *Gaining Ground: Tailoring Social Programs to American Values* (University of California Press, 1989), p. 22.

23. Himmelfarb, *The De-Moralization of Society*, p. 246.

24. Jeff Faux, "The Myth of the New Democrat," *The American Prospect* 15 (1993), pp. 20–29, and Jeff Faux, "The Evasion of Politics," *The American Prospect* 16 (1994), pp. 14–18.

25. Will Marshall, "Friend or Faux?" *The American Prospect* 16 (1994), p. 14.

26. For a good exposition, see Amitai Etzioni, *The Spirit of Community: Rights, Responsibilities, and the Communitarian Agenda* (New York: Crown Publishers, 1993).

27. David Blankenhorn, "Conclusion: The Possibility of Civil Society," in *Seedbeds of Virtue: Sources of Competence, Character, and Citizenship in American Society*, edited by Mary Ann Glendon and David Blankenhorn (Lanham, Md.: Madison Books, 1995), pp. 280, 279.

28. William A. Galston, *Liberal Purposes: Goods, Virtues, and Diversity in the Liberal State* (Cambridge University Press, 1991), p. 236.

29. Philip Selznick, *The Moral Commonwealth: Social Theory and the Promise of Community* (University of California Press, 1992), p. 371; see also Christopher Lasch, *The Revolt of the Elites and the Betrayal of Democracy* (New York: W.W. Norton, 1995), p. 101.

30. David Kirp, *Almost Home: America's Love-Hate Relationship with Community* (Princeton University Press, 2000), p. 331.

CHAPTER ELEVEN

1. In each of the four debates, there is a side that one can readily identify as arguing for a more generous, less restrictive and stigmatizing approach to the particular policy at hand, and a side that argues for a more stringent and stigmatizing, less open-handed stance. It seems reasonable to call the first the more *liberal* side and the second the more *conservative*. It is generally the case that specific individuals who take the conservative side in any one of the four debates will do so in the others, and that these individuals would label themselves, or be labeled by others, as conservatives. Likewise for the liberal side. But nothing in what follows rests on this being the case, since the object here is to look at the structure of debates, not the ideologies of individuals.

2. Mimi Abramovitz, *Regulating the Lives of Women: Social Welfare Policy from Colonial Times to the Present* (Boston: South End, 1996), p. 360.

3. Interview, Chuck Damschen, October 18, 2007.

4. Interview, Todd Porter, October 20, 1997.

5. Interview, Larry Mumper, October 16, 2007.

6. Tommy G. Thompson, "The Good News about Welfare Reform: Wisconsin's Success Story," Heritage Lecture 593 (Washington: Heritage Foundation, March 6, 1997), p. 3.

7. David T. Ellwood, "Conclusion," in *Welfare Policy for the 1990s,* edited by Phoebe H. Cottingham and David T. Ellwood (Harvard University Press), p. 274.

8. Joanna K. Weinberg, "Dilemmas of Welfare Reform: Workfare Programs and Poor Women," *New England Law Review* 26 (1991), p. 418.

9. Interview, Ron Stoker, October 16, 2007.

10. Sarah K. Gideonse, and R. William Meyers, "Why the Family Support Act Will Fail," *Challenge* (Sept./Oct. 1989), p. 33.

11. Mildred Rein, *Dilemmas of Welfare Policy* (New York: Praeger, 1982), p. 156.

12. Porter interview.

13. Tommy G. Thompson, "Continuing to Transform Welfare: The Next Bold—and Compassionate—Step," Heritage Lecture 747 (Washington: Heritage Foundation, May 29, 2002), pp. 2, 3; see also Neil Gilbert, *Welfare Justice* (Yale University Press, 1995), p. 167.

14. Interview, Bill Seitz, October 20, 2007.

15. University Consortium on Welfare Reform, *Illinois Family Study: The Two Worlds of Welfare Reform in Illinois,* July 2004 (Northwestern University Institute for Policy Research, 2004).

16. Lawrence M. Mead, "The Work Obligation," in *Points of Light: New Approaches to Welfare Dependence,* edited by Tamar Ann Mehuron (Washington: Ethics and Public Policy Center, 1991), p. 69; see also Lawrence M. Mead, "The Politics of Conservative Welfare Reform," in *The New World of Welfare,* edited by Rebecca Blank and Ron Haskins (Brookings, 2001), p. 218.

17. Interview, Randy McNally, October 16, 2007.

18. Jason Turner, "Hearing on TANF Reauthorization," in *Welfare: A Documentary History of U.S. Policy and Politics,* edited by Gwendolyn Mink and Rickie Solinger (New York University Press, 2003), pp. 770, 769; see also Robert Rector, "Congress Re-Starts Welfare Reform," Web Memo 991 (Washington: Heritage Foundation, February 7, 2006).

19. Gary Bryner, *Politics and Public Morality: The Great American Welfare Reform Debate* (New York: Norton, 1998), p. 226.

20. Martha Minow, "The Welfare of Single Mothers and Their Children," *Connecticut Law Review* 26 (1994), p. 818.

21. Pamela A. Holcomb, "State Welfare-to-Work Waiver Demonstrations," in *Families, Poverty, and Welfare Reform*, edited by Lawrence B. Joseph (Chicago: Harris Graduate School of Public Policy Studies, 1999), pp. 222, 223.

22. Joel F. Handler and Yeheskel Hasenfeld, *The Moral Construction of Poverty: Welfare Reform in America* (New York: Sage, 1991), p. 171.

23. Chad Alan Goldberg, "Welfare Recipients or Workers? Contesting the Workfare State in New York City," *Sociological Theory* 19 (2001), p. 207.

24. Leonard Goodwin, *Causes and Cures of Welfare* (Lexington: Heath, 1983), p. 140. See also Donna Shalala, "Hearings on the Work and Responsibility Act" (July 14, 1994), in *Welfare: A Documentary History*, edited by Mink and Solinger, p. 578.

25. Interview, Sharon Spencer, October 16, 2007.

26. Interview, Gilda Jacobs, October 19, 2007.

27. See some of the discussion in Glenn C. Loury, "Comment," in *Work and Welfare*, by Robert M. Solow, edited by Amy Guttman (Princeton University Press, 1998), p. 47.

28. Interview, Don Perdue, October 16, 2007.

29. Gordon Lafer, "Job Training for Welfare Recipients," in *Work, Welfare, and Politics*, edited by Frances Fox Piven and others (University of Oregon Press, 2002), p. 185.

30. Interview, Linda Coleman, October 16, 2007.

31. Interview, Shalonn Curls, October 16, 2007.

32. Ifie Okwuje and Nicholas Johnson, "A Rising Number of State Earned Income Tax Credits Are Helping Working Families Escape Poverty" (Washington: Center on Budget and Policy Priorities, October 20, 2006), p. 1.

33. Christopher Howard, *The Hidden Welfare State: Tax Expenditures and Social Policy in the United States* (Princeton University Press, 1997), p. 71.

34. Dennis J. Ventry, "The Collision of Tax and Welfare Politics: The Political History of the Earned Income Tax Credit," in *Making Work Pay: The Earned Income Tax Credit and Its Impact on America's Working Families*, edited by Bruce D. Meyer and Douglas Holtz-Eakin (New York: Russell Sage, 2001), p. 37.

35. House of Representatives, *Welfare Reform Is Working: A Report on State and Local Initiatives*, Hearings before the Committee on Government Reform, 106 Cong., 1 sess. (April 22, 1999), p. 60; see also David Firestone, "Fight or Flight? GOP Split over Tax Credits," *New York Times*, June 8, 2003, p. A30.

36. Interview, Patricia Serpa, October 17, 2007.

37. Interview, Dave Syverson, October 18, 2007.

38. Lawrence E. Lynn, "Public Policy and Poverty," in *Families, Poverty, and Welfare Reform*, edited by Joseph, p. 54.

39. Mary Jo Bane and David T. Ellwood, *Welfare Realities: From Rhetoric to Reform* (Harvard University Press, 1994), p. 149. See also Charles Karelis, *The Persistence of Poverty* (Yale University Press, 2007), p. 136; and Human Services Committee (Con-

necticut Senate), *Joint Favorable Report: An Act Creating an Earned Income Credit against the Personal Income Tax,* 2/27/2007, pp. 2, 7, 8, 14.

40. Jacobs interview.

41. Interview, William E. Peterson, October 17, 2007.

42. Interview, Al Riley, October 18, 2007.

43. Joel F. Handler and Yeheskel Hasenfeld, *The Moral Construction of Poverty: Welfare Reform in America* (New York: Sage, 1991), p. 142.

44. Interview, Ana Sol Gutierrez, October 15, 2007.

45. Interview, Edward Flanagan, October 18, 2007.

46. Ron Haskins, "Making Ends Meet: Challenges Facing Working Families in America," testimony before the House Committee on the Budget, 107 Cong., 1 sess., August 1, 2001, p. 17; William Julius Wilson, *When Work Disappears: The World of the New Urban Poor* (New York: Knopf, 1996), p. 222.

47. Riley interview.

48. Bryner, *Politics and Public Morality,* p. 285.

49. Blanche Bernstein, *The Politics of Welfare: The New York City Experience* (Boston: Abt Books, 1982), p. 40.

50. Brian Steensland, "Cultural Categories and the American Welfare State: The Case of Guaranteed Income Policy," *American Journal of Sociology* 111 (2006), p. 1295.

51. Syverson interview.

52. Interview, Anne Donahue, October 20, 2007.

53. *In re Dickerson,*. 227 B.R. 742 B.A.P. 10th Circuit (1998).

54. House of Representatives, *Effects of Welfare Reform.* Hearing before the Subcommittee on Human Resources of the Committee on Ways and Means, 106 Cong., 1 sess., May 27 1999, p. 105.

55. Carl P. Chelf, *Controversial Issues in Social Welfare Policy* (New York: Sage, 1992), p. 145. It is of course true that much of what the welfare recipient spends on training, nutrition, and housing can be interpreted as preparing the recipient to enter the workforce, but none of these expenditures would be regarded as work expenses in the conventional IRS definition, because they would also double as personal consumption.

56. Interview, Barb Caruso, September 26, 2007.

57. Interview, George Cahlandt, September 26, 2007.

58. Interview, Cherie Jamason, September 27, 2007. See also Robert Lerman and C. Eugene Steuerle, "Structured Choice versus Fragmented Choice: Bundling of Vouchers," *Vouchers and the Provision of Public Services,* edited by C. Eugene Steuerle, Van Dorn Ooms, George Peterson, and Robert D. Reischauer (Brookings, 2000), p. 477: "High-quality child care may produce external benefits (lower social costs because of reduced crime and reduced spending on schooling) as great as improved housing."

59. Interview, Celia Hagert, September 26, 2007.

60. Interview, Barbara Van Burgel, September 26, 2007.

61. Interview, Sandra Hamill, September 27, 2007.

62. Deanna Lyter, Melissa Sills, Gi-Taik Oh, and Avis Jones-Deweever, *The Children Left Behind: Deeper Poverty, Fewer Supports* (Washington: Institute for Women's Policy Research, 2004), p. 4.

63. See also Michael H. Schill, "Privatizing Federal Low Income Housing Assistance: The Case of Public Housing," *Cornell Law Review* 75 (1990), p. 893.

64. Douglas Besharov and Peter Germanis, *Full Engagement Welfare in New York* (Washington: American Enterprise Institute, 2004), p. 81.

65. Martin Anderson, *Welfare: The Political Economy of Welfare Reform in the United States* (Stanford, Calif.: Hoover Institution, 1978), p. 33.

66. Interview, Ken Furr, September 27, 2007.

67. Interview, Sara Mims, September 25, 2007.

68. Robert E. Rector and Kirk A. Johnson, *Understanding Poverty in America* (Washington: Heritage Foundation, 2004), p. 3, n. 3.

69. Marc Bendick Jr., "Privatization of Public Services," in *Public-Private Partnership: New Opportunities for Meeting Social Needs,* edited by Harvey Brooks, Lance Liebman, and Corinne S. Schelling (Cambridge, Mass.: Ballinger, 1984), p. 161.

70. Christine K. Ranney and John E. Kushman, "Cash Equivalence, Welfare Stigma, and Food Stamps," *Southern Economic Journal* 53 (1987), p. 1012.

71. Interview, Lynn M. Luker, September 28, 2007.

72. Interview, Linda Miller, September 28, 2007.

73. Chelf, *Controversial Issues in Social Welfare,* p. 37; see also some of the discussion in R. Shep Melnick, *Between the Lines: Interpreting Welfare Rights* (Brookings, 1994), pp. 192–93.

74. Anne Kim, "Fixing Food Stamps," Policy Brief (Washington: Progressive Policy Institute, September 2002), p. 4. See also Jeffrey Berry, *Feeding Hungry People: Rulemaking in the Food Stamp Program* (Rutgers University Press, 1984), p. 31: "As one of the early administrators argued many years later, 'The basic thing was that in spite of all the things you heard about hunger, these families didn't feel the need for more food. They felt the need for more money.'"

75. Interview, Gina Cornia, September 27, 2007.

76. See also Michael Wiseman, "Food Stamps and Welfare Reform," Policy Brief 19 (Washington: Brookings, 2002), p. 4.

77. Interview, Matt Habash, September 28, 2007.

78. Interview, Berry Friesen, September 28, 2007.

79. Interview, Kevin Seggelke, September 27, 2007. For families who would "spend more on food than the face value of their food coupons," Gary Burtless writes, "the major effect of the coupons is to displace cash to other uses, and the utility value of the coupons is nearly the same as an equivalent amount of cash"; see "The Economist's Lament: Public Assistance in America," *Journal of Economic Perspectives* 4 (1990), p. 76. But even if most families remain unconstrained in this way (and in-kind aid is as good as cash), that need not preclude (and indeed does not preclude) the ongoing in-principle argument about in-kind aid. Conservatives are those who simply want it to be, or regret that it often is not, constraining—as it would be, say, if income eligibility limits were lowered—while liberals are happy with that reality.

80. Morton Paglin, "Our Multiple-Benefit Antipoverty Program," in *Welfare Reform in America,* edited by Paul M. Sommers (Boston: Kluwer-Nijhoff, 1984), pp. 84–85.

81. Interview, Mark Anderson, September 28, 2007.

82. See testimony of Wendell Primus, House of Representatives, *Effects of Welfare Reform,* Hearing before the Subcommittee on Human Resources of the Committee on Ways and Means, May 27, 1999.

83. Interview, Patty Whitney Wise, September 28, 2007.

84. Interview, Lucy Nolan, September 28, 2007.

85. Seggelke interview.

CHAPTER TWELVE

1. Charles Leslie Glenn, *The Ambiguous Embrace: Government and Faith-Based Schools and Social Agencies* (Princeton University Press, 2000), p. 84; John J. DiIulio, "Symposium: Public Values in an Era of Privatization: Response Government by Proxy," *Harvard Law Review* 116 (2003), pp. 1360–61.

2. Mark Ragan and David J. Wright, *The Policy Environment for Faith-Based Social Services in the United States: What Has Changed since 2002? Results of a 50-State Study* (Albany, N.Y.: Roundtable on Religion and Social Welfare Policy, December 2005), p. 1.

3. I will leave aside the question of religious discrimination in hiring by charitable choice organizations, which raises many employment-law issues apart from the constitutional questions being discussed here.

4. *Witters* v. *Washington Department of Services for the Blind,* 474 US 481 (1986).

5. Interview, Paula Parker Sawyers, December 4, 2007.

6. As does the nine-month program offered by Faith Works to parolees; Faith Works, though, is not the sort of local-church-based social service provider—the kind vulnerable to short-term fluctuations in funding—whose support was the primary concern of the charitable choice law. See *Freedom from Religion Foundation* v. *McCallum,* 179 F. Supp. 2d 950 (WD Wisconsin 2002); see also the discussion in Glenn, *The Ambiguous Embrace,* p. 113.

7. Interview, Janet Scott, December 6, 2007.

8. Interview, Tiffany Fisher, December 3, 2007.

9. Interview, Cheryl Swartley, November 27, 2007; see also Michele Estrin Gilman, "Fighting Poverty with Faith: Reflections on Ten Years of Charitable Choice," *Journal of Gender, Race and Justice* 10 (2007), p. 409: "Regardless of the constitutional appeal of voucher programs, most welfare-related programs are still structured as direct aid programs."

10. Susan Dokupil, "A Sunny Dome with Caves of Ice: The Illusion of Charitable Choice," *Texas Review of Law and Politics* 5 (2000), p. 196: "The direct contract perspective does not survive constitutional scrutiny so easily."

11. Parker Sawyers interview.

12. Interview, Holly Hollman, November 28, 2007; see also Jo Renee Formicola, Mary C. Segers, and Paul Weber, *Faith-Based Initiatives and the Bush Administration: The Good, the Bad, and the Ugly* (Lanham, Md.: Rowman & Littlefield, 2003), p. 66.

13. See, for example, remarks of Ira C. Lupu, professor of law at George Washington University, "The Role of Faith-Based Organizations in the Social Welfare System,

Plenary Session—Private Choice of Public Services: Vouchers and Government Funding of Faith-Based Social Service Organizations" (Albany, N.Y.: Roundtable on Religion and Social Welfare Policy, Spring Research Forum, March 6, 2003), p. 4.

14. See, for example, Lewis D. Solomon, *In God We Trust: Faith Based Organizations and the Quest to Solve America's Ills* (Lanham, Md.: Lexington Books, 2003), p. 235.

15. Isaac Kramnick and R. Laurence Moore, "Can the Churches Save the Cities? Faith Based Services and the Constitution," *American Prospect*, November/December 1997, p. 52. See also Sheila Seuss Kennedy and Wolfgang Bielefield, *Charitable Choice at Work: Evaluating Faith-Based Job Programs in the States* (Georgetown University Press, 2006), p. 159; and Christopher L. Eisgruber and Lawrence G. Sager, *Religious Freedom and the Constitution* (Harvard University Press, 2007), p. 235.

16. Interview, Wade Matthews, December 3, 2007.

17. Interview, Suzanne Yack, November 30, 2007.

18. Interview, Robert Linthicum, November 29, 2007.

19. John J. DiIulio, "With Ben Franklin's Blessings: A Primer on the Faith-Based Initiative," Event Transcript, Pew Forum on Religion and Public Life, Key West, Fla., May 23, 2005, p. 27.

20. Ibid.

21. Melissa Rogers, "The Breaking Points: When Consensus Becomes Conflict," in *Sacred Places, Civic Purposes: Should Government Help Faith-Based Charity?* edited by E. J. Dionne Jr. and Ming Hsu Chen (Brookings, 2001), p. 323; see also Formicola, Segers, and Weber, *Faith-Based Initiatives and the Bush Administration*, p. 146.

22. Interview, Sydney Hoffman, December 3, 2007.

23. Interview, Kathy Myers, November 24, 2007. See also John J. DiIulio, "Not by Faith Alone," *Sacred Places, Civic Purposes?* edited by Dionne and Chen, p. 87; and Fred Davie, Suzanne Le Menestrel, and Richard Murphy, "Promises and Perils: Faith-Based Involvement in After-School Programs," in *Sacred Places, Civic Purposes*, p. 240.

24. Stanley Carlson-Thies, "More Religion, Please," *Capital Commentary* (Annapolis: Center for Public Justice, August 27, 2000).

25. Formicola, Segers, and Weber, *Faith-Based Initiatives and the Bush Administration*, pp.145, 173; Dennis R. Hoover, "Yes to Charitable Choice," *The Nation*, July 14, 2000, pp. 6–7, 28.

26. E. J. Dionne Jr. and Ming Hsu Chen, "When the Sacred Meets the Civic: An Introduction," in *Sacred Places, Civic Purposes*, edited by Dionne and Chen, p. 10.

27. Interview, Shelley Appel, November 26, 2007. See also Stephen Monsma and Christopher Soper, *Faith, Hope, and Jobs: Welfare-to-Work in Los Angeles* (Georgetown University Press, 2006), p. 97.

28. John P. Bartkowski, *Charitable Choices: Religion, Race, and Poverty in the Post Welfare Era* (New York University Press, 2003), p. 167.

29. DiIulio, "With Ben Franklin's Blessings," p. 3.

30. Interview, Andy Aldrich, November 30, 2007.

31. Interview, James Sell, November 30, 2007.

32. Interview, Lori Wiersma, November 26, 2007.

33. Hoffman interview.

34. Interview, John Baumann, November 26, 2007.

35. Matthews interview; Gilman, "Fighting Poverty with Faith, p. 418; Amy Sherman, "Should We Put Faith in Charitable Choice?" *Responsive Community*, Fall 2000, p. 3; Robert Wuthnow, *Saving America? Faith-Based Services and the Future of Civil Society* (Princeton University Press, 2004), pp. 34–36, 172; and Mark Chaves, *Congregations in America* (Harvard University Press, 2004), ch. 3.

36. Interview, David Spickard, November 26, 2007; see also Carmen M. Guerricagoitia, "Innovation Does Not Cure Constitutional Violation: Charitable Choice and the Establishment Clause," *Georgetown Journal on Poverty Law and Policy* 8 (2001), p. 454.

37. "In Good Faith: Government Funding of Faith-Based Social Services: A Statement Arising from Discussions Convened by the American Jewish Committee and the Feinstein Center for American Jewish History at Temple University," in *Sacred Places, Civic Purposes*, edited by Dionne and Chen, p. 308.

38. DiIulio, "With Ben Franklin's Blessings," p. 3.

CHAPTER THIRTEEN

1. For recent examples, see Ted Halstead and Michael Lind's description of American political conflict in *The Radical Center* (New York: Doubleday, 2001), p. 14; Michael Tomasky, *Left for Dead* (New York: Free Press, 1996), p. 99; and the introduction in Neil Jumonville and Kevin Mattson, eds., *Liberalism for a New Century* (University of California Press, 2007), p. 3.

2. I note here that, by and large, I did not focus on debates over user fees, which arise when a private consumer pays a public provider for services (for example, tolls paid by drivers for the use of public highways), or contracting out, which occurs when a public provider—government—pays a private provider to furnish the services in question (for example, governments engaging private companies to build and manage prisons). Instead, and there is a reason for this, the debates analyzed in the previous chapters fall into two different classes. One of these can loosely be described as cases in which the public provider—the state—pays not a private provider, as in contracting out, but rather a private consumer, who then uses those public funds in the private market to purchase goods and services such as street repair, education, health care, or food. Falling into this class are the controversies I analyze over government's giving residents of private communities tax deductions for their road maintenance payments, for example, or furnishing vouchers for private school parents.

The other class of topics I examine distinguishes itself from user fees, in which private consumers pay the public provider. Instead, they involve private *providers* taking over a certain degree of financial responsibility from, and sometimes even paying, the public provider. Examples here include private named donations to support public spaces in universities and museums or parents setting up a private booster club to provide extra teachers or equipment at their children's public schools. In none of these cases can the private provider's relationship with the public provider be characterized as a user fee; instead, it takes the form of donations or contributions, not fees.

I have chosen to look at these two classes of debates because they engage a much wider array of constituencies, get debated with far greater passion, and implicate a broader range of political values than do contracting out and user fees. The latter (as a relative, certainly not an absolute, statement) tend to be of interest to narrower business or client constituencies, get engaged at a more technical level, and focus preponderantly more heavily on criteria of economic efficiency.

3. See, for example, John G. Gunnell, "Louis Hartz and the Liberal Metaphor: A Half-Century Later," *Studies in American Political Development* 19 (2005), p. 204.

4. Or consider how the approach I am advancing might apply to an important judicial debate beyond the realms discussed here: the constitutional question of state action; that is, the issue of whether a particular private entity has crossed the border into the public sphere, hence becoming subject to constitutional constraints.

One leg of state action doctrine, the so-called "public function" theory, brands as a state actor any private entity to which the state has substantially abdicated a core public responsibility. An example would be the company town that the Supreme Court, in *Marsh* v. *Alabama*, 326 U.S. 501 (1946), held to have assumed so many responsibilities and characteristics of the absent state—including fire, police, and sewer services—that it became a state actor, falling under the constitutional obligation to allow the distribution of leaflets within its perimeters. The other leg of state action doctrine, the so-called "nexus" theory, brands as state actors private entities that fall into just the opposite class: entities for which the state is all too present as a funder or a regulator, vitally necessary for their very functioning. An example would be the coffee shop that the Supreme Court, in *Burton* v. *Wilmington Parking Garage*, 365 U.S. 715 (1961), held to be so dependent on and infused by the state (a public parking garage was its lessor) that the coffee shop, too, became a state actor, falling under the constitutional obligation to serve African Americans; see some of the discussion in Jody Freeman, "The Private Role in Public Governance," *New York University Law Review* 75 (2000), p. 543.

Because of the availability of these two converse doctrines, those endeavoring to claim that a private entity is a state actor often find themselves simultaneously depicting it as both falling substantially within the ambit of the public sphere, relying on or being controlled by a very present state, and wholly within the private realm, substantially unregulated by a very absent state. For example, in *Jackson* v. *Metropolitan Edison Co.*, 419 U.S. 345 (1974), the argument that an electrical utility, Metropolitan Edison, was a state actor is based equally on the contrary claims that the "pattern of cooperation between Metropolitan Edison and the State [had] led to significant state involvement in virtually every phase of the company's business" (p. 368) and that the state had allowed the company to "substitute" for itself in an area "traditionally associated with sovereignty" (p. 353); see also the dissent in *Rendell-Baker* v. *Kohn*, 457 U.S. 830, 844, 849 (1982), where the state is described as both "delegating" substantial public functions to the private entity, and extensively "regulat[ing]" the entity.

5. Richard A. Epstein, *Overdose: How Excessive Government Regulation Stifles Pharmaceutical Innovation* (Yale University Press, 2006). See also Lawrence D. Brown and Lawrence R. Jacobs, *The Private Abuse of the Public Interest: Market Myths and Policy Muddles* (University of Chicago Press, 2008), pp. 121, 127.

6. As Carol Nackenoff puts it, for Hartz, "American political thought was remarkably homogeneous and consensual"; see "Locke, Alger, and Atomistic Individualism Fifty Years Later: Revisiting Louis Hartz's Liberal Tradition in America," *Studies in American Political Development* 19 (2005), p. 206. Seymour Martin Lipset and Samuel P. Huntington each has his own list of five different basic American values, although for both scholars, these values can easily be reclassified into *public* and *private* as I understand those terms here. And Lipset, in discussing America's "fundamental ideals" or "basic value[s]," describes them as "solidified" and finds an "intimate connection between" them. Huntington, too, finds American creedal values to be "singular" and to "reinforce" one another, while commanding "consensus," indeed "unanimity." See Seymour Martin Lipset, *The First New Nation* (New York: Basic Books, 1963), pp. 104, 106, 118; Samuel P. Huntington, *American Politics: The Promise of Disharmony* (Harvard University Press, 1981), pp. 14, 16, 18.

7. Louis Hartz, *The Liberal Tradition in America* (New York: Harcourt, Brace, 1955), p. 89; Bernard Sternsher, *Consensus, Conflict and American Historians* (Indiana University Press, 1975), pp. 5, 80; Karen Orren and Stephen Skowronek, *The Search for American Political Development* (Cambridge University Press, 2004), p. 59; and Herbert McClosky and John Zaller, *The American Ethos: Attitudes toward Capitalism and Democracy* (Harvard University Press, 1984), p. 17.

8. Huntington, *American Politics*, pp. 16, 17, 18.

9. See, as well, James A. Morone's apt discussions in "The Other's America: Notes on Rogers Smith's *Civic Ideals*," *Studies in American Political Development* 13 (1999), p. 188; and in *The Democratic Wish: Popular Participation and the Limits of American Government* (Yale University Press, 1998), pp. 16–19. Other scholars, more generally, have noted that Americans hold contradictory political values. But the question here has to do not with individuals and their ideologies but with debates and their structures: with how these values are marshaled in particular arguments.

10. Public interest and pro-private-market groups—groups whose views normally conflict on almost every issue—can occasionally find that their positions cohere on a particular matter. For example, in the 2005 Supreme Court case of *Kelo* v. *New London*, 545 U.S. 469 (2005), in which a municipal government sought to expropriate residential property in a working-class neighborhood and then turn it over to a high-end private developer, opponents spanned the spectrum from the libertarian, pro-property-rights Cato Institute to the progressive National Association for the Advancement of Colored People. See, for example, Peter S. Wenz, *Beyond Red and Blue: How Twelve Political Philosophies Shape American Debates* (MIT Press, 2009), p. 14. This "strange bedfellows" kind of occurrence, part and parcel of democratic coalition making, is a different phenomenon from the one I have been analyzing here. In many of the debates I have examined, a particular group, such as a homeowners association, which normally takes a coherent position on any number of matters—or groups whose views do not normally conflict, such as advocates for insurance coverage of particular health conditions—can find themselves relying on conflicting public sphere and private realm norms in the debate at hand.

11. Or consider, to take an example drawn from a policy domain beyond the ones

discussed here, the debates over the proper governmental response to the decline of defined benefit and the rise of defined contribution private pensions. Defined benefit plans, in which employers promise a certain amount upon retirement, honor public sphere norms in that they retain some semblance of a welfare-state-style guaranteed income. Defined benefit plans embody private market values, though, in that they are available not to all adult citizens universally at all times, but only to those who possess an ongoing job; to change or lose one's job often means forgoing part, or all, of the value of one's defined benefit pension.

By contrast, defined contribution plans—in which the individual beneficiary controls the investments—reflect private market values in that they force the individual to rely on his or her own investing acumen to secure a decent pension, and so their value is more threatened by the ups and downs of the financial markets. Defined contribution accounts reflect public sphere values, however, in that—because of their ready portability—one can hold on to them regardless of one's employment status, and so they are less threatened by the ups and downs of the labor market: precisely the same public sphere values lie behind (for example) the desire to move from employer-based to universal health insurance.

Accordingly, attempts at consensus—at finding policy responses that forge common ground between defined benefit and defined contribution pensions—rely on bringing together the public sphere values to be found on either side. For example, Teresa Ghilarducci, an economist at the New School for Social Research, suggests a "Guaranteed Retirement Account," which, like "defined benefit plans [offer] benefits . . . guaranteed for life" and, like "defined-contribution plans, . . . are fully portable"; see Teresa Ghilarducci, *Guaranteed Retirement Accounts*, Briefing Paper 204 (Washington: Economic Policy Institute, November 20, 2007), p. 8.

12. Catharine A. MacKinnon, *Toward a Feminist Theory of the State* (Harvard University Press, 1989), p. 168.

13. See also Jean Bethke Elshtain's full treatment of these issues in *Public Man, Private Woman* (Princeton University Press, 1981).

14. See, for example, Jeff Weintraub, "The Theory and Politics of the Public/Private Distinction," in *Public and Private in Thought and Practice: Perspectives on a Grand Dichotomy*, edited by Jeff Weintraub and Krishan Kumar (University of Chicago Press, 1997), pp. 15, 37.

15. Michael J. Sandel, "Bad Bidding," *New Republic*, April 13, 1998, p. 9; also in *Public Philosophy* (Harvard University Press, 2006). See, as well, the discussion in Martha Minow, *Partners, Not Rivals* (Boston: Beacon Press, 2002), pp. 29–30.

16. S. I. Benn and G. F. Gaus, *Public and Private in Social Life* (New York: St. Martin's Press, 1983); and Alan Wolfe, "Public and Private in Theory and Practice: Some Implications of an Uncertain Boundary," in *Public and Private in Thought and Practice*, edited by Weintraub and Kumar, p. 196. The state of course exerts claims of secrecy with respect to the rest of society, but these are not the same things as claims of privacy. *Privy* and *private* are different notions. The state, on the general social theory understanding that I am describing here, is thus not seen as a "private realm" by comparison with any other social sphere or institution.

INDEX

DATE DUE